Mandatory Non-financial Risk-Related Disclosure

Stefania Veltri

Mandatory Non-financial Risk-Related Disclosure

Measurement Problems and Usefulness for Investors

Springer

Stefania Veltri
Department of Business Administration and Law
University of Calabria
Rende, Italy

ISBN 978-3-030-47920-6   ISBN 978-3-030-47921-3 (eBook)
https://doi.org/10.1007/978-3-030-47921-3

This Springer imprint is published by the registered company Springer Nature Switzerland AG.
The registered company address is: Gewerbestrasse 11, 6330 Cham, Switzerland

Foreword

In October 2014, the European Union adopted Directive 2014/95/EU (hereafter EU Directive), which mandates companies of a certain size to draft and publish a non-financial declaration related to the disclosure of corporate non-financial information (NFI) about society and the environment, with the ultimate aim to enhance the consistency and comparability of corporate NFI disclosed throughout the EU. NFI refers to a broad range of themes and issues such as environmental and social policies, impacts, and long-term risks related to these policies, which allows stakeholders to draw a more comprehensive and realistic picture of a company.

The book focuses specifically on the mandatory disclosure of non-financial (NF) risks as required by the EU Directive for listed Italian companies, investigating both the state of the art of its disclosure and its usefulness for investors. Risk disclosures are among the most important types of NFI valued by investors, and the author investigates a relevant question: whether this information is useful for investors or not, i.e., if it is a substantive or symbolic practice. To address the research aim, the book adopts a two-staged research approach. In the first stage, the author employed a manual meaning-oriented content analysis to investigate the NF declarations of the listed Italian companies mandated to disclose the NFI, returning a quality NF risk disclosure index. In the second stage, the author used the value relevance methodology to investigate whether the NF risk information disclosure affects the levels of equity prices, in particular employing a modified Ohlson (1995) model in which the risk-related information is added to the basic model as a proxy for the non-accounting information.

The research shows several original points with respect to other empirical researches on the issue. It is the first study to examine the association between NF risk disclosure and firm market value, the first study to investigate the relationships between two different kinds of risk disclosures, financial and non-financial, and the first to examine the usefulness for investors of a complete risk profile of a firm, taking into consideration backward-looking and forward-looking information disclosures. Furthermore, it is the first research study investigating the value relevance of NF risk disclosure in a mandatory context (the Italian one) after the adoption of

EU Directive and testing the mediating role of NF risks in the financial risks/market value association.

The empirical part focuses on Italy, a country that provides a unique opportunity to examine the impact of mandatory NF risk disclosure on firm market value, being one of the biggest industrial European countries that does not have mandatory legislation for NFI disclosure, and also one of the leading countries in voluntary corporate social responsibility (CSR) reporting at an international level.

Several are the expected contributions of the book. First, it expands the field of application of value relevance analysis, providing evidence of the usefulness of accounting and non-accounting risk measures and whether shareholders consider both in their investment decisions. Second, it enriches the literature addressing the measurement of the NF risk disclosure by employing a manual meaning-oriented content analysis and providing a quality NF risk disclosure index, whereas the majority of existing researches focus on coverage indexes. Furthermore, it provides empirical evidence of the state of the art of NF risk-related information disclosure and of the risk-related information value relevance in a context other than traditional US institutional setting. Finally, it investigates whether quality NF risk disclosure is value relevant in a mandatory context, in order to support or not mandatory disclosure of NFI and to evaluate whether the choices made by the Italian legislator in implementing the EU directive have been able to support an NF risk disclosure value relevant for investors.

Department of Business Administration and Law, University of Calabria
Rende, Italy
Franco Rubino

Preface

This book focuses on the impact of the disclosure of non-financial risk, which could be seen as the most relevant non-financial information (NFI), in the aftermath of the 2014/95/EU Directive. The author analyzes whether the switch from voluntary to mandatory NFI enhances the quality of disclosed non-financial (NF) risk-related information and the usefulness of the risk disclosure for investors. The book focuses specifically on the mandatory disclosure of NF risks as required by the EU Directive for listed Italian companies, investigating both the state of the art of its disclosure and its usefulness for investors.

In doing so, the book contributes to fill two relevant gaps in the risk literature. The first research gap is related to the insufficient investigation of the disclosure of NF risks. Companies mandated to disclose risk-related information focused mainly on financial risks, in spite of the width of the definition of risk, conceived as information about any opportunity, danger, threat, or exposure that has or could impact the company in the future. The second gap is that empirical evidence about the effects of corporate risk disclosures is still limited, and the potential benefits of the disclosure of information on risks have not been fully explored. In particular, the relationship between risk disclosures and firm value is under-researched, as the risk literature mainly focuses on the incentives question, related to the motives for which companies decide to disclose.

The research in this book focuses on Italy, a country that provides a unique opportunity to examine the impact of mandatory NF risk disclosure on firm market value, being one of the biggest industrial European countries that does not have mandatory legislation for NFI disclosure, and also one of the leading countries in voluntary corporate social responsibility (CSR) reporting at an international level. It has been carried out in the fiscal year 2017, the first year of the application of the mandatory NF disclosure for obliged Italian listed public interest entities (PIEs).

The research could be divided into two main parts. Part I focuses on the measurement problems of NF risks, i.e., a timely argument due to the mandatory adoption in Europe of the EU Directive on non-financial and diversity information (Directive 2014/95/EU). This part focuses on the significance of the non-financial risks disclosure, on the theoretical lens of the study, on the main content of the EU Directive and of Legislative Decree 254/2016 that enacted the EU Directive in the Italian context, and on the tool used to measure the state of the art of NF risk-related disclosure in the Italian context, i.e., a meaning-oriented manual content analysis, and ends with a self-constructed quality index NF risk disclosure, applied to the Italian sample. This is an original point of the book because, as far as we are aware, this is the first quality NF risk disclosure self-constructed on the basis of the NF categories identified by the EU Directive and the Legislative Decree 54/2016.

The second part investigates the usefulness of NF risk information in the Italian context using the value relevance analysis and a modified Ohlson Model (1995). This part tests in detail the association between financial and non-financial risks and separately the usefulness of financial and NF risks for Italian investors (after having provided a literature review of existing empirical studies). Then, in the final chapter, the mediation role of NF risks in the association between financial risks and firm market value is tested and evidence of it is provided. Several are the original points of this part. The first is related to the financial risk value relevance analysis, as the existing empirical studies are mostly focused on the US context, so the book adds knowledge on the usefulness of financial risk information for investors operating in a context other than the USA. Secondly, as far as we are aware, it is the first value relevance analysis expressly focused on a specific kind of NFI, i.e., the NF risks. Third, it is the first study, as far as we are aware, hypothesizing a relationship between financial and non-financial risks, a hypothesis that is on the basis of another original point of our research, i.e., the NF risk disclosure plays a role in the association between financial risk disclosure and firm market value.

The book contributes both to the measurement literature, as it presents a self-constructed quality NF risks, and to the value relevance analysis literature, providing evidence of the usefulness of financial and non-financial risk-related disclosures in the Italian context. The final chapter also provides the main limitations, the future research directions, and the main implications of the book.

Rende, Italy
April 2020

Stefania Veltri

Contents

Part I Measuring Non-Financial Risk Disclosure

1 A Brief Overview of the Book . . . 3
1.1 The Main Aim of the Book . . . 3
1.2 The Shared Notion of Risk . . . 3
1.3 Financial and Non-financial Risk . . . 4
1.4 The Risk Perspective of the Book . . . 5
1.5 The Association Between Financial and Non-financial Risk . . . 5
1.6 The Risk Literature and the Gaps Addressed . . . 6
1.7 The Theoretical Lens . . . 7
1.8 The Research Design . . . 7
1.9 The Italian Context . . . 7
1.10 The Summary of the Results . . . 8
1.11 The Originality Cues of the Work . . . 8
1.12 The Contributions of the Work . . . 8
1.13 The Structure of the Book . . . 9
References . . . 9

2 Risk-Related Disclosure . . . 11
2.1 Introduction . . . 11
2.2 The Significance of Risk Disclosure . . . 11
2.3 The Financial Risk Disclosure and Its Determinants . . . 12
2.4 The Non-financial Risk Disclosure . . . 15
2.5 The Character of Risk Disclosure Around the World . . . 19
2.6 Mandatory Versus Voluntary Non-financial Risk Disclosure . . . 21
2.7 The Theoretical Underpinnings of the Sampled Studies . . . 23
2.8 The Theoretical Lens of This Work . . . 23
References . . . 26

3 The Mandatory Non-financial Disclosure in the European Union . . . 31
3.1 Introduction . . . 31
3.2 The Historical Milestones Towards the EU Directive . . . 31
3.3 The EU Directive: Main Content . . . 32
3.4 The GRI Initiative and the Relationships with the EU Directive . . . 36
3.5 The IIRC Initiative and the Relationships with EU Directive . . . 38
3.6 Comparing the Three Initiatives . . . 40
3.7 The EU Directive and the Reporting Frameworks . . . 42
3.8 The Italian Legislative Decree 254/2016 . . . 44
3.9 Italy and the Non-financial Information Disclosure Practices . . . 47
3.10 The Sample . . . 51
References . . . 52

4 Measuring the Quality of Non-financial Risk-Related Disclosure . . . 57
4.1 Introduction . . . 57
4.2 The Main Non-financial Risk-Related Disclosure Frameworks . . . 57
4.3 The Non-financial Risk Disclosure Categories According to the Decree . . . 61
4.4 The Content Analysis . . . 65
4.5 Form-Oriented Versus Meaning-Oriented Content Analysis . . . 67
4.6 Content Analysis Studies on Risk Disclosure . . . 68
4.7 Going Beyond the Content Analysis: The Risk Disclosure Indexes . . . 69
4.8 The Centrality of Quality of Mandatory Non-financial Disclosure . . . 71
4.9 The Quality of Risk Disclosure in Empirical Studies . . . 72
4.10 The Notion of Quality Shared in the Book . . . 75
4.10.1 Unidimensional Measures . . . 76
4.10.2 Multidimensional Measures . . . 77
4.11 Objective/Subjective Quality Indices and Theories Behind . . . 78
4.12 The Non-financial Quality Risk Disclosure Index . . . 79
References . . . 81

Part II Testing the Usefulness of Non-Financial Risk Disclosure

5 The Relationship Between Financial and Non-financial Risk . . . 89
5.1 Introduction . . . 89
5.2 The Literature on the Relationship Between Financial and Non-financial Risk Disclosure . . . 89
5.3 The First Research Hypothesis . . . 92

5.4 Measuring the Financial Risk 93
5.5 Analysing the Relationship Between Financial and Non-financial Risk in the Italian Context 94
References 96

6 The Value Relevance Analysis 99
6.1 Introduction 99
6.2 The Semi-strong Market Efficiency Theory 99
6.3 The Value Relevance Analysis (VRA) and the Ohlson Model (OM) (1995) 100
6.4 OM (1995): From the Three Main Assumptions to the Market Value of the Firm 101
6.5 Critically Considering the Three OM (1995) Assumptions 103
6.6 OM (1995): The Simplified Model Used in Empirical Studies 105
6.7 OM (1995): Examining the Deflators 106
6.8 OM (1995): Focusing on the 'ν' Variable 107
6.9 OM (1995): Simplifying Assumptions and Further Models 108
6.10 The Modified OM (1995) Employed in the Research 109
References 110

7 The Value Relevance of Financial Risk 115
7.1 Introduction 115
7.2 The Risk Informativeness Literature 115
7.3 The Second Research Hypothesis 122
7.3.1 The Convergence Hypothesis 122
7.3.2 The Divergence Hypothesis 123
7.4 Analysing the Value Relevance of Financial Risk in the Italian Context 126
References 129

8 The Value Relevance of Non-financial Risk 133
8.1 Introduction 133
8.2 The Non-financial Risk Informativeness Literature 133
8.3 The CSR Value Relevance Literature 134
8.4 The Environmental Value Relevance Literature 137
8.5 The Third Research Hypothesis 143
8.6 Analysing the Value Relevance of the Non-financial Risk in the Italian Context 146
References 149

9 The Mediating Role of Non-financial Risk 153
9.1 Introduction 153
9.2 The Mediating Effect in Non-financial Information Literature 153
9.3 Hypothesizing a Mediating Effect in our Research 155
9.4 The Design of the Research 156

9.5 Main Results 158
9.5.1 Descriptive Statistics 159
9.5.2 Regression Results 159
9.6 Testing the Mediation Effect 162
9.7 Discussions of Results 162
9.8 Main Limitations of the Study and Future Research Directions 164
9.9 Main Implications of the Study 165
References 165

About the Author

Stefania Veltri is a senior lecturer in accounting and Assistant Professor teaching business economics. She is department member at the Department of Business Administration and Law, University of Calabria. Her main research interests are related to the value relevance of accounting and extra-accounting information and the systems of measurement, management, and reporting of intellectual capital. All these arguments are pursued employing both quantitative and qualitative methods. On these research themes, she has published books, book chapters, and journal articles (such as *Journal of Intellectual Capital*, *Corporate Communications*, and *Journal of Management and Governance*), and she has presented papers to national and international congresses.

Part I
Measuring Non-Financial Risk Disclosure

Chapter 1
A Brief Overview of the Book

1.1 The Main Aim of the Book

In October 2014, the European Union adopted Directive 2014/95/EU (hereafter EU Directive), which mandates companies of a certain size to draft and publish a non-financial declaration (NFD) related to the disclosure of corporate non-financial information (NFI) about society and the environment, with the ultimate aim to enhance the consistency and comparability of corporate NFI disclosed throughout the EU. NFI refers to a broad range of themes and issues such as environmental and social policies, impacts and long-term risks related to these policies and allows stakeholders to draw a more comprehensive and realistic picture of a company. In the book we intend to focus specifically on the mandatory disclosure of non-financial (NF) risks as required by the EU Directive for listed Italian companies, investigating both the *state of the art of NF risk-related information disclosure* and its *usefulness for investors*.

1.2 The Shared Notion of Risk

It is thus necessary to define the notion of risk shared in the book. Table 1.1 summarizes some definitions of risk.

In the book, we accept the *definition of risk* of Linsley and Shrives (2005), as information about any opportunity, danger, threat, or exposure that has or could impact the company in the future.

S. Veltri, *Mandatory Non-financial Risk-Related Disclosure*,
https://doi.org/10.1007/978-3-030-47921-3_1

Table 1.1 Some definitions of risk

Authors (year)	Risk definitions
Linsley and Shrives (2005)	Information about any opportunity, danger, threat or exposure that has or could impact the company in the future
Linsley and Shrives (2006)	The positive or negative outcome of events
Abraham and Cox (2007)	An uncertainty, a threat, a volatility or an opportunity that must be managed by companies
Solomon et al. (2000)	Uncertainty associated with potential gain and loss

Source: our elaboration

1.3 Financial and Non-financial Risk

Risk is a *complex concept and has a multi-faceted nature*. There are many taxonomies of risk proposed in the literature (De Luca and Phat 2019; Leopizzi et al. 2020). In our book, we distinguish between financial risks and NF risks that in turn could be articulated into several categories.

In our research, the distinction between financial and NF risks is really important, because we believe that, notwithstanding usefulness and materiality being key issues that relate to both financial and non-financial information, financial information has a different nature (the result of past events and measurable in terms of financial consequences and impacts) with respect to NFI (more forward-looking and less measurable). This dichotomy leads to a more difficult judgement about the materiality grade of information and, as a consequence, to a not foreseeable perception by users of that information (Van Der Lugt and Malan 2012).

Financial information relies on the concept of recognition and on the related probability that any future economic benefit associated with the assessed item will flow to or from the entity with a reliably measurable value, and financial risks could be identified as risks that incorporate backward-looking information and that therefore can be included within the annual report following the book-keeping rules.

On the contrary, NF risk is related to NF information, that is, essentially information to the extent necessary for an understanding of the development, performance, position and impact of the activity of the undertaking, relating to, as a minimum, environmental, social and employee matters, respect for human rights, anti-corruption and bribery matters, including (a) a brief description of the business model of the undertaking; (b) a description of the policies pursued by the undertaking in relation to those matters; (c) the outcome of these policies; (d) the principal risks related to these matters including how the undertaking manages those risks; and (e) relevant NF key performance indicators (Leopizzi et al. 2020).

By nature, NF risk-related information is qualitative, mainly disclosed in narrative form, forward-looking, not unequivocally measurable and not following the book-keeping rules.

1.4 The Risk Perspective of the Book

The adopted definition of risk as information is functional to the perspective used in the book, that is, one of the *risk disclosures*, leaving aside the risk management perspective in the sense of the activities carried out at the organizational level to face corporate risks. In other words, it is an external, communicational perspective. More precisely, in the book the concept of risk disclosure adopted is the one proposed by Linsley and Shrives (2006), according to which a firm provides an efficient risk disclosure 'if the reader is informed of any opportunity or prospect, or of any hazard, danger, harm, threat or exposure, which has already impacted upon the company or may impact upon the company in the future or of the management of any such opportunity, prospect, hazard, harm, threat or exposure'.

1.5 The Association Between Financial and Non-financial Risk

In recent years, several factors (i.e. changing economic and regulatory environments, more complex capital structures, increasing reliance on financial instruments, the growth of international funding transactions and prominent corporate crises) have all focused increasing attention on financial risk reporting (Beretta and Bozzolan 2004; Linsley and Shrives 2006; Mazumder and Hossain 2018). At the same time, stakeholders, researchers, practitioners and standards setters have become increasingly interested in the disclosure of NF risk-related information. In other words, firm survival has to be included in a broader discourse encompassing the way in which the firm manages the risks arising from the social and environmental impacts of its medium- and long-term activities and demonstrates itself to be socially responsible (Milne and Gray 2007).

In spite of the width of the definition of corporate risk, companies mandated to disclose (or voluntary disclosing) risk-related information focused mainly on financial risks (Dobler et al. 2014; Elshandidy et al. 2018), and the extant literature on risk reporting is largely dominated by the accounting standards for financial instruments issued by the FASB and the IASB (Tahat et al. 2019). Nevertheless, risk disclosures are among the most important type of NFI valued by investors (Bozzolan and Miihkinen 2019), and company reporting is progressively incorporating NF risk disclosure. It is thus worth asking to what extent the latter is related and consistent with the already standardized financial information (IIRC 2013) and provide useful information to stakeholders. In the book we aim to investigate the possible association and interaction between financial risk disclosure and NFI from the investors' perspective.

We aim to investigate the usefulness for investors of a complete corporate risk-related information, being aware that financial and NF risk-related information have different features and are interconnected. As far as we are aware, our research is the first to explicitly distinguish between financial and NF risks and to take into consideration that financial risk-related disclosure affects NF risk-related disclosure.

1.6 The Risk Literature and the Gaps Addressed

There are three research areas within risk disclosure literature: the determinants of risk disclosures (incentives); the extent (financial versus NF) risk disclosure; and the informativeness of risk disclosures (Elshandidy et al. 2018). Among these three research areas, theoretical and empirical studies focused on incentives question are largely predominant (Leopizzi et al. 2020).

As our research focuses on the mandatory NF risk disclosure, the incentives question lacks relevance.

As for the second research area, the majority of studies focused on financial risk disclosure (i.e. Beretta and Bozzolan 2004; Lajili and Zeghal 2005; Linsley and Shrives 2005), whilst there is a paucity of studies focusing on NF risk disclosure (Leopizzi et al. 2020; De Luca and Phat 2019). This identifies the existence of a gap in academic research, and our study tries to fill this gap, through investigating the level of risk disclosure, focusing on NF risks. As in the other studies, we use the content analysis methodology, but we went beyond a mechanical content analysis focused on counting the disclosed items within a text; instead, we employed a meaning-oriented type of content analysis, carried out manually, focused on the nature of themes disclosed, with a greater level of interpretation of the content rather than just counting the disclosure index. The features which determine a quality disclosure have been identified by carefully analysing a related literature review (Beretta and Bozzolan 2004; Boesso and Kumar 2007).

As for the third research area, empirical evidence about the effects of corporate risk disclosures is still limited, and the potential benefits of the disclosure of information on risks have not been fully explored. In particular, the relationship between risk disclosures and firm value is under-researched (Bravo 2017). The literature provides evidence of a scarcity of studies focused on the association between financial risk disclosure and firm value and is even more rarely focused on the association between NF risk disclosure and firm value. The existing studies focus on the NF (environmental) risks answering to book-keeping requirements, which is included in the annual accounts according to the IAS 37 standard. No study, as far as we are aware, investigated before the association between the NF risk-related information disclosure (related to a forward-looking, narrative disclosure) and the firm market value. Our research would like to fill this research void. Furthermore, by taking into account the complete (financial and NF) risk profile of a company and the association between these two different kinds of risk, our research also fills another gap in the risk literature research.

1.7 The Theoretical Lens

As for the theoretical foundations of the study, our paper is embedded within the *material legitimacy theory*, meaning that, in a context of mandatory reporting, the coercive force of the law prevails, companies disclose because they must and disclose information relevant (material) both for the company and for the stakeholders (Dumay et al. 2015), so providing a quality NF risk-related information disclosure.

In our research, we aim to investigate whether this information is useful for investors or not, i.e. if it is a substantive or symbolic practice. As the legitimacy theory make no assumption of the rational, wealth-maximizing individuals behaviour operating in markets, we also rely on the *semi-strong theory of market efficiency*, according to which share prices – on average – are assumed to reflect all publicly available information, that is, they are value relevant for investors (Beaver 1981; Fama 1970, 1991; Fama et al. 1969).

1.8 The Research Design

To address the research aim, this paper adopts a two-staged research approach. In the first stage, we employed a manual meaning-oriented content analysis to investigate the NF declarations of the listed Italian companies mandated to disclose the NFI, returning a quality NF risks disclosure index.

In the second stage, we used the value relevance methodology to investigate whether the NF risk information disclosed affects the levels of equity prices. In detail, we employed a modified Ohlson model (Ohlson 1995) in which the risk-related information is added to the basic model to proxy the non-accounting information.

1.9 The Italian Context

A number of studies have examined risk reporting throughout the world, focusing on financial risk reporting, and there are several studies providing a review of the literature (Elshandidy et al. 2018; Tahat et al. 2019). The studies focused on the mandatory disclosure of NF risks that is under-researched with respect to the financial risks disclosure. The existing researches focus on NFI information voluntarily disclosed and on the determinants of such disclosure. The compulsoriness of NFI disclosure in Europe in compliance to the 2014/95/EU Directive led researchers to focus on the level of mandatory NFI disclosure and thus also of NF risk-related information disclosure (De Luca and Phat 2019; Leopizzi et al. 2020). Our research focuses on Italy, a country that provides a unique opportunity to examine the impact of mandatory NF risk disclosure on firm market value, being one of the biggest industrial European countries that did not have mandatory legislation for NFI disclosure and also one of the leading countries in voluntary corporate social responsibility (CSR) reporting at an international level (Rossi and Tarquinio 2017). In detail, the research focuses on Italian large listed public-interest entities (PIEs). To be classified as large PIEs, a company must exceed on its balance sheet data the criterion of the average number of 500 employees and either (a) a balance sheet total exceeding EUR 20 million or (b) a net turnover exceeding EUR 40 million.

1.10 The Summary of the Results

The research was carried out in 2017, the first year of the application of the mandatory NF disclosure for obliged Italian listed PIEs.

The main findings provide support for a positive association between NF risk information disclosure levels and company's market value. Moreover, the research provides evidence of a significant mediating effect played by the NF risk on the relationship between financial risks and market value.

1.11 The Originality Cues of the Work

The research shows several original points with respect to other empirical researches on the issue. As far as we are aware, it is the first study to examine the association between NF risk disclosure and firm market value. It is also, to the best of our knowledge, the first study to investigate the relationships between two different kinds of risk disclosures, financial and non-financial, and the usefulness for investors of a complete risk profile of a firm, taking into consideration backward-looking and forward-looking information disclosures. Furthermore, as far as we are aware, it is the first research investigating the value relevance of NF risk disclosure in a mandatory context (the Italian one) after the adoption of the EU Directive. Finally, as far as we are aware, our research is also the first hypothesizing a mediating effect of NF risk disclosure on the association between financial risks disclosure and market value.

1.12 The Contributions of the Work

The results offer several contributions to the literature. First, they provide empirical evidence of the state of the art of NF risk-related information disclosure and of the risk-related information value relevance in a context other than traditional US institutional setting. Second, they enrich the literature addressing the measurement of the NF risk disclosure by employing a manual meaning-oriented content analysis and providing a quality NF risk-disclosures index. Third, they complement the literature providing evidence not only of the direct effect of NF risks disclosure on the company market value but also of its fully mediating effect on the association between financial risks disclosure and share prices. Fourth, they enrich the empirical literature on the value relevance of NF variables in a mandatory context, allowing an understanding of whether the choices made by the Italian legislator in implementing the EU directive have been able to support an NF risks disclosure value relevant for investors. Fifth, they provide insight into what role the state can play (or is willing to play) in the regulation of NFIand in detail of NF risk disclosure.

1.13 The Structure of the Book

The remainder of this work is organized as follows: Sect. 1.2 provides a brief review of the NF risk disclosure; Sect. 1.3 illustrates the compulsoriness of the NF risks within the Italian setting; Sect. 1.4 focuses on the measurement issues related to the NF risks disclosure; Sect. 1.5 concentrates on the association between financial and NF risks; Sect. 1.7 focuses on the value relevance model; Sect. 1.7 focuses on the main empirical studies on the value relevance of financial risks and on the usefulness of financial risks disclosure for Italian investors; Sect. 1.8 focuses on the main empirical studies on the value relevance of NF risks and on the usefulness of NF risks disclosure for Italian investors; Sect. 1.9, finally, focuses on the mediating role played by NF risks on the association between the financial risks/firm market value association in the Italian context. The section also discusses the main results, the limits, the future research directions and the main implications of the present work.

References

Abraham, S., & Cox, P. (2007). Analysing the determinants of narrative risk information in UK FTSE 100 annual reports. *The British Accounting Review, 39*(3), 227–248.

Beaver, W. H. (1981). Market efficiency. *The Accounting Review, 56*(1), 23–37.

Beretta, S., & Bozzolan, S. (2004). A framework for the analysis of firm risk communication. *The International Journal of Accounting, 39*, 265–288.

Boesso, G., & Kumar, K. (2007). Drivers of corporate voluntary disclosure: A framework and empirical evidence from Italy and the United States. *Accounting, Auditing & Accountability Journal, 20*(2), 269–296.

Bozzolan, S., & Miihkinen, A. (2019). *The quality of mandatory non-financial (risk) disclosures: The moderating role of audit firm and partner characteristics*. SSRN. Accessed January 10, 2020, from https://ssrn.com/abstract=3342703

Bravo, F. (2017). Are risk disclosures an effective tool to increase firm value? *Managerial and Decision Economics, 38*(8), 1116–1124.

De Luca, F., & Phat, H. (2019). Informativeness assessment of risk and risk-management disclosure in corporate reporting: An empirical analysis of Italian large listed firms. *Financial Reporting, 2*, 9–41.

Dobler, M., Lajili, K., & Zéghal, D. (2014). Environmental performance, environmental risk and risk management. *Business Strategy and the Environment, 23*, 1–17.

Dumay, J., Frost, G., & Beck, C. (2015). Material legitimacy. *Journal of Accounting and Organizational Change, 11*(1), 2–23.

Elshandidy, T., Shrives, P. J., Bamber, M., & Abraham, S. (2018). Risk reporting: A review of the literature and implications for future research. *Journal of Accounting Literature, 40*, 54–82.

European Union. (2014). *Directive as regards disclosure of non-financial and diversity information by certain large undertakings and groups, 2014/95/EU*. Accessed March 25, 2019, from http://eur-lex.europa.eu/legalcontent/EN/TXT/PDF/?uri=CELEX:32014L0095&from=EN/

Fama, E. F. (1970). Efficient capital markets: A review of theory and empirical work. *Journal of Finance, 25*(2), 383–417.

Fama, E. F. (1991). Efficient capital markets: II. *Journal of Finance, XLVI*(5), 1575–1617.

Fama, E. F., Fisher, L., Jensen, M. C., & Roll, R. (1969). The adjustment of stock prices to new information. *International Economic Review, 10*(1), 1–21.

International Integrated Reporting Council (IIRC). (2013). *The International <IR> framework, London*. Retrieved from https://integratedreporting.org/resource/international-ir-framework/

Lajili, K., & Zeghal, D. (2005). A content analysis of risk management disclosure in Canadian annual reports. *Canadian Journal of Administrative Sciences, 22*(2), 125–142.

Leopizzi, R., Iazzi, A., Venturelli, A., & Principale, S. (2020). Nonfinancial risk disclosure: The 'state of the art' of Italian companies. *Corporate Social Responsibility and Environmental Management, 27*(1), 358–368.

Linsley, P., & Shrives, P. (2005). Examining risk reporting in UK public companies. *The Journal of Risk Finance, 6*(4), 292–305.

Linsley, P., & Shrives, P. (2006). Risk reporting: A study of risk disclosure in the annual reports of UK companies. *The British Accounting Review, 38*(4), 387–404.

Mazumder, M. M. M., & Hossain, D. M. (2018). Research on corporate risk reporting: Current trends and future avenues. *Journal of Asian Finance, Economics and Business, 5*(1), 29–41.

Milne, M. J., & Gray, R. (2007). Future prospects for corporate sustainability reporting. *Sustainability Accounting and Accountability, 1*, 184–207.

Ohlson, J. A. (1995). Earnings, book values, and dividends in equity valuation. *Contemporary Accounting Research, 11*(2), 661–687.

Rossi, A., & Tarquinio, L. (2017). An analysis of sustainability report assurance statements: Evidence from Italian listed companies. *Managerial Auditing Journal, 32*(6), 578–602.

Solomon, J. F., Solomon, A., Norton, S. D., & Joseph, N. L. (2000). A conceptual framework for corporate risk disclosure emerging from the agenda for corporate governance reform. *The British Accounting Review, 32*(4), 447–478.

Tahat, Y., Dunne, T., Fifield, S., & Power, D. (2019). Risk related disclosure: A review of the literature and an agenda for future research. *Accounting Forum, 43*, 193. https://doi.org/10.1080/01559982.2019.1584953.

Van Der Lugt, C., & Malan, D. (2012). *Making investment grade: The future of corporate reporting: New trends in capturing and communicating strategic value*. Cape Town: Published by United Nations Environment Programme.

Chapter 2
Risk-Related Disclosure

2.1 Introduction

The chapter focuses on risk disclosure, stressing the significance of risk disclosure (and the difference with reporting), and then separately investigates the main studies on financial and NF risk disclosure, examined under three relevant points: the determinants of disclosure, the character of disclosure (voluntary/mandatory) and the theoretical underpinning. The chapter ends illustrating the theoretical underpinning of the book, focused on the mandatory disclosure of NF risk-related information.

2.2 The Significance of Risk Disclosure

In the book the concept of risk disclosure adopted is the one proposed by Linsley and Shrives (2006), according to which a firm provides an efficient risk disclosure 'if the reader is informed of any opportunity or prospect, or of any hazard, danger, harm, threat or exposure, which has already impacted upon the company or may impact upon the company in the future or of the management of any such opportunity, prospect, hazard, harm, threat or exposure'. Consistently with Dumay (2016), we believe that disclosure is different from reporting, even if the terms are mostly used synonymously. In detail, disclosure is 'the revelation of information that was previously secret or unknown', whilst reporting is a 'detailed periodic account of a company's activities, financial condition and prospects that is made available to shareholders and investors' (Dumay 2016). In this context, disclosures are thus more useful than reports because investors are always looking for more timely and important information, especially if it is secret or unknown.

S. Veltri, *Mandatory Non-financial Risk-Related Disclosure*,
https://doi.org/10.1007/978-3-030-47921-3_2

Stakeholders such as investors, regulators and financial analysts consider risk disclosure very useful to deal with uncertainties, and they need corporate risk disclosure to make informed investment decisions (Epstein and Buhovac 2006). Risk disclosure is also necessary to managers to go for better operational and investment decisions, and it also can help enhancing corporate reputation. Louhichi and Zreik (2015) found that risk disclosure affects corporate reputation in a positive manner. According to the two authors, disclosing risk information is a part of social contract, meaning that, if a company discloses more on risk, it will be rewarded with enhanced reputation.

In the book we adopt the users' perspective, that is, the investors' perspective, as one of the main aims of the research is the usefulness of NF risk-related information for investors.

In the chapter, we take into consideration studies dealing with external risk reporting as part of a firm's disclosure strategy focused on the underlying drivers and determinants (the main incentives) that motivate firms to provide risk information. We also consider only articles that have appeared in internationally recognized peer-reviewed journals.

In detail, there are three main features that we examine in the chapter: the extent of risk disclosure (financial versus NF risk disclosure), the determinants of the disclosure (and the theories behind the choice to disclose) and the nature (voluntary or mandatory) of the disclosure.

2.3 The Financial Risk Disclosure and Its Determinants

The first important discerning criterion is that which distinguishes between financial and NF risk disclosure, as almost the totality of the existing literature is focused on the disclosure of financial risk, and three recent large reviews on risk reporting focus on financial risk reporting (Elshandidy et al. 2018; Mazumder and Hossain 2018; Tahat et al. 2019).

The reviews of Elshandidy et al. (2018) and Mazumder and Hossain (2018) have been analysed to retrieve and examine the most influential studies focused on the determinants of the mandatory and voluntary financial risk disclosure, summarized below.[1]

Beretta and Bozzolan (2004) propose a framework comprising four dimensions, to analyse firms' risk disclosures, namely, quantity, density, depth and outlook profile. The authors find that the quantity of risk disclosure for their sample of Italian firms is mainly driven by firm size and that the quality of risk disclosure is affected by how size and industry type vary across the four dimensions.

[1]The Tahat et al. (2019) review has not been taken into consideration, as it is expressly focused on risk disclosure related to financial instruments.

Ali (2005) finds corporate size to be the determinant of voluntary corporate risk disclosure, meaning that larger companies disclose on a larger extent.

Linsley and Shrives (2005) find that size has significant effect on corporate risk disclosure in the UK.

Linsley and Shrives (2006) analyse the risk disclosure under four categories: financial/non-financial, monetary/non-monetary, good news/bad news and forward-looking/historic. They find that firm size and to a lesser extent environmental risk are statistically associated with risk disclosure, whereas gearing, asset cover, and other measures of risk (i.e. beta and the book-to-market value of equity) are not.

Abraham and Cox (2007) identify four categories of risk: total, business, financial, and internal control. The authors investigate the impact of corporate governance factors on risk disclosure, finding that the number of executive directors and the number of independent non-executive directors is significantly positively related to higher levels of aggregated risk reporting. Other factors which are also positively and significantly related are lower institutional ownership and dual-listing (UK/US).

Konishi and Ali (2007) find that company size is positively related to risk disclosure. However, they did not find any relationship between the risk disclosure and other corporate characteristics.

Deumes and Knechel (2008) employ a risk reporting disclosure index based on six separately identifiable internal control factors. They find that there are economic incentives for voluntary internal control reporting in a low-regulation environment. They also find a negative relationship between the extent of internal control disclosure and block holder ownership and a positive relationship between the extent of risk disclosure and financial leverage.

Amran et al. (2008) find that the extent of risk disclosure by Malaysian companies is low and that size has significant effect on corporate risk disclosure.

Hill and Short (2009) identify seven categories of risk: (1) internal risks; (2) external risks; (3) corporate development; (4) third-party risks; (5) information risks; (6) ongoing claims and disputes; and (7) 'boiler plate' disclosures, analysed along five dimensions: (1) time orientation; (2) financial/non-financial; (3) quantitative/qualitative; (4) economic sign; and (5) risk management strategies. They find that firms tend to reveal a high (low) proportion of forward-looking information (risk management disclosure) but also that they tend to reveal a low proportion of information on internal controls and risk management. Their results document that managerial ownership is negatively associated with risk disclosure.

Hassan (2009) finds that leverage and industry-type significantly influence risk disclosure by the United Arab Emirates (UAE) firms.

Taylor et al. (2010) find that corporate governance strength, the need to raise capital and being locally listed influence Australian firms' decision to reveal a high level of financial risk management information, both mandatorily and voluntarily. They also document a significant impact of IFRS adoption on the revealing of that information, finding that larger and highly leveraged firms tend to provide more risk information than others.

Dobler et al. (2011) find that observed variations in the quantity of risk disclosure are partially associated with domestic regulation, which plays an important role in firm incentives. The impacts of risk factors vary by country, as US and Canadian firms' risk disclosures are positively associated with their risk levels, German firms' negatively, and UK firms not significantly related at all.

Oliveira et al. (2011) find a non-significant impact of regulations on risk-reporting practices. Risk disclosure practices are likely to be categorized as generic, qualitative and backward-looking. It finds (consistent with the agency theory) significant impacts of leverage and the board of directors on risk-reporting practices.

Mihikinen (2012) finds an increase in the quantity of risk disclosure, with more extensive and more comprehensive information following the release of a new Finnish risk reporting standard. He also finds larger firms that are cross-listed in the USA tend to provide more quantitative risk disclosure and observes that the quality has increased over the years.

Barakat and Hussainey (2013) investigate the direct and joint effects of governance, regulation and supervision on the quality of operational risk disclosure. They find that bank governance has a significant positive impact on operational risk disclosure and that supervision is an essential element of that impact.

Elshandidy et al. (2013) find that firms characterized by higher levels of systematic risk, financing risk and risk-adjusted returns, and those with lower levels of stock return variability exhibit higher levels of aggregated and voluntary risk disclosure. They also find mandatory risk disclosure to be influenced positively by firm size, dividend yield and board independence and negatively by high leverage.

Ntim et al. (2013) find that corporate risk disclosure is negatively related to block ownership and institutional ownership and positively related to board diversity, board size and independent non-executive directors.

Probohudono et al. (2013) find a significant positive relationship between size and risk disclosure. The other variable that was positively related to risk disclosure was board independence. However, it was found that leverage is significantly negatively associated with voluntary risk disclosure.

Mokhtar and Mellett (2013) examined the impact of corporate governance, competition and ownership structure on risk disclosure. They find that the main determinants of risk disclosure are competition, role duality, ownership concentration, board size and type of auditor.

Elshandidy et al. (2015) find that mandatory and voluntary risk reporting are influenced by systematic risk, the legal system and cultural values. They also find that country and firm characteristics have higher explanatory power over the observed variations in mandatory risk reporting than over those in voluntary risk reporting. They find that the legal system and cultural values have high explanatory power over mandatory risk reporting variations over time.

Malafronte et al. (2016) find that the amount of risk information provided in the annual report is significantly affected by insurers' characteristics such as size and technical provision and country-level characteristics.

Al-Hadi et al. (2016) find that firms with a separate risk committee are likely to exhibit more market risk disclosure than other firms. The decision of these firms to provide risk information is also influenced by risk committee characteristics including size and qualification.

Nahar et al. (2016a) conducted a longitudinal study examining the determinants of risk disclosure in the annual reports (from 2007 to 2012) of Bangladeshi banks. The authors conducted the study from the perspective of five types/categories of financial institutions risk: market, credit, liquidity, operational and equity. It was found that the determinants of disclosure vary across these different categories of risk. The following variables, "the number of risk committees, leverage, company size, the existence of risk management unit, board size and a Big4 affiliate auditor, remained as 'significant determinants of at least one category of financial risk disclosure'.

Nahar et al. (2016b), in another study on Bangladeshi banks, examined the relationship among risk disclosure, cost of capital and bank performance. They find that cost of capital and risk disclosure are negatively related and also that there is an inverse relationship between risk disclosure and bank performance.

Allini et al. (2016) examined the determinants of risk disclosure of the listed state-owned enterprises of Italy. They find that company size, Internet visibility, women's presence on the board and age of board members affect risk disclosure. However, the presence of directors with accounting/finance/business qualification is negatively related to risk disclosure.

Table 2.1 provides details of the studies investigated in terms of the journal receiving the study (and year of publication), the country where the research was carried out, and the sample.

From the analysis of the studies reported in Table 2.1 and of their findings, it emerges that company size remain one of the main factors influencing risk disclosure: in most of the studies, it was found that larger companies are reporting more on risk related issues. Moreover, it emerges that risk disclosures are often more extensive in companies with superior corporate governance. Furthermore, most of the studies conducted are based on developed economies such as the UK, Canada, Japan, Singapore and Australia.

2.4 The Non-financial Risk Disclosure

Stakeholders, researchers, practitioners and standard setters have become increasingly interested in the inclusion of NFI in annual reports. NFI refers to a broad range of themes and issues such as environmental and social policies, impacts and long-term risks related to these policies and allows stakeholders to draw a more comprehensive and realistic picture of a company (Manes Rossi et al. 2018). In other words, firm survival can no longer be traced back only to an economic dimension of profit maximization, but it has to be included in a broader discourse encompassing the way in which the firm manages the risks arising from the social and environmental impacts of its activities in the medium and long term and demonstrates itself to be socially responsible (Milne and Gray 2007). Economic sustainability is no longer enough because it does not ensure a company's future success; rather it requires a holistic approach. To be considered sustainable, companies have to achieve all three

Table 2.1 Main articles focused on the determinants of risk disclosure

Authors (year)	Journal	Country	Sample
Beretta and Bozzolan (2004)	IJOA	Italy	Non-financial firms listed on the Italian (ordinary) market in 2001
Ali (2005)	JJAIAS	Japan	90 non-financial companies in the Japanese Stock Exchange
Linsley and Shrives (2005)	JRF	UK	79 FTSE 100 non-financial firms in 2001
Linsley and Shrives (2006)	BAR	UK	79 FTSE 100 non-financial firms in 2000
Abraham and Cox (2007)	BAR	UK	71 FTSE 100 non-financial firms in 2002
Konishi and Ali (2007)	IJAAPE	Japan	100 companies listed in the Tokyo Stock Exchange
Deumes and Knechel (2008)	AJPT	Netherlands	192 non-financial listed firms from 1997 to 1999
Amran et al. (2008)	MAJ	Malaysia	Annual reports of 100 Malaysian companies
Hill and Short (2009)	AF	UK	420 IPO listed firms from 1991 to 2003
Hassan (2009)	MAJ	United Arab Emirates	41 firms from the year 2005
Taylor et al. (2010)	AF	Australia	Sample of 111 listed resource firms from 2002 to 2006
Dobler et al. (2011)	JIAR	Canada, Germany, UK, USA	160 firm-year observations from the year 2005
Oliveira et al. (2011)	MAJ	Portugal	81 non-financial firms from the year 2005
Miihkinen (2012)	IJOA	Finland	99 non-financial firms listed on the OMX Helsinki between 2005 and 2007
Barakat and Hussainey (2013)	IRFA	Europe	85 banks from 20 EU member countries over three years (2008, 2009 and 2010)
Elshandidy et al. (2013)	IRFA	UK	1216 firm-year observations for FTSE all-share non-financial firms from 2005 to 2008
Ntim et al. (2013)	IRFA	South Africa	50 firms from 2002 to 2011
Probohudono et al. (2013)	SRJ	Cross country	Indonesia, Malaysia, Singapore and Australia listed firms
Mokhtar and Mellett (2013)	MAJ	Egypt	105 firms from the year 2007
Elshandidy et al. (2015)	BAR	Germany, UK, USA	3685 firm-year observations for Frankfurt (CDAX), FTSE and NASDAQ all-share non-financial firms from 2005 to 2010
Malafronte et al. (2016)	IRFA	Europe	231 firm-year observations from 2005 to 2010

(continued)

Table 2.1 (continued)

Authors (year)	Journal	Country	Sample
Al-Hadi et al. (2016)	CGIR	Gulf Cooperation Council	677 firm-year observations of financial firms from 2007 to 2011
Nahar et al. (2016a)	IJAIM	Bangladesh	Bangladeshi banks from 2007 to 2012
Nahar et al. (2016b)	ARA	Bangladesh	Bangladeshi banks from 2007 to 2012
Allini et al. (2016)	PMM	Italy	Listed state-owned enterprises

Source: our elaboration from Elshandidy et al. (2018) and Mazumder and Hossain (2018)

dimensions of sustainability: their operations should have no negative impact on the environment; they have to match the expectations of society; and they should be financially sound (Dyllick and Hockerts 2002).

Thus, over time, corporate disclosures have evolved from solely disclosing economic risk to also disclosing social and environmental risk. Disclosing all forms of sustainability risk is high on the international agenda and is also evidenced by the emerging risk accounting, reporting and disclosure literature.

Dyllick and Hockerts (2002) in their article outline that many companies address sustainability risks in their business strategies and issue sustainability performance to report on how well they achieve these strategies.

According to Benn et al. (2006), environmental awareness is one of the elements that is raising increasing concerns about the fair treatment of social and environmental measures—and the risks associated with these concerns are driving corporate sustainability practices.

Christofi et al. (2012) in their writings emphasize that growing pressure to regulate social justice, economic growth and environmental change has led to an evolution in corporate sustainability risk management practices and reporting.

Dumay and Hossain (2019) investigated the extent to which Australian listed companies disclosed their sustainability risk information under Recommendation 7.4 (after changes in 2014 to the *Corporate Governance Principles and Recommendations*). The findings show that the most disclosed sustainability risk is still the economic sustainability risk, followed by environmental and social sustainability risk.

The most common NF risks are environmental risks and social risks, often included on the same label of sustainability risks. Among these, environmental risk is the area which received most attention from scholars, as confirmed by the literature (Matten 1995; Weinhofer and Busch 2013; Clarkson et al. 2013; Plumlee et al. 2015). Recent environmental disasters emphasize the need for a better way to forecast and mitigate social and environmental risks (Truant et al. 2017). The Financial Stability Board in 2016 issued a report, the Task Force on Climate-related Financial Disclosure, which renews the pressure on companies in Europe to disclose specifically climate-related financial risks because 'it has been difficult for investors to know which companies are most vulnerable to climate change, which are best prepared, and which are taking action' (TCDF 2016). The TCDF divided climate-related risks into two major categories: risks related to the transition to a lower-carbon economy and risks related to the physical impacts of climate change. The former may include extensive policy, legal, technology and market changes to address mitigation and adaptation requirements related to climate change. The latter results in event-driven (acute) or longer-term shifts (chronic) in climate patterns. Both categories may also have direct and indirect financial and social impacts. In the survey conducted by KPMG, carbon-related risks are the most reported sustainability issues (KPMG 2015).

As for the determinants of NF risk-related disclosure, we can refer to studies focused on sustainability reporting, which found as the most important determinants company size, profitability, industry and country. As far as we are aware, only the study of Truant et al. (2017) is explicitly focused on the determinants of sustainability risks. The authors conducted their work on a sample of large Italian organizations that issued sustainability disclosure in accordance with the Global Reporting Initiative (GRI), G4 guidelines, which requires companies to provide a detailed narrative of the risks identification, impact and opportunities over a wide range of social, ethical and environmental topics. The authors tested the level of sustainability risk disclosure by sampled companies with three variables hypothesized in the literature to affect the risk disclosure level positively, namely, the international presence, the sustainability experience and the external assurance. Consistently with the literature, the authors find that 'experienced' sustainable reporters provide a significant volume of disclosure and that disclosure quality on risk is positively influenced by their international presence and reporting experience. However, when accounting for specific risk-related areas of disclosure, only a few of them seem to adopt a managerial perspective linking strategy, risk metrics, and disclosure.

Overall, sustainability risk has also found a spotlight in corporate governance practices, meaning that several corporate governance guidelines now include recommendations that advise listed companies to report on their economic, social and sustainability risks (Dumay and Hossain 2019). For example, the King IV guidelines require listed South African companies to expand their risk disclosure much further than was previously required under the King III guidelines of 2009 in the light of changing weather conditions and the pressure on the population and natural resources. In Australia, the third edition of the Corporate Governance Principles and Recommendations incorporates a new sub-section 7.4, which states that 'A listed entity should disclose whether it has any material exposure to economic, environmental and social sustainability risks and, if it does, how it manages or intends to manage those risks'.

However, even though there is a general consensus on the need for effective risk management and its disclosure, there is less agreement on how, and to what extent, environmental, social, and economic sustainability risk should be disclosed. In other words, there is a lively debate in the literature focused on the effectiveness of compulsoriness to disclose corporate, financial and NF risk-related information (Ioannou and Serafeim 2015), and the effect of mandatory disclosure of NFI in relation to an enhancement of corporate transparency and stakeholders' engagement in corporate governance is controversial (Hess 2007).

The next section highlights the character, mandatory or voluntary, of risk reporting regulations in different countries.

2.5 The Character of Risk Disclosure Around the World

The regulations on corporate risk disclosure around the world vary greatly in nature from merely discretionary to rigidly mandatory (Mazumder and Hossain 2018).

In the USA there is an important distinction between financial risks, whose disclosure is mandatory, and NF risk that companies voluntarily disclose. As for the financial risks, until 2005, US companies were required to provide risk disclosures in registration statements for equity and debt offerings (Campbell et al. 2014). Starting from 2005, the Securities and Exchange Commission (SEC) mandated listed firms to provide risk disclosures under 'Item 1A-Risk Factor' section of form of 10-K (Wahlen et al. 2014). The SEC's Regulation S-K (Item 305c) provided under the Securities Exchange Act of 1934 requires companies to disclose 'the most significant factors' that make the offering of securities speculative or risky. As per the requirement of SEC, every listed company in the USA must file a comprehensive summary of company financial performance in the format prescribed in form 10-K. For a non-US company that lists securities in the USA, a required format is 'Form 20-F' which includes 'Item 3DRisk Factors' for risk disclosures (Wahlen et al. 2014). The SEC requires that every listed company must disclose significant risk information in a concise, firm-specific and organized way rather than just disclosing risk factors which are generic in nature for all companies. Along with mandatory risk disclosures, some firms voluntarily provide NF risk information in Management Discussion & Analysis (MD&A) disclosure (Campbell et al. 2014).

In Canada, similar to the USA, disclosure of financial and market risk and their management is regulated to a large extent (Dobler et al. 2011; Lajili and Zeghal 2005), whilst NF risks are disclosed on a discretionary basis, mostly in the MD&A section under the condition of 'materiality' and 'significant risk exposure', giving management a chance to exercise their discretion in choosing to disclose publicly potentially important risk information (Lajili and Zeghal 2005).

The South African context is a mandatory context for risk reporting. The first attempt to emphasize risk management and reporting was made by the King Report (King II) in 2002. King II provided explicit guidance on risk definition, identification, classification, governance and reporting (Ntim et al. 2013). King II recommended that a company must assess risk and related control activities on an ongoing basis and disclose in the annual report such risk management policies, contingency plan, internal control and reporting system along with a statement admitting the board's responsibility for overall risk management and control (Ntim et al. 2013).

In Japan the disclosure of corporate risk could be considered almost voluntary. A small initiative was taken by Financial Service Agency (FSA), which mandates all listed companies to disclose risk related information in their annual security reports starting from April 2003. However, such guidance lacks necessary directions regarding the content and structure of risk disclosures, so Japanese companies have been voluntarily reporting risk information (Ali 2005; Konishi and Ali 2007).

In the context of other developing countries, such as Bangladesh, risk reporting is quasi-voluntary in nature, owing to very minimum as well as vague regulatory guidance regarding risk reporting. Moreover, regulatory enforcement is extremely fragile, owing to poor or no monitoring mechanism. In Bangladesh, until 2012, there were no explicit guidelines for the listed companies to provide risk-related information in the corporate disclosures (except disclosures in 'corporate prospectus' for IPO). Bangladesh Securities and Exchange Commission (BSEC) issued Corporate Governance Code (revised)-2012 which requires listed companies to disclose information on 'Risk and Concern' in the 'Directors' Report to the Shareholders' section of corporate annual reports. However, guidelines which could direct the company regarding the nature, extent and format of risk disclosures are missing.

In the Indian context, also, Securities and Exchange board of India (SEBI) issued Revised Clause 49 listing agreement to the Indian stock exchange on 31 Dec 2005 which requires that company should also talk about risk as part of the director's report or Management discussion and analysis report under the heading 'Risk and Concerns' (Saggar and Singh 2017).

In Europe, except for the UK, corporate risk disclosure is mandatory. In the UK setting, risk reporting is voluntary, and listed companies are encouraged to disclose business risk information in the Operating and Financial Review (OFR). Since 1997, the Institute of Chartered Accountants in England and Wales (ICAEW) has been trying to guide and motivate the UK firms to voluntarily provide information about risk in their annual reports. The Institute has published several discussion papers on risk reporting covering prospects and problems of risk reporting along with the guidance on how firms can report risk information in their annual report narratives (ICAEW 1997, 1999, 2002, 2011).

In Italy, risk reporting had been voluntary in the Italian institutional setting (Beretta and Bozzolan 2008) until 2007, when following the European Union (EU) Transparency Directive (Directive 2004/109/EC) aimed to harmonize the transparency in corporate disclosures among EU listed firms, a new requirement was added in the Civil Code of Italy in 2007. This requirement forces firms to include a description of their risks and management responses in the MD&A section of their annual reports (Elshandidy and Neri 2015).

In Spain, similarly to Italy, the Capital Firms Law (Article no. 262) establishes the obligation of listed firms to disclose information on main risks and uncertainties in the management reports along with a description of management policies and procedures to cope with them (Domínguez and Gámez 2014).

In Germany, the German Accounting Standards Board (GASB) has published a comprehensive risk reporting standard (GAS 5) which requires companies to disclose information on all risk categories and risk management (Miihkinen 2013).

GAS 5 requires that all risk-related disclosures should be made in a specific section (preferably under "Risk and Opportunities or Outlook") of the annual report narrative (Elshandidy et al. 2015).

In Finland, similarly to Germany, risk reporting is highly regulated and guided. In 2006, the Finnish Accounting Practice Board issued a detailed risk disclosure standard in order to develop best practices among companies in risk reporting. The standard is considered to be very unique in a sense that includes not only extensive guidance on expected risk reporting but also several illustrative disclosure examples (Miihkinen 2012). Prior to this standard, the Finish Accounting Act required the company to provide risk disclosures, but the requirements were very general and without implementation guidance (Miihkinen 2013).

As regards the NF risks disclosure, in 2014 Europe introduces a mandatory legislation for NFI disclosure (among which NF risk disclosure) with the 2014/95/EU Directive (hereafter EU Directive), and countries belonging to Europe enacted laws to implement the EU Directive.

However, there are some elements that could row against the effectiveness of a mandatory regime for NFI disclosure, becoming barriers that impede a mandatory, legislative approach from being an effective tool to foster corporate transparency and accountability (Chauvey et al. 2015; Costa and Agostini 2016). The first element is that the EU Directive does not impose a specific content, a definitive method of reporting, or a valid enforcement system for the provision of NFI. The coexistence of voluntary and mandatory items in the EU Directive could thus lead to a limited influence of the mandatory EU Directive on NFI disclosure (Dumay et al. 2019). The second element is related to the consideration that the EU Directive operates in a supranational context, characterized by different degrees of sensibility to these practices. This obviously could lead to different types of transposition of the EU Directive into the national legal systems (La Torre et al. 2018; Venturelli et al. 2017). Furthermore, the different sensibilities of the countries involved in the EU Directive regarding non-financial reporting could represent a determining factor for the adoption by the companies of the comply-or-explain principle. This principle, admitted by the EU Directive, allows the companies involved in the EU Directive to exclude certain information from their non-financial statement through an explanation regarding the reason behind the choice (Quinn and Connolly 2017).

2.6 Mandatory Versus Voluntary Non-financial Risk Disclosure

In the literature, there are at least two competing positions related to the effectiveness of a mandatory NFI disclosure. The first one, in support of the voluntary character of NFI disclosure, highlighted that the birth and the development of CSR took place in the context of voluntariness, owing to the managers' recognition of its strategic value (Venturelli et al. 2019), and empirical researches provided evidence that, for listed

Table 2.2 Pros and cons of voluntary and mandatory risks disclosure

	Voluntary disclosure	Mandatory disclosure
Pros	• Enhanced credibility and improved investor relations • Access to more liquid markets • Improved pricing and decision-making capabilities • A reduction in perceived risk, increased reputations and a lower cost of capital • Reduced litigation risk	• Providing stakeholders, especially investors and analysts, with information to aid them to enforce management's fiduciary duties and thus contribute to the alleviation of agency problems • Providing a level of public accountability and/or enforceability that would increase the credibility of disclosure • Helping ease information asymmetry • Enhancing transparency and in turn more difficult for controlling insiders to consume private benefits
Cons	• Competitive disadvantage if sensitive information is disclosed • Bargaining weaknesses related to stakeholders • Increased litigation risk • Preparation and audit costs	• Engendering competitive disadvantages as companies are forced to release sensitive information • The loss of potentially useful voluntarily disclosed information • The potential loss of meaning due to the production of boilerplate information

Source: our elaboration of Elshandidy et al. (2018)

companies, the quality of NFI disclosure positively affect the company equity value (Wang and Li 2015; Godfrey et al. 2009). The alternative position views the mandatory disclosure of NFI through more complete, accurate, neutral and objective regulation and comparable with respect to the voluntary disclosure (Deegan 2002; Crawford and Williams 2010). This position was at the basis of the introduction of mandatory disclosure of NFI in the European countries of Spain, France, Portugal, Finland, Sweden and Denmark, but recent studies underlined that regulation had as a consequence the short-term standardization of practice because of its coercive nature (Husted and De Jesus Salazar 2006) and impacted more on quantity (number of reports produced), instead of quality (Bebbington et al. 2012; Chauvey et al. 2015; Locke and Seele 2016; Costa and Agostini 2016; Ioannou and Serafeim 2014; Luque-Vílchez and Larrinaga 2016).

Table 2.2 highlights the main pros and cons of both voluntary and mandatory corporate disclosure.

The scientific debate has not led to a consensus regarding whether the regulation is preferable to voluntary disclosure of NFI (Venturelli et al. 2017).

Nevertheless, consistently with Elshandidy et al. (2018), we believe that mandating disclosure is to incentivize, as it encourages higher levels of it when there is no other incentives to disclose and therefore helps to reduce information asymmetry (Dobler 2008). Furthermore, the incentives to voluntarily disclose information appear to be relatively low precisely when they might be most desirable, for example, when financial risks are high (Marshall and Weetman 2007). On the contrary, theories of voluntary disclosure struggle to explain why firms are incentivized to reveal risk information (Abraham and Shrives 2014). Our position is thus towards the usefulness of the mandatory NFI disclosure but only if this translates into a quality NFI disclosure.

2.7 The Theoretical Underpinnings of the Sampled Studies

In the existing risk reporting literature, different strands of theories have been used to justify the incentives and/or disincentives of risk-related disclosures. These different strands could be summarized into two major streams (Mazumder and Hossain 2018). One stream of theories argues for the enhancement of risk-related information in the corporate disclosures. To this stream belong the agency theory, the stakeholder theory, the legitimacy theory, the resource-dependence theory and the signalling theory. Another stream of theories is used to justify the disincentives of risk-related disclosure. To this stream belong the institutional theory, which urges for symbolic disclosure for the sake of minimum compliance with social or regulatory pressure, and the proprietary cost theory, which rationalizes the reasons behind corporate reluctance in reporting risk-related information.

Table 2.3 summarizes the most applied perspectives in the literature, together with the studies using that perspective. It also should be underlined that (1) often the researchers do not declare the theoretical underpinning of the research and (2) several studies used a multi-theoretical perspective.

2.8 The Theoretical Lens of This Work

In the book we refer to a peculiar version of legitimacy theory, named material legitimacy theory (Dumay et al. 2015).

Legitimacy is defined by Suchman (1995, p. 574) as 'a generalized perception or assumption that the actions of an entity are desirable, proper, or appropriate within the same socially constructed system of norms, values, beliefs and definitions'.

Basically, legitimacy theory—as typically applied within the social and environmental accounting literature—adopts a central assumption that the maintenance of successful organizational operations requires managers to ensure that their organization appears to be operating in conformance with community expectations and therefore is attributed the status of being 'legitimate'. Within the legitimacy theory, organizations are viewed as being part of a broader social system. Researchers applying legitimacy theory also typically assume (albeit, typically an unstated assumption) a dichotomous state for 'legitimacy'. That is, there will either be compliance with community expectations (a legitimate organization) or non-compliance (an illegitimate organization). An organization, which is not deemed to be legitimate, and therefore fails to comply with community expectations, will have sanctions imposed upon it by society, for example, restrictions imposed on

Table 2.3 Most applied perspectives in risk-related information disclosure

Theories	Objectives	Arguments	Studies
Agency theory (Jensen and Meckling 1976)	To enhance risk disclosure	Risk disclosure minimizes information asymmetries, reduces agency costs, and shareholder interferences. Corporate governance structure plays a crucial role in enhancing risk disclosure	Abraham and Cox (2007); Deumes and Knechel (2008); Taylor et al. (2010); Oliveira et al. (2011); Miihkinen (2012); Elshandidy et al. (2013); Ntim et al. (2013); Mokhtar and Mellett (2013); Nahar et al. (2016a); Al-Hadi et al. (2016)
Stakeholder theory (Freeman 1984)	To enhance risk disclosure	Risk disclosure satisfies the information needs of the various corporate stakeholders. Greater stakeholders' interest motivates the firms to disclose more on risk	Amran et al. (2008); Oliveira et al. (2011); Mokhtar and Mellett (2013); Ntim et al. (2013); Barakat and Hussainey (2013)
Legitimacy theory (Shocker and Sethi 1973)	To enhance risk disclosure	Risk disclosure is necessary for firms to gain social acceptance and legitimate their operations	Oliveira et al. (2011); Ntim et al. (2013); Barakat and Hussainey (2013); Al-Hadi et al. (2016)
Signalling theory (Spence 1973)	To enhance risk disclosure	Irms disclose risk information to differentiate them from other companies having poor or no risk mechanism	Miihkinen (2012); Elshandidy et al. (2013); Mokhtar and Mellett (2013)
Resource dependence theory (Pfeffer and Salancik 2003)	To enhance risk disclosure	Risk disclosure helps to gain access to critical resources	Oliveira et al. (2011); Barakat and Hussainey (2013); Al-Hadi et al. (2016)
Institutional theory (Di Maggio and Powell 1983)	To comply with social or regulatory pressure	Firms disclose risk-related information to mimic other companies or because are obliged by institutions, returning boilerplate disclosures	Ntim et al. (2013); Elshandidy et al. (2015)
Proprietary cost theory (Verrecchia 1983)	To rationalize the reasons behind corporate reluctance in disclosing risk	There is a natural reluctance to disclose risk-related information or to manipulate it for the firms' benefits	Miihkinen (2012); Mokhtar and Mellett (2013)

Source: our elaboration on Mazumder and Hossain (2018) and Elshandidy et al. (2018)

its operations, difficulty in securing necessary resources inclusive of labour, reduced demand for its goods and services and so forth.

Societal expectations are considered likely to change across time so that 'legitimacy' is seen to be a concept that is relative to the social system in which the organization operates and is time and place specific.

Legitimacy as explained within the legitimacy theory is often linked to the idea of a 'social contract' (Patten 1992) wherein the social contract represents the multitude of implicit and explicit expectations that society has about how an organization should conduct its operations. The legitimacy of an organization is considered likely to be challenged when an organization does not comply with the terms of the 'social contract' and therefore with the expectations of the society in which it operates (creating what is known as "legitimacy gap").

Legitimacy theory is thus grounded in the notion that there is an implicit contract between individual organizations and the society in which they operate (Chen and Rothschild 2010). Societal expectations are based upon numerous agreed-upon social norms; thus the survival an organization depends on its ability to meet society's expectations in the fulfilment of this implicit contract (Cho et al. 2015). According to the legitimacy theory, corporate disclosure strategies are therefore used by companies to gain social acceptance (Deegan 2002, 2019).

The shift from mainly voluntary to more mandatory NFI disclosure means the theoretical motivations behind sustainability reporting need to be reconsidered. Legitimacy theory is widely acknowledged as a socio-political theoretical foundation to justify voluntary sustainability reporting (Cho et al. 2012). This theoretical base comes out of a democratic view of the way organization is run, where groups of stakeholders are able to judge and influence an organization's decisions and actions (Archel et al. 2009). Companies voluntarily disclose social and environmental information so their activities will be socially perceived as legitimate (Deegan 2002). Thus, the voluntary adoption of NFI disclosure is a response to stakeholders' expectations and their demand for information so as to confer legitimacy to organizations (O'Donovan 2002).

In a context of mandatory reporting, where the coercive force of the law prevails, companies disclose NFI because they must, and the State plays a role in supporting the ideology for legitimizing NFI (Archel et al. 2009).

In this context, a new theoretical development, that is, material legitimacy, emerged (Dumay et al. 2015). It is a form of legitimacy that blends what is important to the organization (strategic legitimacy) with the primary concerns of the corporate major stakeholders (institutional legitimacy). Under a material legitimacy approach, therefore, organizations try to achieve a mutually beneficial "win-win" outcome for themselves and their stakeholders.

The material legitimacy approach is in our opinion the right theoretical approach to apply in a mandatory context, as the material legitimacy is a model of legitimacy-influenced disclosure based on material legitimacy and transparency to explain what and how NFI is disclosed and in a mandatory context to understand how and what NFI has reported becomes more significant than explaining the motivations and drivers behind NFI disclosure adoption.

In such a context, the EU Directive could be seen as a policy action that provides legitimacy to the NFDs of companies. Coherently with the material legitimacy approach, in the book we argue that companies mandated to communicate NFI to their stakeholders disclose relevant NFI, material for both company and stakeholders.

References

Abraham, S., & Cox, P. (2007). Analysing the determinants of narrative risk information in UK FTSE 100 annual reports. *The British Accounting Review, 39*(3), 227–248.

Abraham, S., & Shrives, P. J. (2014). Improving the relevance of risk factor disclosure in corporate annual reports. *The British Accounting Review, 46*(1), 91–107.

Al-Hadi, A., Hasan, M. M., & Habib, A. (2016). Risk committee, firm life cycle, and market risk disclosures. *Corporate Governance: An International Review, 24*(2), 145–170.

Ali, M. M. (2005). Corporate risk reporting practices in annual reports of Japanese companies. *Journal of Japanese Association for International Accounting Studies, 3*, 113–133.

Allini, A., Rossi, F. M., & Hussainey, K. (2016). The board's role in risk disclosure: An exploratory study of Italian listed state-owned enterprises. *Public Money & Management, 36*(2), 113–120.

Amran, A., Bin, A. M. R., & Hassan, B. C. H. M. (2008). Risk reporting: An exploratory study on risk management disclosure in Malaysian annual reports. *Managerial Auditing Journal, 24*(1), 39–57.

Archel, P., Husillos, J., Larrinaga, C., & Spence, C. (2009). Social disclosure, legitimacy theory and the role of the state. *Accounting, Auditing & Accountability Journal, 22*(8), 1284–1307.

Barakat, A., & Hussainey, K. (2013). Bank governance, regulation, supervision, and risk reporting: Evidence from operational risk disclosures in European banks. *International Review of Financial Analysis, 30*, 254–273.

Bebbington, J., Kirk, E. A., & Larrinaga, C. (2012). The production of normativity: A comparison of reporting regimes in Spain and the UK. *Accounting, Organizations and Society, 37*(2), 78–94.

Benn, S., Dunphy, D., & Griffiths, A. (2006). Enabling Change for Corporate Sustainability: An Integrated Perspective. *Australasian Journal of Environmental Management, 13*(3), 156–165.

Beretta, S., & Bozzolan, S. (2004). A framework for the analysis of firm risk communication. *The International Journal of Accounting, 39*(3), 265–288.

Beretta, S., & Bozzolan, S. (2008). Quality versus quantity: The case of forward-looking disclosure. *Journal of Accounting, Auditing & Finance, 23*(3), 333–376.

Campbell, J. L., Chen, H., Dhaliwal, D. S., Lu, H. M., & Steele, L. B. (2014). The information content of mandatory risk factor disclosures in corporate filings. *Review of Accounting Studies, 19*(1), 396–455.

Chauvey, J., Giordano-Spring, S., Choand, C. H., & Patten, D. M. (2015). The normativity and legitimacy of CSR disclosure: Evidence from France. *Journal of Business Ethics, 130*, 789–803.

Chen, C. F., & Rothschild, R. (2010). An application of hedonic pricing analysis to the case of hotel rooms in Taipei. *Tourism Economics, 16*(3), 685–694.

Cho, C. H., Freedman, M., & Patten, D. M. (2012). Corporate disclosure of environmental capital expenditures. *Accounting, Auditing & Accountability Journal, 25*(3), 486–507.

Cho, C. H., Laine, M., Roberts, R. W., & Rodrigue, M. (2015). Organized hypocrisy, organizational façades, and sustainability reporting. *Accounting, Organizations and Society, 40*, 78–94.

Christofi, A., Christofi, P., & Sisaye, S. (2012). Corporate sustainability: historical development and reporting practices. *Management Research Review, 35*(2), 157–172.

Clarkson, P. M., Fang, X., Li, Y., & Richardson, G. (2013). The relevance of environmental disclosures: Are such disclosures incrementally informative? *Journal of Accounting and Public Policy, 32*(5), 410–431.

Costa, E., & Agostini, M. (2016). Mandatory disclosure about environmental and employee matters in the reports of Italian- listed corporate groups. *Social Environmental and Accountability Journal, 36*, 10–33.

Crawford, E. P., & Williams, C. C. (2010). Should corporate social reporting be voluntary or mandatory? Evidence from the banking sector in France and the United States. *Corporate Governance, 10*, 512–526.

Deegan, C. (2002). The legitimising effect of social and environmental disclosures – a theoretical foundation. *Accounting, Auditing & Accountability Journal, 15*(3), 282–311.

Deegan, M. (2019). Legitimacy theory. *Accounting, Auditing & Accountability Journal, 32*(8), 2307–2329.

Deumes, R., & Knechel, W. R. (2008). Economic incentives for voluntary reporting on internal risk management and control systems. *Auditing: A Journal of Practice & Theory, 27*(1), 35–66.

Di Maggio, P., & Powell, W. (1983). The iron cage revisited: Institutional isomorphism and collective rationality in organizational fields. *American Sociological Review, 48*(2), 147–160.

Dobler, M. (2008). Incentives for risk reporting –a discretionary disclosure and cheap talk approach. *The International Journal of Accounting, 43*, 184–206.

Dobler, M., Lajili, K., & Zéghal, D. (2011). Attributes of corporate risk disclosure: An international investigation in the manufacturing sector. *Journal of International Accounting Research, 10*(2), 1–22.

Domínguez, L. R., & Gámez, L. C. N. (2014). Corporate reporting on risks: Evidence from Spanish companies. *Revista de Contabilidad, 17*(2), 116–129.

Dumay, J. (2016). A critical reflection on the future of intellectual capital: From reporting to disclosure. *Journal of Intellectual Capital, 17*(1), 168–184.

Dumay, J., & Hossain, M. D. A. (2019). Sustainability risk disclosure practices of listed companies in Australia. *Australian Accounting Review, 29*(2), 343–359.

Dumay, J., Frost, G., & Beck, C. (2015). Material legitimacy. *Journal of Accounting and Organizational Change, 11*(1), 2–23.

Dumay, J., La Torre, M., & Farneti, F. (2019). Developing trust through stewardship: Implications for intellectual capital, integrated reporting, and the EU directive 2014/95/EU. *Journal of Intellectual Capital, 20*(1), 11–39.

Dyllick, T., & Hockerts, K. (2002). Beyond the business case for corporate sustainability. *Business Strategy and the Environment, 11*(2), 130–141.

Elshandidy, T., & Neri, L. (2015). Corporate governance, risk disclosure practices, and market liquidity: Comparative evidence from the UK and Italy. *Corporate Governance: An International Review, 23*(4), 331–356.

Elshandidy, T., Fraser, I., & Hussainey, K. (2013). Aggregated, voluntary, and mandatory risk reporting incentives: Evidence from FTSE all-share. *International Review of Financial Analysis, 30*, 320–333.

Elshandidy, T., Fraser, I., & Hussainey, K. (2015). What drives mandatory and voluntary risk reporting variations across Germany, UK, and US? *The British Accounting Review, 47*(4), 376–394.

Elshandidy, T., Shrives, P. J., Bamber, M., & Abraham, S. (2018). Risk reporting: A review of the literature and implications for future research. *Journal of Accounting Literature, 40*, 54–82.

Epstein, M. J., & Buhovac, A. R. (2006). *The reporting of organizational risks for internal and external decision making*. Canada: CMA Canada, AICPA and CIMA. Accessed July 13, 2019, from http://www.zdruzenje-ns.si/db/doc/upl/risk_reporting_epstein_rejc_buhovac.pdf

Freeman, R. E. (1984). *Strategic planning: A stakeholder approach*. Boston, MA: Pitman.

Godfrey, P. C., Merrill, C. B., & Hansen, J. M. (2009). The relationship between corporate social responsibility and shareholder value: An empirical test of the risk management hypothesis. *Strategic Management Journal, 30*(4), 425–445.

Hassan, M. K. (2009). UAE corporation-specific characteristics and level of risk disclosure. *Managerial Auditing Journal, 24*(7), 668–687.

Hess, D. (2007). Social reporting and new governance regulation: The prospects of achieving corporate accountability through transparency. *Business Ethics Quarterly, 17*(3), 453–476.

Hill, P., & Short, H. (2009). Risk disclosures on the second-tier markets of the London Stock Exchange. *Accounting and Finance, 49*(4), 753–780.

Husted, B., & De Jesus Salazar, J. (2006). Taking Friedman seriously: Maximizing profits and social performance. *Journal of Management Studies, 43*(1), 75–91.

ICAEW. (1997). *Financial reporting of risk: Proposals for a statement of business risk*. London: Institute of Chartered Accountants of England and Wales.

ICAEW. (1999). *No surprises: The case for better risk reporting*. London: Institute of Chartered Accountants of England and Wales.

ICAEW. (2002). *No surprises: Working for better risk reporting*. London: The Institute of Chartered Accountants in England and Wales.

ICAEW. (2011). *Reporting business risks: Meeting expectations*. London: Institute of Chartered Accountants of England and Wales.

Ioannou, I., & Serafeim, G. (2014). The impact of corporate social responsibility on investment recommendations: Analysts perceptions and shifting institutional logics. *Strategic Management Journal, 36*(7), 1053–1081.

Ioannou, I., & Serafeim, G. (2015). *The consequences of mandatory corporate sustainability reporting*. Harvard Business School: Boston, MA.

Jensen, M. C., & Meckling, W. H. (1976). Theory of the firm: Managerial behavior, agency costs and ownership structure. *Journal of Financial Economics, 3*(4), 305–360.

Konishi, N., & Ali, M. M. (2007). Risk reporting of Japanese companies and its association with corporate characteristics. *International Journal of Accounting, Auditing and Performance Evaluation, 4*(3), 263–285.

KPMG. (2015). *Currents of change; The KPMG survey of corporate responsibility reporting 2015*. Amstelveen: KPMG.

La Torre, M., Sabelfeld, S., Blomkvist, M., Tarquinio, L., & Dumay, J. (2018). Harmonising non-financial reporting regulation in Europe: Practical forces and projections for future research. *Meditari Accountancy Research, 26*(4), 598–621.

Lajili, K., & Zeghal, D. (2005). A content analysis of risk management disclosure in Canadian annual reports. *Canadian Journal of Administrative Sciences, 22*(2), 125–142.

Linsley, P. M., & Shrives, P. J. (2005). Examining risk reporting in UK public companies. *The Journal of Risk Finance, 6*(4), 292–305.

Linsley, P., & Shrives, P. (2006). Risk reporting: A study of risk disclosure in the annual reports of UK companies. *The British Accounting Review, 38*(4), 387–404.

Locke, I., & Seele, P. (2016). The credibility of CSR (corporate social responsibility) reports in Europe: Evidence from a quantitative content analysis in 11 countries. *Journal of Cleaner Production, 122*, 186–200.

Louhichi, W., & Zreik, O. (2015). Corporate risk reporting: A study of the impact of risk disclosure on firms reputation. *Economic Bulletin, 35*(4), 2395–2408.

Luque-Vílchez, M., & Larrinaga, C. (2016). Reporting models do not translate well: Failing to regulate CSR reporting in Spain. *Social and Environmental Accountability Journal, 36*(1), 56–75.

Malafronte, I., Porzio, C., & Starita, M. G. (2016). The nature and determinants of disclosure practices in the insurance industry: Evidence from European insurers. *International Review of Financial Analysis, 45*, 367–382.

Manes Rossi, F., Tiron-Tudor, A., Nicolò, G., & Zanellato, G. (2018). Ensuring more sustainable reporting in Europe using non-financial disclosure—De Facto and De Jure evidence. *Sustainability, 10*(1162), 1–20.

Marshall, A., & Weetman, P. (2007). Modelling transparency in disclosure: The case of foreign exchange risk management. *Journal of Business Finance & Accounting, 34*(5–6), 705–738.

Matten, D. (1995). Strategy follows structure: Environmental risk management in commercial enterprises. *Business Strategy and the Environment, 4*, 107–116.

Mazumder, M. M. M., & Hossain, D. M. (2018). Research on corporate risk reporting: Current trends and future avenues. *Journal of Asian Finance, Economics and Business, 5*(1), 29–41.
Miihkinen, A. (2012). What drives the quality of firm risk disclosure? *The International Journal of Accounting, 47*(4), 437–468.
Miihkinen, A. (2013). The usefulness of firm risk disclosures under different firm riskiness, investor-interest, and market conditions: New evidence from Finland. *Advances in Accounting, 29*(2), 312–331.
Milne, M. J., & Gray, R. (2007). Future prospects for corporate sustainability reporting. *Sustainability Accounting and Accountability, 1*, 184–207.
Mokhtar, E. S., & Mellett, H. (2013). Competition, corporate governance, ownership structure and risk reporting. *Managerial Auditing Journal, 28*(9), 838–865.
Nahar, S., Azim, M., & Jubb, C. A. (2016a). Risk disclosure, cost of capital and bank performance. *International Journal of Accounting and Information Management, 24*(4), 476–494.
Nahar, S., Azim, M., & Jubb, C. (2016b). The determinants of risk disclosure by banking institutions: Evidence from Bangladesh. *Asian Review of Accounting, 24*(4), 426–444.
Ntim, C. G., Lindop, S., & Thomas, D. A. (2013). Corporate governance and risk reporting in South Africa: A study of corporate risk disclosures in the pre-and post-2007/2008 global financial crisis periods. *International Review of Financial Analysis, 30*, 363–383.
O'Donovan, G. (2002). Environmental disclosures in the annual report. *Accounting, Auditing & Accountability Journal, 15*(3), 344–371.
Oliveira, J., Lima Rodrigues, L., & Craig, R. (2011). Risk-related disclosures by non-finance companies: Portuguese practices and disclosure characteristics. *Managerial Auditing Journal, 26*(9), 817–839.
Patten, D. (1992). Intra-industry environmental disclosures in response to the Alaskan oil spill: A note on legitimacy theory. *Accounting, Organisations and Society, 17*(5), 471–475.
Pfeffer, J., & Salancik, G. R. (2003). *The external control of organizations: A resource dependence perspective*. Stanford, CA: Standard University Press.
Plumlee, M., Brown, D., Hayes, R. M., & Marshall, R. S. (2015). Voluntary environmental disclosure quality and firm value: Further evidence. *Journal of Accounting and Public Policy, 34*(4), 336–361.
Probohudono, A. N., Tower, G., & Rusmin, R. (2013). Risk disclosure during global financial crisis. *Social Responsibility Journal, 9*(1), 124–137.
Quinn, J., & Connolly, B. (2017). The non-financial information directive: An assessment of its impact on corporate social responsibility. *European Company Law, 14*(1), 15–21.
Saggar, R., & Singh, B. (2017). Corporate governance and risk reporting: Indian evidence. *Managerial Auditing Journal, 32*(4/5), 378–405.
Shocker, A. D., & Sethi, S. P. (1973). An approach to incorporating societal preferences in developing corporate action strategies. *California Management Review, 15*(4), 97–105.
Spence, M. (1973). Job market signaling. *The Quarterly Journal of Economics, 87*(3), 355–374.
Suchman, M. C. (1995). Managing legitimacy: Strategic and institutional approaches. *Academy of Management Review, 20*(3), 571–610.
Tahat, Y., Dunne, T., Fifield, S., & Power, D. (2019). Risk related disclosure: A review of the literature and an agenda for future research. *Accounting Forum, 43*, 193. https://doi.org/10.1080/01559982.2019.1584953.
Task Force on Climate-related Financial Disclosures (TCFD). (2016). *Recommendations of the task force on climate related financial disclosures*. Basel: Financial Stability Board.
Taylor, G., Tower, G., & Neilson, J. (2010). Corporate communication of financial risk. *Accounting and Finance, 50*(2), 417–446.
Truant, E., Corazza, L., & Scagnelli, D. S. (2017). Sustainability and risk disclosure: An exploratory study on sustainability reports. *Sustainability, 9*(636), 1–20.
Venturelli, A., Caputo, F., Cosma, S., Leopizzi, R., & Pizzi, S. (2017). Directive 2014/95/EU: Are Italian companies already compliant? *Sustainability, 9*(1385), 1–20.

Venturelli, A., Caputo, F., Leopizzi, R., & Pizzi, S. (2019). The state of art of corporate social disclosure before the introduction of non-financial reporting directive: A cross country analysis. *Social Responsibility Journal, 15*(4), 409–423.

Verrecchia, R. E. (1983). Discretionary disclosure. *Journal of Accounting and Economics, 5*, 179–194.

Wahlen, J., Baginski, S., & Bradshaw, M. (2014). *Financial reporting, financial statement analysis and valuation*. Boston, MA: Nelson Education.

Wang, K. T., & Li, D. (2015). Market reactions to the first-time disclosure of corporate social responsibility reports: Evidence from China. *Journal of Business Ethics, 138*(4), 1–22.

Weinhofer, G., & Busch, T. (2013). Corporate strategies for managing climate risks. *Business Strategy and the Environment, 22*, 121–144.

Chapter 3
The Mandatory Non-financial Disclosure in the European Union

3.1 Introduction

In the chapter we focus on the path that led to the issuing of the 2014/95/EU Directive (hereafter EU Directive), and then we deeply analyse two important supranational initiatives, GRI and Integrated Reporting, and their relationships with the EU Directive. The chapter also provides a brief analysis of EU Directive, before examining deeply the Italian Legislative Decree 254/2016 which enacted the EU Directive in the Italian context. The chapter ends with the analysis of the sample on which we carried out our research, preceded by a summary of the main studies on the mandatory NFI disclosure in the Italian context.

3.2 The Historical Milestones Towards the EU Directive

In Europe, until recently, NF risk information was provided largely voluntarily (Dobler 2008), steering literature mainly to investigating why, and to what extent, firms disclose risk information (Elshandidy et al. 2018). With the issuing of the EU Directive in 2014, and its following adoption within EU countries, large public interest entities (PIEs) have been obliged to disclose, in their annual report or in a separate document, some important NF information, among which NF risk-related information.

The 2014/95/EU Directive could be seen as a key milestone in the NFI disclosure. With the EU Directive, the disclosure become mandatory, introducing a novelty for the European countries, where NFI disclosure was voluntary and the practices in relation to this disclosure were diverse in each European country. Before the EU Directive came into force, a quite long history of voluntary and semi-compulsory

S. Veltri, *Mandatory Non-financial Risk-Related Disclosure*,
https://doi.org/10.1007/978-3-030-47921-3_3

schemes enacted by international organizations and governments has covered the last three decades.

Table 3.1 shows the milestones of this path with regard to both the international and European scenario (Herzig and Kühn 2017).

In Table 3.1 *Character* defines whether the initiative establishes voluntary (V) or mandatory (M) requirements. *NF themes addressed* defines the NF topics covered by the initiative, namely, P (Policies and/or processes); Env (Environment); S (Social); E (Employee and labour); H (Human rights); A (Anti-corruption); and D (Diversity). *Scope* defines if the scope of the initiative is global (GL) or only related to the European Union (EU).

Table 3.1 shows clearly that Directive 2014/95/EU cannot be considered a sporadic intervention by the EU, but the outcome of a systematic process addressed to harmonize the accountability practices.

The main aim of the EU Directive is, in fact, to create an increasingly transparent European economic area to guarantee the interests of all stakeholders who are concerned with the behaviour of corporations and to prevent the risk of any abuse of power or conflicts of interest (La Torre et al. 2018).

The EU Directive is an act of policy to legitimize NFI disclosure with two main aims, that is, improve the comparability of information and enhance corporate accountability among European countries answering to the stakeholders' needs.

3.3 The EU Directive: Main Content

The European Union Directive 2014/95 on non-financial and diversity information was issued by the European Parliament to establish the mandatory 'disclosure of non-financial information (NFI) in respect of certain large undertakings [which] is of importance for the interests of undertakings, shareholders and other stakeholders' (European Union 2014).

Thus, the EU Directive represents an important regulatory move towards harmonizing the non-financial reporting (NFR) practices of all European Member States and marks a shift in NFR from a voluntary exercise to one that is mandatory for the undertakings concerned.

In the intention of the Legislator, the introduction of mandatory requirements by the Directive 2014/95/EU and the related guidelines issued in 2017 that operationalize how to prepare mandatory non-financial information can improve the quality and credibility of non-financial information and increase the comprehensiveness of non-financial information (EU Commission 2017). Table 3.2 highlights the main phases of the EU Directive.

The term 'non-financial information' is ambiguous and really wide, as it specifically refers to disclosing information about society and the environment (Haller et al. 2017). The Directive requires certain companies to produce an annual non-financial statement that divulges 'information on sustainability, such as social and environmental factors, with a view to identifying sustainability risks and

Table 3.1 Historical milestones towards the Directive 2014/95/EU

Year	Initiative	Character	NF themes addressed	Scope
1993	Eco-Management and Audit Scheme (EMAS)	V	P, Env	EU
1996	ISO 14001	V	P, Env	GL
1999	AA1000 Framework Standard	V	P, Env, S, E	GL
2000	GRI Sustainability Reporting Guidelines	V	P, Env, S, E	GL
2000	EU Financial Reporting Strategy: The Way Forward COM(2000)359	M	P	GL
2000	United Nations Global Compact (UNGC) Foundation	V	Env, S, E, H, A	GL
2000	Carbon Disclosure Project (CDP) Foundation	V	Env	GL
2001	GHG Protocol Standards	V	P, Env	GL
2001	Commission Recommendation on the recognition, measurement and disclosure of environmental issues in the annual accounts and annual reports of companies (2001/453/EC)	M	Env	EU
2001	SA8000	V	P, S, E, H, A, D	GL
2001	EMAS revision (EC No 761/2001)	V	P, Env	EU
2002	GRI G2 Guidelines (update)	V	P, Env, S, E, H, A, D	GL
2003	Accounts Modernization Directive (2003/51/EC)	M	P, Env, S, E	EU
2003	AA1000 Assurance Standard	V	P	GL
2004	GHG Protocol Standards (update)	V	P, Env	GL
2004	ISO 14001 (update)	V	P, Env	GL
2005	AA1000 Stakeholder Engagement Standard	V	P	GL
2006	GRI G3 Guidelines (update)	V	P, Env, S, E, H, A, D	GL
2008	AA1000 Assurance Standard (update)	V	P	GL
2008	AA1000 AccountAbility Principles Separate Standard	V	P	GL
2008	SA8000: 2008 (update)	V	Env, E, H, D	GL
2009	EMAS revision (EC No 1221/2009)	V	P, Env	EU
2010	ISO 26000	V	P, Env, S, E, H, A, D	GL
2011	GRI G3.1 Guidelines (update)	V	P, Env, S, E, H, A, D	GL
2011	Guiding Principles on Business and Human Rights	V	P, S, E, H, D	GL
2012	Rio + 20 Declaration explicit references to nonfinancial reporting paragraph 47	V	P, Env, S, E, H, A	GL

(continued)

Table 3.1 (continued)

Year	Initiative	Character	NF themes addressed	Scope
2013	GRI G4 Guidelines (update)	V	P, Env, S, E, H, A, D	GL
2013	Directive 2013/34/EU	M	P	EU
2013	International Integrated Reporting Framework	V	P, Env, S, E, H, A, D	GL
2014	Directive 2014/95/EU	M	P, Env, S, E, H, A, D	EU

Source: our elaboration from Mion and Loza Adaui (2019)

Table 3.2 The main phases of the EU Directive

Ex ante phases	Type	Content
Phase 1	Public consultations	(a) Public consultation on disclosure of NFI (b) Multi-stakeholder roundtables (c) Constitution of expert group (d) External study on the topic
Phase 2	Problem definition	(a) Inadequate transparency of NFI (in terms of both quantity and quality) (b) Lack of diversity in the board
Phase 3	Policy objectives	(a) To increase the number of companies reporting on sustainability issues (b) To increase the quality of information (c) To enhance the board diversity
Phase 4	Regulatory policy options	(a) No policy change (b) NF statement in the annual report with minimum requirements on the content (c) Detailed reporting (mandatory, report or explain, voluntary) (d) Creation of an EU reporting standard
Phase 5	Analysis of the impact assessment of the regulatory policy chosen (b)	(a) Expected benefit (b) Estimated costs (c) Other impacts (social, environmental, etc.)
EU Directive	Directive 2014/95/EU	Non-financial and diversity disclosure
Ex post phase		Implementation in each Member State compliance with EU requirements
Phase 6	Monitoring and evaluation	

Source: our elaboration from Carini et al. (2018)

increasing investor and consumer trust' (European Union 2014, p. 2). The annual non-financial statement receiving the NFI could be included in the management commentary or be an autonomous document, assuming the form of a sustainability or an integrated report.

Table 3.3 Matters and issues to disclose following the EU Directive

General matters	Issues to disclose
Business model	A brief description of the undertaking's business model
Comply or explain	The explanation for not having a relevant sustainability policy or for not disclosing certain information
Assurance	The information of the use (or not) of external assurance
Sustainability matters	
Environmental Social Employee Human rights Anti-corruption and bribery	• The description of the policies (including due diligence process implemented) • The outcomes of these policies • The risks related to these matters (and how the company manage those risks)
Diversity matters	
Diversity	• The information relating to age, gender, educational and professional backgrounds • The policy objectives of the diversity and their implementation • The results of this implementation in the reporting period

Source: our elaboration

The purpose of the Directive is thus to harmonize the laws of each Member State by establishing some minimum requirements for the types of NFI that larger companies (undertakings) and public interest entities (PIEs) must publicly divulge to their investors, consumers and other stakeholders, with the aim to 'enhance the consistency and comparability of NFI disclosed' (European Union 2014).[1]

According to the EU Directive, the NFI to be included is essentially 'information to the extent necessary for an understanding of the development, performance, position and impact of the activity of the undertaking, relating to, as a minimum, environmental, social and employee matters, with respect for human rights, anti-corruption and bribery matters, including (European Union 2014, pp.4–5; Leopizzi et al. 2020): '(a) a brief description of the business model of the undertaking; (b) a description of the policies pursued by the undertaking in relation to those matters, including due diligence processes implemented; (c) the outcome of those policies; (d) the principal risks related to those matters linked to the operations of the undertaking, including, where relevant and proportionate, its business relationships, products or services which are likely to cause adverse impacts in those areas, and how the undertaking manages those risks; (e) non-financial key performance indicators important to the particular business".

Table 3.3 summarizes the EU Directive's matters and issues to disclose.

[1]It is important to underline that harmonization differs from standardization, as international standardization pushes countries to share the same accounting standards, whilst accounting harmonization results in 'pressures to bring the accounting standards of different countries into closer harmony with one another' (Thorell and Whittington 1994).

It remains debated in the literature whether making mandatory the NFI disclosure for large companies effectively enhances corporate accountability and transparency, favouring stakeholders' trust. Regulating NFI does not always mean better reporting or improvements to corporate accountability. The question as to whether NF disclosure is actually a reflection of corporate reality or mere rhetoric to manipulate stakeholders, that is, if is used in a substantive or symbolic form (Merkl-Davies and Brennan 2007; Michelon et al. 2015), continues to persist in the context of the Directive (La Torre et al. 2018).

In our study we thus want to fill the gap, if any, between NF disclosure talk and corporate action by questioning the usefulness of mandatory NFI disclosure (in detail NF risk-related information disclosure) by classifying risk-related information disclosure to assess its quality and then investigating the usefulness of such information disclosure for stakeholders in making investment decisions.

3.4 The GRI Initiative and the Relationships with the EU Directive

The issuing of the GRI guidelines was the turning point for the development of sustainability disclosure (Manes Rossi et al. 2018). GRI guidelines pushed NFI disclosure practices from a spot phenomenon to a systematic activity involving strategic aspects, such as corporate risk and opportunities, anti-corruption, corporate governance and fraud matters management (Milne and Gray 2007; Cho and Patten 2007; Patten et al. 2015).

By following GRI guidelines, disclosing organizations provided their stakeholders with reliable, important and standardized NFI (GRI 2013). As the GRI states, 'by using the GRI guidelines, reporting organizations disclose their most critical impacts—be they positive or negative—on the environment, society and the economy. They can generate reliable, relevant and standardized information with which to assess opportunities and risks, and enable more informed decision-making—both within the business and among its stakeholders' (GRI 2013).

As for the relationship between EU Directive and GRI standards, we can say that both consider the disclosure of NFI separately from financial information and both are stakeholder oriented.[2]

Table 3.4 compares GRI and EU Directive under five different profiles that are the materiality principle, impacts in the value chain, the exception and omission, the external assurance and the continuous improvement. The concept of materiality is

[2]For a description of the common themes, the areas of alignment between EU Directive and GRI standards and the possibility to use GRI standards to comply with EU Directive requirements, see GRI (2017).

Table 3.4 Areas of alignment between EU Directive and GRI standards

Areas	EU Directive	GRI standards
The significance of materiality	The EU Directive requires undertakings to provide adequate information in relation to matters that stand out as being most likely to bring about the materialization of principal risks of severe impacts, along with those that have already materialized	Under the materiality principle of the GRI, material topics are determined as those which reflect the organization significant economic, environmental and/or social impacts or which substantially influence the assessments and decisions of its stakeholders
Impacts in the value chain	The severity of an actual or potential impact of a material sustainability subject should be judged by their scale and gravity. The risks of adverse impact may stem from the undertaking's own activities or may be linked to its operations and, where relevant and proportionate, its products, services and business relationships, including its supply and subcontracting chains	The GRI standards place a great emphasis on due diligence processes and the value chain. Organizations are asked to report on not only impacts they cause directly but also those they contribute to or are linked to via business relationships, such as with suppliers or customers
Exceptions and omissions	The EU Directive gives governments the option to allow companies not to disclose information related to impending developments or matters under negotiation (comply or explain principle)	GRI recognizes that in exceptional cases it may not be possible to disclose certain information. In those cases, a report is expected to clearly identify the information that has been omitted, along with the specific reason for omission
External assurance	The EU Directive allows Member States to decide whether independent assurance of the disclosed information is a requirement	GRI recommends external assurance, but it is not required for a report to be considered in accordance with the GRI standards
Continuous improvement	The Directive is careful to encourage further improvements to the transparency of the NFI of undertakings	The GRI standards offer the flexibility needed to support organizations as they transition from being first-time reporters to developing a more comprehensive and meaningful sustainability reporting practice

Source: our elaboration based on GRI (2017)

the basis of NF disclosure[3] and means that information should be provided in 'relation to matters that stand out as being most likely to bring about the materialization of principal risks of severe impacts, along with those that have already materialized' (EU Directive 2014). Extending a materiality assessment to include the value chain helps an organization to understand where its biggest impacts occur, regardless of whether those impacts are within its direct control. This principle, heavily influenced by the UN Guiding Principles on Business and Human Rights,

[3]The other principles are 'fair, balanced and understandable'; 'comprehensive but concise'; 'strategic and forward-looking'; 'stakeholder oriented'; and 'consistent and coherent' (EU Commission 2017).

aims to ensure that the outsourcing of production does not permit the outsourcing of responsibility. The exception and omission refers to acknowledging circumstances in which it may not be possible to disclose certain information. The external assurance analyses whether the two initiatives impose or not to assure the NF statement, whilst the continuous improvement analyses the attitude towards the NFI disclosure of the two initiatives.

Conversely, the GRI framework appears to be more demanding than the EU Directive, containing a long list of requirements that preparers have to fulfil. Differences could also be underlined in the significance of the materiality principle, in the importance given to the business model (not so important for GRI guidelines) and in the key performance indicators and human right policies, much more detailed in GRI guidelines than in the EU Directive (Manes Rossi et al. 2018).

3.5 The IIRC Initiative and the Relationships with EU Directive

Both EU Directive and IIRC initiative date back to the end of the 2000s. The origins of the EU Directive date back to the EU Workshops on ESG disclosure hosted by DG Enterprise between September 2009 and February 2010. These workshops constituted the first tangible sign that the EU Commission had changed strategy on CSR and regulation, as a consequence of the financial crisis. For the first time, the Barroso Commission opened the discussion on CSR highlighting that all stakeholders—not just investors and businesses—should participate in the workshops (Commission 2009).

As for the IIRC initiative, the origin could be dated back to a meeting that was held in London in December 2009, hosted by The Prince of Wales' organization, and Accounting for Sustainability Project (A4S), to which intervened some of the key actors in the field of both financial and non-financial accounting. In this meeting emerged the plan to establish the International Connected Reporting Committee, the first embryo of the future International Integrated Reporting Council (IIRC).

Since the beginning, the two set of reporting rules have advanced in parallel, dealing with the same major questions in different ways, maintaining a hidden dialogue but also formal distance (Monciardini et al. 2017).

The year 2011 was important for both initiatives. As for the EU Directive, following a public consultation (November 2010 and February 2011), which attracted over 300 responses, in April 2011, the EU Commission officially announced that it 'will present a legislative proposal on the transparency of the social and environmental information provided by companies in all sectors' (Commission 2011). As for the IIRC initiative, in November 2011, the IIRC started to operate through a not-for-profit company, established under the same name with the purpose to develop an internationally accepted integrated reporting framework (IIRF) by 2014.

Table 3.5 The main landmarks of EU Directive and IIRF

Years	EU Directive	IIRF
2009/ 2010	September 2009 and February 2010: two EU Workshops on ESG disclosure hosted by DG Enterprise, in which for the first time, the discussion on CSR was opened to all stakeholders	December 2009: meeting held in London, hosted by The Prince of Wales' organization, and Accounting for Sustainability Project (A4S), aiming to establish the International Connected Reporting Committee
2011	April 2011: The EU Commission officially announced that it 'will present a legislative proposal on the transparency of the social and environmental information provided by companies in all sectors'	November 2011: started to operate through a not-for-profit company, established under the same name, with the purpose to develop an internationally accepted integrated reporting framework (IIRF) by 2014
2013/ 2014	April 2014: The EU parliament backed by the EU Directive	December 2013: the IIRC published the IIRF

Source: our elaboration based on Monciardini et al. (2017)

The year 2013 saw the two initiatives progressing in parallel. In April 2013, the IIRC's consultation draft framework was published on the same day as the draft EU Directive proposal on company non-financial reporting was presented by the EU Commission. The final acts were the publication, in December 2013, of the International Integrated Reporting Framework (IIRF), and, in April 2014, the EU non-financial Directive was backed by the EU parliament. Table 3.5 synthesizes the main landmarks of the two initiatives.

We briefly illustrated the EU Directive in the 3.3 section, whilst we need to pinpoint the main features of IIRF to compare the two initiatives.

The purpose of the IIRF is to establish Guiding Principles and Content Elements that govern the overall content of an integrated report. Seven are the IIRF principles, (A) strategic focus and future orientation; (B) connectivity of information; (C) stakeholder relationships; (D) materiality; (E) conciseness; (F) reliability and completeness; and (G) consistency and comparability, among which materiality plays the most relevant role. The focus of IIRF is to focus on the value creation processes of the company, that is, to explain how an entity creates value, increasing decreasing and transforming its capitals (financial, manufactured, intellectual, human, social, natural). This means that the disclosure of the corporate strategy and of its business model is at the heart of the IIRF.

IIRF and EU Directive are distinct yet complementary initiatives, characterized by similarities but also differences. The main similarity point is that both aim to expand the boundaries of corporate accounting regulation, including the environment in which the firm operates. Anyway, the EU Directive is a public law, which mandates to disclose NFI, whilst the IR initiative is a market-driven initiative; it is not prescriptive; it is not a set of rules; it is not about compliance (KPMG 2013). Table 3.6 highlights the main differences between the two initiatives in relation to the rationale, the aim, the audience, the focus and the NFI to disclose.

Table 3.6 The main differences between EU Directive and IIRF

	EU Directive	IIRF
Rationale	It is based on the *right to know* about the positive or negative impact that large corporations have on the environment and local communities in which they operate	It is in line with the Anglo-American approach to accounting and business economics, seen as a true and fair view of the financial performance and position of an entity
Aim	To address the failure of existing accounting rules to respond to *broader societal, environmental and economic needs* that go beyond shareholder interests	To enable a more efficient and productive allocation of capital
Audience	All entity stakeholders	Providers of financial capital
Focus	The capacity of the firm to create (shareholder) value exploiting internal and external social, natural and economic resources (capitals)	The internal and external social, natural and economic impacts of the activities of the firm
NFI to disclose	The EU Directive focuses on environmental and social disclosures	Integrated reporting is about the integration by companies of financial, environmental, social and other information in a comprehensive and coherent manner

Source: our elaboration based on Monciardini et al. (2017)

3.6 Comparing the Three Initiatives

The three initiatives (EU Directive, GRI standards and IR framework) could be compared under five different profiles: the relationship between financial and NFI disclosure, the location of NF information, the audience, the rigidity of the content and the materiality principle (Manes Rossi et al. 2018).

The EU Directive requires large undertakings either to disclose non-financial information in the management commentary or to include the required information 'in a separate report' (EU Commission 2017). The GRI suggests preparing a Sustainability Report, by following principles provided in its standards. Essentially, both the EU Directive and the GRI consider the disclosure of non-financial information separately from financial information. Instead the IR framework requires companies to issue a combined report about 'how the strategy, governance, performance and prospects of an organization, in the context of its external environment, lead to the creation of value over the short-, medium- and long-term' (IIRC 2013). Following this approach, a combination of financial and non-financial information of the performance of a company should be provided by preparing an integrated report (Eccles and Saltzman 2011; Jensen and Berg 2012).

The aim of the EU Directive is 'to help companies disclose high quality, important, useful, consistent and more comparable non-financial (environmental, social and governance-related) information in a way that fosters resilient and sustainable growth and employment, and provides transparency to stakeholders' (European Commission 2017). In the same vein, the purpose of the GRI 4 guidelines is to

Table 3.7 Comparing EU Directive, GRI standards and IR framework

Areas	EU Directive	GRI standards	IR framework
Financial and NFI disclosure	Separate	Separate	Combined
Location of NFI	In the management commentary or in a separate report	Sustainability report according to GRI standards	Integrated report
Audience	Stakeholder oriented	Stakeholder oriented	Investor oriented
Content	Flexible	Rigid (strict lists to respect)	Flexible
Materiality principle	A company should focus on providing an information that useful for stakeholders to understand its development, performance, position and activities' impact	A material information is an information based on a wide range of impacts and stakeholders	A material information is an information focused on fewer and more strategic issues

Source: our elaboration

'offer Reporting Principles, Standard Disclosures and an Implementation Manual for the preparation of sustainability reports by organizations, regardless of their size, sector or location. The GRI guidelines also offer an international reference for all those interested in the disclosure of governance approach and of the environmental, social and economic performance and impacts of organizations' (GRI 2013). Differently, the IIRF focuses on investors and aims to improve the 'quality of information available to providers of financial capital to enable a more efficient and productive allocation of capital' (IIRC 2013).

The most 'demanding' framework is that one proposed by the GRI, as it contains a long list of requirements that must be fulfilled by the preparers, whilst the other two frameworks do not set detailed requirements about the information to disclose (Skouloudis et al. 2009). Finally, there is a principle of NFI disclosure that deserves specific attention for its importance and because it differentiates its meaning along the three initiatives, the materiality principle. According to the GRI 4 guidelines (GRI 2013), materiality should include all aspects reflecting the significant economic, environmental and social impacts of the organization or substantially influencing the assessments and decisions of stakeholders (Lai et al. 2017). The concept of materiality in the EU Directive refers to the importance of the impact (positive or adverse) on the activity of the company, and it requires consideration of the specific context and circumstances of the company. For the IR framework, materiality means to focus on 'fewer and more strategic issues' (Stubbs and Higgins 2014). The IR framework proposes a four-step process of identification of those important matters that have, or may have, an effect on the ability of the organization to create value by considering their effects on the strategy, governance, performance or prospects of the organization (IIRC 2013).

Table 3.7 summarizes the differences between these three initiatives.

3.7 The EU Directive and the Reporting Frameworks

From a practical perspective, the Directive establishes that, to comply with the law, undertakings can either produce a new standalone non-financial statement or disclose the required NFI in their annual report (European Union 2014). The Directive mostly focuses on the type of information that must be disclosed, but includes very little information about the positioning of NFI disclosure, which is a significant acknowledgement of the importance of information over reporting (La Torre et al. 2018).

In detail, the EU Directive requires the non-financial statement to be included in the management report. However, this claim is not final because the EU Directive also makes it possible to use a separate report, but 'the report must be published at the same time as the management report or not later than 6 months after the balance sheet date and is referred to in the management report'. In other words, the external reader must understand clearly the path to follow for gaining access to the information. In conclusion, the EU Directive allows two reporting systems to be maintained, with a reference in the management report to publication of the autonomous report. On this point the EU Guidelines (2017) clarify that this approach is based on the connectivity of information, so there could be different sources of information but they must be inter-related.[4]

Despite the Directive of the EU promise of harmonizing NFI in practice, undertakings can choose from a multitude of international and national reporting frameworks to comply with the law, which is unlikely to improve the comparability of information.

A recent position paper by the Federation of European Accountants (FEE) (2016) acknowledges nine international frameworks and guidelines as appropriate for complying with the Directive, over more than 30 international frameworks for sustainability reporting (Brown et al. 2009). These frameworks also are the Global Reporting Initiative (GRI), the International Integrated Reporting Council (IIRC), the Sustainability Accounting Standards Board (SASB), AccountAbility (AA), the United Nations Global Compact (UNGC), the Organisation for Economic Co-operation and Development (OECD), the European Federation of Financial Analysts Societies (EFFAS), the International Standards Organisation (ISO) and a recent framework, named 'Core and More' for integrating NFI into corporate reporting, promoted by FFE (2015).

Table 3.8 presents these nine frameworks/guidelines together with their main aims.

[4]The NF stated the NFS 'may include internal cross-references or signposting in order to be concise, limit repetition, and provide links to other information ... but cross-referencing and signposting should be smart and user-friendly, for instance, by applying a practical rule of "maximum one 'click' out of the report"' (EU Commission 2017).

Table 3.8 The international frameworks/guidelines for NFI disclosures

Frameworks/guidelines	Main aims
GRI (since 1997)	To provide a harmonized and clear methodology for reporting of NFI To make information comparable
IIRC (since 2010)	To integrate financial with NFI that would show how value-relevant information fits into the operations of organizations
SASB (since 2011)	To develop sustainability standards consistent with financial regulation
AA (since 1999)	To provide organizations with a set of principles to frame and structure the way in which they understand, govern, administer, implement, evaluate and communicate their accountability
UNGC (since 2000)	To embed the 10 UNGC principles in markets and corporate board-rooms, for the benefit of both businesses and society around the world
OECD (since 1999)	To provide non-binding principles and standards for responsible business conduct in a global context consistent with applicable laws and internationally recognized standards
EFFAS (since 2010)	To provide a basis for the integration of CSR data into corporate performance reporting
ISO 26000 (since 2010)	To improve the reliability of undertakings' CSR communication and transparency and to give a common and universal basis of CSR concepts and methodologies
FEE core and more (since 2015)	To enable corporate reporting in a smarter way, organizing financial and NFI based on the interests of users

Source: our elaboration from FFE (2016)

Among these frameworks, the EU Directive specifically mentions (in paragraph no. 9 of the preamble) the Global Reporting Initiative G.R.I. G4; the UN's Global Compact; and the OECD's Guidelines for Multinational Enterprises.

For their relevance, as companies mostly use GRI guidelines or IRC framework when deciding to disclose NFI with an autonomous document, we briefly comment in the section the GRI framework and the IRC framework.

The GRI guidelines were one of the earliest frameworks. After the first GRI guidelines were released in 2000, the number of standalone GRI reports increased steadily and significantly (Crisóstomo et al. 2017). The GRI established itself as the best standard for sustainability reporting (Tschopp and Nastanski 2014), and it is widely chosen by companies as the reference standard for their sustainability reports as it is a multi-stakeholder-oriented framework. The GRI guidelines were in fact developed for the purpose of extending a legitimate financial accounting framework to encompass NFI and, thereby, address a broader audience of stakeholders. By addressing a broader stakeholder audience in sustainability reports, companies aim to gain or repair legitimacy (Buhr et al. 2014).

Frameworks for integrated reporting, such as IIRF, evolved as a response to criticisms of standalone sustainability reporting (Stubbs and Higgins 2015). The IIRF provides a principles-based framework for an integrated form of reporting where the links between a company's strategy, its business model, its governance and its performance reveal how a company creates value over time (IIRC 2013).

The IIRF framework is supported by the policymakers and politicians involved in the enactment of the EU Directive, even if the lack of prescriptions and disclosure rules in the IIRF represents a significant barrier in the process of implementing the goal of the Directive to harmonize NF disclosure and make NFI comparable across European companies (Dumay et al. 2017).

As a principles-based framework, the IIRF only provides general principles and content elements, which companies might interpret differently (Flower 2015). Examples of this are the different interpretations in practice of the materiality principle (Lai et al. 2017) and of the conciseness principle, which can be misinterpreted by companies in the sense of not disclosing important information when producing integrated reports (du Toit et al. 2017).

3.8 The Italian Legislative Decree 254/2016

The EU Directive is now in force, and each Member State has completed the process of transposing the Directive into its own local laws and, in 2018, each impacted undertaking had to produce a non-financial statement to comply. As for the reporting form, the EU Directive is flexible in terms of how it can be transposed into different local contexts by the States. Thus, there is no particular guidance regarding which frameworks and guidelines should be used for the NF Directive. The next section explores the implementation of EU Directive in a big European industrialized country, Italy, one of the leading countries in voluntary corporate social responsibility (CSR) reporting at an international level (Rossi and Tarquinio 2017).

Table 3.9 highlights the main milestones in the Italian context which led to the enactment of the Legislative Decree 254/2016.

As we can see in the table, Italy is a country in which there was a mandatory legislation for NFI before the adoption of the EU Directive. National standards to guide companies to disclose social issues have been enacted by the GBS (Gruppo di studio per il Bilancio Sociale), whose mission is related to the development and promotion of scientific research on the Social Report and on issues linked to responsible management processes of companies in order to encourage the dissemination of corporate social responsibility and its application in national and international contexts (GBS 2019).

On June 8, 2001, Italian legislators enacted Legislative Decree number 231 (Decree 231/2001), which introduced the principle of administrative liability, by which Italian companies and select employees (e.g. managers) are held directly (personally) liable for corporate crimes in Italy or abroad, whether committed or attempted as a result of the self-interest of corporate executives, employees and external collaborators of the company. Companies were encouraged to voluntarily disclose organizational, managerial and internal control models that are likely to prevent corporate crime. Decree 231/2001 thus urged companies to adopt corporate governance structures to address agency problems and risk prevention systems, in

Table 3.9 Historical milestones towards the Legislative Decree 254/2016

Year	Initiative	Character	NF themes addressed	Scope
2001	Standard GBS 2001—Principi di redazione del bilancio sociale	V	P, Env, S, E	IT
2001	Legislative Decree 231/2001	V	P, A	IT
2007	Legislative Decree 32/2007 (implementing Directive 2003/51/EC)	M	P, Env, S, E	IT
2013	Standard GBS 2001—Principi di redazione del bilancio sociale	V	P, Env, S, E	IT
2014	Directive 2014/95/EU	M	P, Env, S, E, H, A, D	EU
2016	Legislative Decree 254/2016, implementing Directive 2014/95/EU	M	P, Env, S, E, H, A, D	IT

Source: our elaboration. *Character* defines if the initiative establishes voluntary (V) or mandatory (M) requirements. *NF themes addressed* defines the NF topics covered by the initiative, namely, P (Policies and/or processes); Env (Environment); S (Social); E (Employee and labour); H (Human rights); A (Anti-corruption); and D (Diversity). *Scope* defines if the scope of the initiative is Italian (IT) or related to the European Union (EU)

order to stop managers, executives, employees and external collaborators from taking excessive risk and committing fraud (Rossi and Harjoto 2019).

The Legislative Decree 32/2007 enacted the 2003/51/EC European Directive. The 32/2007 Decree represents the first Italian law to recommend the provision of employee and environmental information through consolidated annual reports. The inclusion of this information recognizes the increasing importance of social and environmental accounting (SEA) and non-financial information (i.e. environmental, social and governance issues), both of which may represent a significant portion of corporate value. Nevertheless, the results of a recent study analysing the impact of Italian Legislative Decree 32/2007 showed that, despite the overall increase in sentences devoted to environmental and employee matters, the completeness of the information provided by Italian companies has not substantially improved after the 2007 regulation, indicating thus that this regulation has been ineffective (Costa and Agostini 2016). Greco (2012) also arrived at similar results, finding that, even in the presence of a significant increase in the quantity of risk-related sentences following the new regulation, the information attributes of the disclosure about risks remained unchanged throughout the period.

The legislative Decree 254/2016 implemented the EU Directive in the Italian context. The Italian Decree introduced several new elements that do not appear in Directive 2014/95/EU and in the other national regulations implementing European legislation. In detail, the Italian regulation differentiates itself for (a) the scope; (b) the content of NF declaration; (c) how to report NFI; (d) the positioning of NFI; and (e) the system of sanctions for missing or inaccurate information (Muserra et al. 2019).

As for the first element (a), we can affirm that the Italian legislature has broadened the scope of the rule in comparison with what is set out in the directive, establishing that entities that are not obliged to draw up the non-financial statement, that is, the small and medium enterprises (SMEs), may prepare it on a voluntary basis. In particular, the legislature has provided for a flexible application of the main regime in the case of voluntary non-financial statements, that is, SMES may avoid applying some aspects of the regulation that involve a particular administrative burden and that they could waive the system of controls required by the Decree, displaying a label of limited conformity because the main aim of the Legislator is to promote the diffusion of NFI disclosure among SMEs providing a proportionality criterion in applying the law.

As for the content of NF declaration (b), the minimum content provided by the Decree is in line, but more articulate, with the content set up by the EU regulation. The Italian Decree, in fact, after referring to the main CSR issues, specifies the aspects to be analysed. For instance, the Decree provides a comprehensive list of NFI, ranging from the use of energy resources to active and passive bribery policies. Moreover, in applying the materiality principle, according to which the matters to be reported in the declaration shall be representative of the individual company, the undertaking could identify matters different from those indicated by the EU Directive, eliminating and/or adding further aspects. The comply or explain principle, instead, allows the companies to avoid providing information about the minimum content specified by the Decree if they do not pursue policies in such fields, but they must clearly and articulately explain the reasons for this choice.

In relation to how Italian companies are obliged to disclose NFI (c), the Decree allows the companies either to adopt one of the national or supranational reporting standards (e.g. GRI 2013; IIRC 2013) or, alternatively, to use an autonomous reporting methodology, which combines several reporting standards.

As regards the positioning of NFI (d), the Decree establishes (Art. 5) that the directors can choose whether to integrate the statement into the management report or, alternatively, to prepare a separate report. Under the latter option, the company may also produce the statement as part of other documents – such as the sustainability report or the integrated report – provided that the words 'non-financial statement drawn up in accordance with Leg. Dec. 254/2016' are added within that document.

Finally, regarding the systems of internal and external controls introduced to verify the NFI disclosed, we can affirm that these controls are more cogent in the Italian context. The Decree explicitly mentions the duty of the board to prepare and publish the NF Declaration. The Decree also establishes that the auditor in charge of the assurance of financial statements, or another body entitled to carry out a statutory audit, must verify the presence of the non-financial statement and that the same entity, or a different auditor, must assess whether the content of the NF declaration is consistent with the regulation and the adopted reporting standard. Finally, the national legislature implemented the directive introducing a system of monetary sanctions, ranging from EUR 20,000 to 150,000, for the omission of important information, non-compliance or failure to submit within the required timeframe.

The analysis of these five features of NF declaration in the Italian context allow us to affirm that the Italian regulation is at the same time more stringent than the EU Directive but also more flexible. The cogent system of external controls, which imposes the assurance of the NFS content and a sanctioning regime for directors and supervisory bodies, provides evidence of the first character. The more flexible approach of the Italian regulation with respect to the EU Directive is instead demonstrated by the circumstance that the Legislator has provided for a wide range of methods of reporting NFI, with the possibility of also using an autonomous reporting methodology.

3.9 Italy and the Non-financial Information Disclosure Practices

Sustainability reporting practices have proliferated significantly among Italian companies in recent decades (Cantele 2014), and the interest of the academic and practitioner communities in these reporting practices has also increased, as is evidenced by the activity of organizations such as the Gruppo per il Bilancio Sociale (Study Group for Social Reporting).

Before European harmonization, in Italy, NFI disclosure was voluntary and the practices in relation to this disclosure were diverse.

There are several empirical studies carried out in the Italian context which have analysed different aspects of sustainability, such as the relationship between the internal corporate governance structure and voluntary disclosure (Patelli and Prencipe 2007); the determinants of disclosure (Prencipe 2004); the process of assurance of NF reporting (Venturelli et al. 2017); the effect of disclosure on customers' behaviour (Gavana et al. 2018); the practitioners' perspective on NF reports (Perrini 2006); and the features of NF disclosures in different industrial sectors (Mio 2010).

In this paragraph, we focus on the studies conducted in the Italian context answering to the legislative requirements and in detail on the empirical studies of mandatory NFI disclosure in Italy in the aftermath of the adoption of the EU Directive to investigate the level of compliance with the legislation.

The researches previously conducted on this issue do not achieve the same results. The research of Venturelli et al. (2017), conducted after the adoption of Directive 2014/95/EU and before its entry into force, provided evidence that demonstrated that Italian-listed corporations were potentially less compliant with the new legislative requirements than corporations in other countries and therefore that the effect of the new regulatory requirements could be important. On the contrary, the research of Costa and Agostini (2016), which analysed the effect of the Italian Legislative Decree (the law concerning the content of consolidated financial statements) on the social and environmental information disclosed in both the annual consolidated reports and the sustainability reports of Italian-listed corporate groups, found a good level of responsiveness to the legislation.

There are several studies conducted in the Italian territory in the aftermath of the enactment of the Legislative Decree 254/2016. Some of these studies focus on the NFI disclosure before the Legislative Decree 254/2016, some others focus on the NFI disclosure after the Decree, and others compare the disclosure before and after the Decree.

Among the studies focused on the NFI disclosure before the Decree, we can quote the studies of Truant et al. (2017); Manes Rossi et al. (2017); Venturelli et al. (2017); Muserra et al. (2019); and Venturelli et al. (2019).

The studies of Truant et al. (2017) and Manes Rossi et al. (2017) are both focused on the NF risk-related information, but the Truant et al. (2017) article focuses on the determinants of the NF risk disclosure in the sustainability report, whilst Manes Rossi et al. (2017) investigated the risk disclosure provided through the integrated report. In detail, the Truant et al. (2017) article, which identified the determinants of NF risk disclosure with international presence, sustainability experience and external assurance, finds that 'experienced' sustainable reporters provide a significant volume of disclosure and that disclosure quality on risk is positively influenced by their international presence and reporting experience. Manes Rossi et al. (2017), investigating risk disclosure throughout three different dimensions, that is, the metrics (monetary or non-monetary), the outlook orientation (past, present or future) and the type of risk news (good or bad news), find that the majority of risk disclosure are non-monetary, backward-looking and neutral and that, at least for Italian companies, a more extended risk disclosure is provided in the integrated report in comparison with the management commentary.

Venturelli et al. (2017) evaluate the existence of an information gap for Italian companies by constructing a non-financial information score on the basis of the requirements set out in the guidelines of the CNDEC (the Italian National Institute of Accountants), published in June 2016, for the following dimensions of information: business model, sustainability policies, sustainability risks, KPIs (key performance indicators) and diversity. The authors find that an information gap remains.

The study of Muserra et al. (2019), which investigated the content and reporting methods of NFI, as specified by the Italian regulation before it came into force through the findings of 17 interviews with preparers and auditors finds that they appreciate many of the requirements introduced by the Italian Legislator, namely, the responsibility of the board for NFI, the flexibility in the content and in the reporting method and the audit of non-financial statements.

Finally, the study of Venturelli et al. (2019), addressed to investigate which factors affect the quality of NFI (in terms of compliance to EU directive requirements) in the UK and Italy before the implementation of the EU Directive, finds that the UK is more compliant than Italy and thus regulation could be important to improve NFI in Italy more than in the UK.

Table 3.10 summarizes the main Italian studies on NFI disclosure before the Decree.

Table 3.10 Main Italian studies on NFI disclosure before the Decree

Authors/ journal (year)	Sample (year)	Main results
Truant et al. *Sustainability* (2017)	30 Italian-listed companies that in 2015 published a sustainability report according to the GRI G4	International presence and sustainability experience affect risk disclosure quality
Manes Rossi et al. *IJBM* (2017)	18 Italian companies publishing in 2015 an IR following IIRC 2015 guidelines	The majority of risk disclosure are non- monetary, backward-looking and neutral
Venturelli et al. *Sustainability* (2017)	223 large companies publishing NFI in their 2015 consolidated or individual financial statement	The Italian context shows an important corporate reporting gap
Muserra et al. *CSREM* (2019)	17 interviews to auditors and preparers of NFI disclosure as specified by Italian regulation	Auditors and preparers appreciate many of the requirements introduced by the Decree 254/2016
Venturelli et al. *SRJ* (2019)	134 large Italian firms and 209 large UK firms consolidated balance sheets for the 2016	The UK is more compliant than Italy and thus regulation could be important to improve NFI in Italy more than in the UK

Source: our elaboration

Three studies focus on the mandatory NFI disclosure in Italy after the enactment of the 254/2016 Decree, namely, the studies of Doni et al. (2019), De Luca and Phan (2019) and Leopizzi et al. (2020). Doni et al. (2019) investigated whether the prior skills and competences on sustainability reporting of companies obliged to disclose NFI can affect the level of compliance with the new mandatory requirements of the 254/2016 Decree. Their evidence confirm that the Italian context shows an important corporate reporting gap. Both the studies of De Luca and Phan (2019) and Leopizzi et al. (2020) focus on the NF risk-related information disclosure. De Luca and Phan (2019) investigated the risk disclosure practices of Italian-listed companies obliged after the enactment of the 254/2016 Decree. In particular, the authors investigate whether the level of risk disclosure is according to the type of information disclosure (risk description or risk management), the industry and the type of risks (financial, strategic, reputation, operation, compliance, reporting). The authors find that companies provide risk-related information at different levels of specificity according to whether the information is risk description or risk management, whether the firms are operating in manufacturing or nonmanufacturing and the type of risk that the firms disclosed in their reports. Leopizzi et al. (2020) analyse the level of NF risk disclosure after the Decree from three perspectives: the types of risk (compliance; strategic; operational; environmental, health and safety; and general), outlook orientation (past, present or future) and approach to risks (positive, negative or neutral), finding that the environmental, health and safety risks are the most disclosed NF risks, that the information is still oriented to the past or present instead of to the future and that companies of the sample disclosed mostly neutral and positive

Table 3.11 Main Italian studies on NFI disclosure after the Decree

Authors/ journal (year)	Sample	Main results
Doni et al. *MEDAR* (2019)	60 Italian-listed companies obliged to disclose NFI for the 2017 year	The Italian context shows an important corporate reporting gap
De Luca and Phan *Financial Reporting* (2019)	60 Italian-listed companies obliged to disclose NFI for the 2017 year	The level of specificity is different: • If the information is risk description or risk management • If the firms belong to manufacturing or nonmanufacturing industry • According to the type of risk disclosed
Leopizzi et al. *CSREM* (2020)	All Italian companies (202) obliged to follow the 254/2016 Decree for 2017	• The environmental, health and safety risks are the most disclosed NF risk • The information is still oriented to the past or present instead of to the future • Companies of the sample disclosed mostly neutral and positive information

Source: our elaboration

information. Table 3.11 summarizes the main Italian studies on NFI disclosure after the 254/2016 Decree.

Four studies compare the NF risk disclosures before and after the Decree, namely, the studies of Leopizzi et al. (2020); Mion and Loza Adaui (2019); Raucci and Tarquinio (2020); and Caputo et al. (2020).

Leopizzi et al. (2020) compare the level of NF risk disclosure in 2016 (before the Decree) and 2017 (after the Decree) finding that the level of NF disclosure is better than before the enactment of the Decree.

Mion and Loza Adaui compare the sustainability reporting practices of 36 Italian and 30 German companies in the top lists of stock exchanges 1 year before (2016) and 1 year after (2017) the implementation of EU Directive. The results provide evidence that the quality of sustainability reporting increased after implementation of the law on mandatory NFI disclosure.

Raucci and Tarquinio (2020) examine the effects produced on sustainability performance indicators (SPIs) after the enactment of the Decree. The authors find that after the introduction of mandatory disclosure of NFI, companies seem to focus only on indicators considered more important according to the EU Directive.

Caputo et al. (2020) compare NFI disclosed by 147 listed Italian companies in 2015 (before the Decree) and 2017 (after the Decree) finding that NFI quality improves and that the use of Integrated Report, the experience years in disclosing sustainability issues and the small number of pages of an NF report affect positively

Table 3.12 Main Italian studies comparing NFI disclosure before and after the Decree

Authors/ journal (year)	Sample	Main results
Leopizzi et al. *CSREM* (2020)	66 Italian companies disclosing NF risk before (2016) and after (2017) the Decree	The level of NF disclosure is better than before the enactment of the Decree
Mion and Loza Adaui *Sustainability* (2019)	36 Italian and 30 German top listed companies 1 year before (2016) and 1 year after (2017) the EU Directive implementation	The quality of sustainability reporting increased after the implementation of NFI mandatory disclosure
Raucci and Tarquinio *Administrative Sciences* (2020)	31 Italian-listed companies which disclosed SPIs before (2012) and after (2017) the Decree	After the introduction of mandatory disclosure of NFI, companies seem to focus only on indicators considered more relevant according to the Directive
Caputo et al. *Sustainability* (2020)	147 Italian-listed companies which disclosed NFI before (2015) and after (2017) the Decree	• The NFI quality improves • IR, experience years and small number of pages positively affect NF report quality (compliance)

Source: our elaboration

the NFI quality (compliance). Table 3.12 summarizes the main Italian studies comparing NFI disclosure before and after the Decree.

3.10 The Sample

Our research is based on a sample of large Italian PIEs mandated, after the enactment of the Legislative Decree No. 254 of 2016, which transposed the EU Directive, to issue NF disclosures in the 2017 fiscal year (first time adoption). Pursuant to Section 2 of the Decree, the new disclosure requirements apply to PIEs meeting the following criteria: exceeding, on an individual or consolidated basis, (1) 500 employees on average during the relevant fiscal year as well as (2) at least one of the following thresholds: total net asset value of €20,000,000 or total net revenues from sales and services of €40,000,000 at the end of the relevant fiscal year. We use AIDA (Bureau Van Dijk) database to filter the list of potential companies for the study. After considering only companies mandated to adopt the new rule and excluding banks and financial institutions, AIDA provides us with a list of 65 listed companies following the aforementioned criteria. Then, we collected non-financial reports from the websites of those companies. Finally, we analysed our research questions on a final sample of 51 companies with available data. Other 14 companies are dropped off the sample for 2 reasons: (1) the publication dates of the report exceed our research timeline and (2) the language used in the reports is not English. This sample size is quite adequate for further empirical inferences about a 65-company

Table 3.13 Sample selection process

	No of companies
Italian-listed companies	358
Non-financial listed companies	283
Non-financial listed companies subjected to Legislative Decree 254	65
Non-financial listed companies subjected to Legislative Decree 254 with available data	51

Source: our elaboration

Table 3.14 Distribution of companies by sector

Sector	NAICS Code	Number of companies	Proportion (%)
Manufacturing	*33*	*23*	*45*
Nonmanufacturing		*28*	*55*
Accommodation and food services	72	1	2
Administrative and support and waste management and remediation services	56	1	2
Construction	23	4	8
Information	51	5	10
Management of companies and enterprises	55	3	6
Other services (except public administration)	81	1	2
Retail trade	45	3	6
Transportation and warehousing	49	2	4
Utilities	22	4	8
Wholesale trade	42	4	8
Total		51	100

Source: our elaboration

population at 95% of confident level and 5% of margin of error. Table 3.13 illustrates the sample selection process.

Table 3.14 presents the distribution of companies in the sample by industry. The industry is determined by first two digits of the North American Industry Classification System (NAICS). In general, the sample comprises of 45% of manufacturing firms and 55% of nonmanufacturing firms.

References

Brown, H. S., De Jong, M., & Lessidrenska, T. (2009). The rise of global reporting initiative as a case of institutional entrepreneurship. *Environmental Politics, 18*(4), 182–200.

Buhr, N., Gray, R., & Milne, M. J. (2014). Histories, rationales, voluntary standards and future prospects for sustainability reporting: CSR, GRI, IIRC and beyond. In J. Bebbington,

J. Unerman, & B. O'Dwyer (Eds.), *Sustainability accounting and accountability* (pp. 51–71). London: Routledge.

Cantele, S. (2014). The trend of sustainability reporting in Italy: Some evidence from the last decade. *International Journal of Sustainable Economics, 6*, 381–405.

Caputo, F., Leopizzi, R., Pizzi, S., & Milone, V. (2020). The non-financial reporting harmonization in Europe: Evolutionary pathways related to the transposition of the directive 95/2014/EU within the Italian context. *Sustainability, 12*(1), 92.

Carini, C., Rocca, L., Veneziani, M., & Teodori, C. (2018). Ex-ante impact assessment of sustainability information- the directive 2014/95. *Sustainability, 10*, 560.

Cho, C. H., & Patten, D. M. (2007). The role of environmental disclosures as tools of legitimacy: A research note. *Accounting, Organizations and Society, 32*(7/8), 639–647.

Commission of the European Communities. (2009). *European workshops in disclosure of environmental, social and governance information*. Workshop 6 – the final workshop. Friday 25 February, Brussels.

Commission of the European Communities (2011*), Disclosure of non-financial information by companies. Directorate general for internal markets and services, Public consultation on disclosure of non-financial information by companies*, Brussels.

Costa, E., & Agostini, M. (2016). Mandatory disclosure about environmental and employee matters in the reports of Italian-listed corporate groups. *Environmental and Accountability Journal, 36*, 10–33.

Crisóstomo, V. L., Prudêncio, P. A., & Forte, H. C. (2017). An analysis of the adherence to GRI for disclosing information on social action and sustainability concerns. In A. Belal & S. Cooper (Eds.), *Advances in environmental accounting & management: Social and environmental accounting in Brazil* (pp. 69–103). Bingley: Emerald Publishing.

De Luca, F., & Phan, H. (2019). Informativeness assessment of risk and risk-management disclosure in corporate reporting: An empirical analysis of Italian large listed firms. *Financial Reporting, 2*, 9–41.

Dobler, M. (2008). Incentives for risk reporting –a discretionary disclosure and cheap talk approach. *The International Journal of Accounting, 43*, 184–206.

Doni, F., Bianchi Martini, S., Corvino, A., & Mazzoni, M. (2019). Voluntary versus mandatory non-financial disclosure: EU directive 95/2014 and sustainability reporting practices based on empirical evidence from Italy. Meditari Accountancy Research, Vol. ahead-of-print No. ahead-of-print. https://doi.org/10.1108/MEDAR-12-2018-0423.

du Toit, E., van Zyl, R., & Schutte, G. (2017). Integrated reporting by South African companies: A case study. *Meditari Accountancy Research, 25*(4), 654–674.

Dumay, J., Bernardi, C., Guthrie, J., & La Torre, M. (2017). Barriers to implementing the international integrated reporting framework. *Meditary Accountancy research, 25*(4), 461–480.

Eccles, R. G., & Saltzman, D. (2011). Achieving sustainability through integrated reporting. *Stanford Social Innovation Review, 9*(3), 56–61.

Elshandidy, T., Shrives, P. J., Bamber, M., & Abraham, S. (2018). Risk reporting: A review of the literature and implications for future research. *Journal of Accounting Literature, 40*, 54–82.

European Commission. (2017). *Guidelines on non-financial reporting (Methodology for reporting non-financial information) (2017/C 215/01)*. Brussels, Belgium: European Commission. Accessed January 23, 2020, from www.ec.europa.eu/antitrafficking/ sites/antitrafficking/files/ guidelines_on_non-financial_reporting.pdf

European Union. (2014). *Directive as regards disclosure of non-financial and diversity information by certain large undertakings and groups, 2014/95/EU*. Accessed March 25, 2019, from http:// eur-lex.europa.eu/legalcontent/EN/TXT/PDF/?uri=CELEX:32014L0095&from=EN/

Federation of European Accountants (FEE). (2015). *The future of corporate reporting – creating the dynamics for change*. Brussels: FEE.

Federation of European Accountants (FEE). (2016). *EU directive on disclosure of non-financial and diversity information: Achieving good quality and consistent reporting*. Brussels: FEE.

Flower, J. (2015). The international integrated reporting council: A story of failure. *Critical Perspectives on Accounting, 27*, 1–17.

Gavana, G., Gottardo, P., & Moisello, A. M. (2018). Do customers value CSR disclosure? Evidence from Italian family and non-family firms. *Sustainability, 10*, 1642.

GBS. (2019). *The SDGs in the reports of the Italian companies* (Research Document no. 16). Milan: Franco Angeli.

Global Reporting Initiative. (2013). *G4 guidelines: Reporting principles and standard disclosures*. Accessed January 12, 2020, from www.globalreporting.org

Greco, G. (2012). The management's reaction to new mandatory risk disclosure: A longitudinal study on Italian listed companies. *Corporate Communications: An International Journal, 17*(2), 113–137.

GRI. (2017). *Linking the GRI standards and the European Directive on non-financial and diversity disclosure*. Accessed January 13, 2020, from www.globalreporting.org

Haller, A., Link, M., & Groß, T. (2017). The term 'non-financial information' – A semantic analysis of a key feature of current and future corporate reporting. *Accounting in Europe, 9480*, 1–23.

Herzig, C., & Kühn, A.-L. (2017). Corporate responsibility reporting. In A. Rasche, M. Morsing, & J. Moon (Eds.), *Corporate social responsibility: Strategy, communication, governance* (pp. 187–219). Cambridge: Cambridge University Press.

International Integrated Reporting Council (IIRC). (2013). *The international integrated reporting framework*. London: International Integrated Reporting Council.

Jensen, J. C., & Berg, N. (2012). Determinants of traditional sustainability reporting versus integrated reporting: An institutionalist approach. *Business Strategy and the Environment, 21*, 299–316.

KPMG. (2013). *Interview with Paul Druckman – CEO of International Integrated Reporting Council*. Accessed February 22, 2020, from https://www.youtube.com/watch?v=ojgzys8l9-Y

La Torre, M., Sabelfeld, S., Blomkvist, M., Tarquinio, L., & Dumay, J. (2018). Harmonising non-financial reporting regulation in Europe: Practical forces and projections for future research. *Meditari Accountancy Research, 26*(4), 598–621.

Lai, A., Melloni, G., & Stacchezzini, R. (2017). What does materiality mean to integrated reporting preparers? An empirical exploration. *Meditari Accountancy Research, 25*(4), 533–552.

Leopizzi, R., Iazzi, A., Venturelli, A., & Principale, S. (2020). Nonfinancial risk disclosure: The 'state of the art' of Italian companies. *Corporate Social Responsibility and Environmental Management, 20*(1), 358–368.

Manes Rossi, F., Nicolò, G., & Levy Orelli, R. (2017). Reshaping risk disclosure through integrated reporting: Evidence from Italian early adopters. *International Journal of Business and Management, 12*(10), 11–23.

Manes Rossi, F., Tiron-Tudor, A., Nicolò, G., & Zanellato, G. (2018). Ensuring more sustainable reporting in Europe using non-financial disclosure—De facto and De jure evidence. *Sustainability, 10*(1162), 1–20.

Merkl-Davies, D., & Brennan, N. (2007). Discretionary disclosure strategies in corporate narratives: Incremental information or impression management? *Journal of Accounting Literature, 26*, 116–196.

Michelon, G., Pilonato, S., & Ricceri, F. (2015). CSR reporting practices and the quality of disclosure: An empirical analysis. *Critical Perspectives on Accounting, 33*, 59–78.

Milne, M. J., & Gray, R. H. (2007). The future of sustainability reporting. In J. Unerman, B. O'Dwyer, & J. Bebbington (Eds.), *Sustainability Accounting and Accountability*. London: Routledge.

Mio, C. (2010). Corporate social reporting in Italian multi-utility companies: An empirical analysis. *Corporate Social Responsibility and Environmental Management, 17*, 247–271.

Mion, G., & Loza Adaui, C. R. (2019). Mandatory nonfinancial disclosure and its consequences on the sustainability reporting quality of Italian and German companies. *Sustainability, 11*(17), 4612.

Monciardini, D., Dumay, J., & Biondi, L. (2017). Integrated reporting and EU law. Competing, converging or complementary regulatory frameworks? *SSRN Electronic Journal*. https://doi.org/10.2139/ssrn.2981674.

Muserra, A. L., Papa, M., & Grimaldi, F. (2019). Sustainable development and the European Union policy on non-financial information: An Italian empirical analysis. *Corporate Social Responsibility and Environmental Management, 27*, 22. https://doi.org/10.1002/csr.1770.

Patelli, L., & Prencipe, A. (2007). The relationship between voluntary disclosure and independent directors in the presence of a dominant shareholder. *The European Accounting Review, 16*, 5–33.

Patten, M. D., Ren, Y., & Zhao, N. (2015). Standalone corporate social responsibility reporting in China: An exploratory analysis of its relation to legitimation. *Social and Environmental Accountability Journal, 35*(1), 17–31.

Perrini, F. (2006). The practitioner's perspective on non-financial reporting. *California Management Review, 48*, 73–103.

Prencipe, A. (2004). Proprietary costs and determinants of voluntary segment disclosure: Evidence from Italian listed companies. *The European Accounting Review, 13*, 319–340.

Raucci, D., & Tarquinio, L. (2020). Sustainability performance indicators and non-financial information reporting. Evidence from the Italian case. *Administrative Sciences, 10*(13), 1–18.

Rossi, F., & Harjoto, M. A. (2019). Corporate non-financial disclosure, firm value, risk, and agency costs: Evidence from Italian listed companies. *Review of Managerial Science*. https://doi.org/10.1007/s11846-019-00358-z.

Rossi, A., & Tarquinio, L. (2017). An analysis of sustainability report assurance statements: Evidence from Italian listed companies. *Managerial Auditing Journal, 32*(6), 578–602.

Skouloudis, A., Evangelinos, K., & Kourmousis, F. (2009). Development of an evaluation methodology for triple bottom line reports using international standards on reporting. *Environmental Management, 44*, 298–311.

Stubbs, W., & Higgins, C. (2014). Integrated reporting and internal mechanisms of change. *Accounting, Auditing & Accountability Journal, 27*, 1068–1089.

Stubbs, W., & Higgins, C. (2015). Stakeholders' perspectives on the role of regulatory reform in integrated reporting. *Journal of Business Ethics, 147*(3), 1–20.

Thorell, P., & Whittington, G. (1994). The harmonization of accounting within the EU-problems, perspectives and strategies. *The European Accounting Review, 3*(2), 215–239.

Truant, E., Corazza, L., & Scagnelli, D. S. (2017). Sustainability and risk disclosure: An exploratory study on sustainability reports. *Sustainability, 9*(636), 1–20.

Tschopp, D., & Nastanski, M. (2014). The harmonization and convergence of corporate social responsibility reporting standards. *Journal of Business Ethics, 125*(1), 147–162.

Venturelli, A., Caputo, F., Cosma, S., Leopizzi, R., & Pizzi, S. (2017). Directive 2014/95/EU: Are Italian companies already compliant? *Sustainability, 9*(8), 1385.

Venturelli, A., Caputo, F., Leopizzi, R., & Pizzi, S. (2019). The state of art of corporate social disclosure before the introduction of non-financial reporting directive: A cross country analysis. *Social Responsibility Journal, 15*(4), 409–423.

Chapter 4
Measuring the Quality of Non-financial Risk-Related Disclosure

4.1 Introduction

In the chapter we introduce the main research question of the book, namely, *RQ: Does quality mandatory NF risk disclosure affect investors' decisions?* The answer to the research question requires a context in which to carry out the research (we justified the choice of Italy in the previous section), the analytical framework for NF risk-related disclosure to employ and an adequate methodology to measure quality NF risk disclosure. As for the framework for the mandatory NF risk disclosure, we focus on the NF risk disclosure categories as provided by the EU Directive implemented by the Legislative Decree 254/2016, preceded by a brief illustration of the other main existing frameworks of NF risk disclosure. As for the methodology, we focus on the most widely used method to measure narrative disclosure, the content analysis, focusing on the main approach that can be followed by researchers to content analyse corporate documents, that is, mechanistic and interpretive content analysis, also presenting the main empirical studies employing automated and manual content analysis. The last sections of the chapter are devoted to the concept of quality of disclosure and how it can be operationalized, to end with the self-constructed quality disclosure index used in our research to measure the mandatory NF risk-related information disclosure.

4.2 The Main Non-financial Risk-Related Disclosure Frameworks

Before the EU Directive (and the enactment of the 254/2016 Decree) that introduced an NF risk disclosure framework, several NF reporting tools dealt with NF risks.

Table 4.1 presents the main NF reporting tools dealing with NF risks.

S. Veltri, *Mandatory Non-financial Risk-Related Disclosure*,
https://doi.org/10.1007/978-3-030-47921-3_4

Table 4.1 Reporting tools and types of NF risks

Reporting tool	Type of risks
GRI (2013)	*Economic*: Market presence, procurement practices, anti-corruption, anti-competitive behaviour *Environmental*: Materials, energy, water, biodiversity, emissions, effluents and waste *Social*: Employment, labour/management relations, occupational health and safety, diversity and equal opportunity, non-discrimination, freedom of association and collective bargaining, child labour, forced or compulsory labour, security practices, rights of indigenous peoples, human rights, local communities, public policy, customer health safety, marketing and labelling, customer privacy, compliance
CDP	Forest, water, Climate change
IIRC (2013)	Market risks and other risks beyond financial reporting
UN global compact	Human rights, occupational health and safety, labour rights, environmental and anti-corruption issues
Total impact measurement & management	Social, environmental, economic, fiscal
Social capital protocol	Contextualized risks without a priori list
Natural capital protocol	Not set a priori
Common good balance sheet	Not set a priori
ICAEW (1997)	Corporate risks are categorized into six risk disclosure categories: financial risk, operations risk, empowerment risk, information processing and technology risk, integrity risk and strategic risk
The Arthur Andersen business risk model	NF risks are articulated into compliance risks; strategic risks; operational risks; environmental, health and safety risks; and general NF risks
COSO (2018) framework	Financial risks, compliance risks, operational risks, strategic risks

Source: our elaboration based on Truant et al. (2017) and Leopizzi et al. (2020)

Also, the empirical studies addressed to measure the NF risks, as part of the more general corporate risks, used diverse frameworks. When the authors distinguish between financial and NF risks, whilst briefly agreeing on the content of financial risks (credit risks, liquidity risks and, more generally, risks related to financial instruments), they greatly differ in relation to the categories (and the content of the categories) to include in the NF risk dimension. This is obviously due to the circumstance that it is not easy to define the NF area, which includes social and environmental issues but not only those, and this difficulty reflects itself in the definition of NF risk area.

Table 4.2 presents some frameworks for NF risks used in the empirical papers dealing with NF risks (we just report the main categories, without highlighting the elements contained in each category and their significance).

Finally, it seems interesting to present in the next tables (from Tables 4.3, 4.4, 4.5, 4.6, 4.7, 4.8, and 4.9) details of some NF risk disclosure used by some empirical papers in Table 4.2 (namely, Linsley and Shrives 2006; Neri and Russo 2013; Truant et al. 2017; Leopizzi et al. 2020; De Luca and Phat 2019), to highlight that often the risks included in the categories identified are not the same for all authors and that the level of risk details provided in the papers is different among the diverse authors.

Table 4.2 NF risk frameworks used in empirical articles

Author(s), journal, year	NF risk framework used
Cabedo and Tirado *Accounting Forum* (2004)	Corporate risks articulated into financial risks (market risks, credit risks, operational risks and liquidity risks) and NF risks (business risks and strategic risks)
Linley and Shrives *The Journal of Risk Finance* (2005)	Following the ICAEW categorization, according to which corporate risks could be articulated into six categories: financial risk, operations risk, empowerment risk, information processing and technology risk, integrity risk and strategic risk
Linley and Shrives *BAR* (2006)	Following the ICAEW categorization, according to which corporate risks could be articulated into six categories: financial risk, operations risk, empowerment risk, information processing and technology risk, integrity risk and strategic risk
Neri and Russo *Financial Reporting* (2013)	Corporate risks identified into four different risks categories to disclose: financial, legal, operational and business
Truant et al. *Sustainability* (2017)	Sustainability risks are articulated into three different disclosure categories: external risk, strategic risk and operational risk
Manes Rossi et al. *IJBM* (2017)	As in Linsley and Shrives (2005, 2006) and ICAEW (1997), corporate risks are categorized into six categories: financial risk, operations risk, empowerment risk, information processing and technology risk, integrity risk and strategic risk
Bravo *MDE* (2017)	Following the Dobler et al. (2011) framework based on prior studies of Cabedo and Tirado (2004) and Linsley and Shrives a review of regulation, the author disclose financial and NF risks
Leopizzi et al. *CSREM* (2020)	COSO (2018) framework, which articulates enterprise risk into financial risks, compliance risks, operational risks and strategic risks
De Luca and Phat *Financial Reporting* (2019)	Corporate risks are categorized into six risk disclosure categories: financial risks, reporting risks, compliance risks, operation risks, reputation risk and strategic risk
Dumay and Hossain *AAR* (2019)	The NF sustainability risk is articulated into three disclosure categories, economic, environmental and social, on the basis of Recommendation 7.4 of the Australian Corporate Governance Guidelines (ASX CGC 2014)

Source: our elaboration

Table 4.3 The risk disclosure framework in Cabedo and Tirado (2004)

Financial risk	Market Credit Operational Liquidity
Operation risk	Business Strategic

Source: our elaboration based on Cabedo and Tirado (2004)

Table 4.4 The risk disclosure framework in Linsley and Shrives (2005, 2006) and Manes Rossi et al. (2017)

Financial risk	Interest rate Exchange rate Commodity Liquidity Credit
Operation risk	Customer satisfaction Product development Efficiency and performance Sourcing Stock obsolescence and shrinkage Product and service failure Environmental Health and safety Brand name erosion
Empowerment risk	Leadership and management Outsourcing Performance incentives Change readiness Communications
Information processing and technology risk	Integrity access Availability Infrastructure
Integrity risk	Management and employee fraud Illegal acts Reputation
Strategic risk	Environmental scan Industry Business portfolio Competitors' pricing Valuation planning

Source: our elaboration from Linsley and Shrives (2006)

Table 4.5 The risk disclosure framework in Neri and Russo (2013)

Financial risk	Market risk Interest risk Credit risk Liquidity risk
Legal risk	Stream of information related to various situations, such as the change that has taken place in the legislation
Operational risk	It is a kind of risk related to the possibility of inadequate internal processes, people and systems or may result from external events
Business risk	It is a kind of risk related to the uncertainties about the demand for product; the price that can be charged for the products; the cost of producing, stocking and delivering the products; but also strategic risk

Source: our elaboration from Neri and Russo (2013)

Table 4.6 The risk disclosure framework in Truant et al. (2017)

External risk	External risks refer to those risks whose manifestation is outside the sphere of influence of the company (pure risks). This category involves risks related to macroeconomic tendencies, changes in demand, competitor actions, technological innovation, new laws and country-specific risks
Strategic risk	Strategic risks are linked to a specific business sector and usually include market risk, product and process innovation risks, human resources risk, price risk, industrial risk and financial risk
Operational risk	It is a kind of risk related to the possibility of inadequate internal processes, people and systems or may result from external events
Social, environmental, business ethics responsibility risks, reputational risks	Social and environmental risks are considered for their transversal impacts over the external, strategic and operational risks, whilst reputational risk is defined as risk deriving from unethical behaviour; thus they have been clustered under ethical risks

Source: our elaboration from Truant et al. (2017)

Table 4.7 The risk disclosure framework in Leopizzi et al. (2020)

Compliance risks	Ethical misconduct Risk of litigation Fiscal risk Corruption Conflict of interest
Strategic risks	Reputation Brand erosion Dependence on third parties Price Stakeholder engagement Competition Politics
Operational risk	Product quality Performance gap Human resource Procurement Product development Obsolescence retire Efficiency Interruption activity Capability Information technology (IT) risks Infrastructure Misleading of the product service
Environmental, health and safety risks	Climate change Health and safety Environment
General NF risks	NF risks not belonging to previous categories

Source: our elaboration from Leopizzi et al. (2020)

Table 4.8 The risk disclosure framework in De Luca and Phat (2019)

Type of risk	Elements	Description
Strategic risk	Macro-environmental	Macro-environmental risk, classified to the level of country risk, includes political/legal, economic, social, demographic, technological and the like
	Industrial	Industry risk refers to the uncertainty that stems from wide-ranging issues involving the entire industry that the company belongs to
	Competitive	Competitors or new entrants to the market take actions to establish and sustain competitive advantage over the organization or even threaten its ability to survive
	Business portfolio	The risk that a firm will not maximize business performance by effectively prioritizing its products or balancing its businesses in a strategic context
	Planning	The business strategies of the organization are out-of-date and unfocused or not realistic, not based on appropriate assumptions, not based on cost drivers and performance measures
	Product lifecycle	The risk threatens the ultimate success of its business strategies in managing the movement of its product lines and evolution of its industry along the life cycle
Reputation risks	Corporate image	The risk that an organization may lose the trust from customers and key employees, or its ability to compete, owing to perceptions that it does not deal fairly with customers, suppliers and stakeholders or know how to manage its business
	Business ethics	The organization, through its actions or inaction, demonstrates that it is not committed to ethical and responsible business behaviour
Operation risk	Customer satisfaction	The organization's processes do not consistently meet or exceed customer expectations
	Product development	The product development process is significantly weaker than more innovative competitors
	Process management and infrastructures	The risk of the capability of the organization to continue critical operations and processes due to the unavailability to the infrastructure of certain raw materials, technologies, infrastructure and other resources
	HR management	The risk that the personnel does not possess the expected knowledge, skills and experience needed to ensure those critical business objectives
	Information systems	The risk that the information technologies used in the business are not efficiently and effectively supporting the business or the risk of theft or damage to the hardware, software or data
	Stock obsolescence and shrinkage	The risk of the shortages of energy, other key commodities and raw materials used in the operations. Shrinkage

(continued)

Table 4.8 (continued)

Type of risk	Elements	Description
	Product and service failure	The risk of faulty or nonperforming products or services
Compliance risks	Health and safety	These risks of the likelihood that a person may be harmed or suffers adverse health effects due to not only the operational process but also the products or services provided by the organization
	Environment	Environmental risks of the liability to third parties for the damage caused by pollution and the liability to governments or third parties for the cost of removing pollutants plus severe punitive damage
	Industry regulation	The risk that changes in regulations and actions by national or local regulators can significantly affect the ability of an organization to conduct business such as antitrust, fair competition efficiently
	Social and employee-related matters	Failure to conform to laws and regulations re gender equality, supranational and international organizations and social dialogue
	Law 231/2001	Liability for crimes committed by representatives of the company
	Human rights	Risk of violations and discrimination in the workforce
	Corruption and bribery	Risk of offering, paying or receiving a bribe through an officer, employee, subsidiary, intermediary or any third party (individual or corporate) acting on behalf of the commercial organization
Reporting risks	Financial accounting and reporting regulation	The risk of the ineffectiveness of disclosure controls and procedures, resulting in material information not being disclosed promptly to certifying officers and in public reports. The risk of publishing material misstatements or omitting material facts, making them misleading
	Law 262/2005	Risks of inadequacy and ineffective application of the financial reporting procedures and that the accounting records are not able to provide a true and fair view of the balance sheet, statement of income and financial position
Financial risks	Credit	The exposure to actual loss or opportunity cost as a result of default or failure by the debtor
	Market (interest rate, exchange rate, market prices)	The exposure of earnings or net worth to changes in market factors (e.g. interest rates, currency rates), which affect income, expense or balance sheet values
	Liquidity	The exposure to loss as a result of the inability to meet cash flow obligations in a timely and cost-effective manner

Source: our elaboration from De Luca and Phat (2019)

Table 4.9 The risk disclosure framework in Dumay and Hossain (2019)

Environmental risks	Risks related to the environmental sustainability, defined as 'the ability of a listed entity to continue operating in a manner that does not compromise the health of the ecosystems in which it operates over the long term' (ASX CGC 2014: 37)
Social risks	Risks related to the social sustainability, defined as 'the ability of a listed entity to continue operating in a manner that meets accepted social norms and needs over the long term' (ASX CGC 2014: 38)
Economic risks	Risks related to the economic sustainability, defined as 'the ability of a listed entity to continue operating at a particular level of economic production over the long term' (ASX CGC 2014: 37)

Source: our elaboration from Dumay and Hossain (2019)

4.3 The Non-financial Risk Disclosure Categories According to the Decree

In Europe, until recently, NF risk information was provided largely voluntarily (Dobler 2008), steering literature mainly in the direction of investigating why, and to what extent, firms disclose risk information (Elshandidy et al. 2018). With the issuing of the EU Directive in 2014, and its subsequent adoption within EU countries members, large public interest entities (PIEs) have been obliged to disclose, in their annual report or in a separate document, some relevant NF information, among which NF risk-related information.

We analysed the content of EU Directive and the Decree 254/2016 which implemented the EU Directive in Italy in the previous chapter. Briefly, there are five NF categories to disclose, identified by the EU Directive (Leopizzi et al. 2020): a) a brief description of the PIE's business model; b) a description of the policies pursued by the PIE in relation to those matters; c) the outcome of these policies; d) the principal risks related to these matters including how the PIE manage those risks; and e) important NF key performance indicators. The same as the EU Directive, Decree 254 does not specify the way to report NFI, and thus NF risks, but it provides for relating NF risks (art 3, subsection 3) to the NF issues (art 3, subsection 1). The NF risks to be disclosed by companies are thus health and safety risks, environmental risks (energy resources, greenhouse gas emissions and air pollution), social and employee risks (gender equality, supranational and international organizations and social dialogue), human rights risks and corruption and bribery risks.

Table 4.10 defines the focused information for the five specific NF risks as identified by the Decree that we employed in our research.

Table 4.10 NF risk factors according to the 254/2016 Decree

Risk factors		Description
Risks subjected to Legislative Decree 254	Health and safety risk	These risks of the likelihood that a person may be harmed or suffers adverse health effects due to not only the operational process but also the products or services provided by the organization
	Environmental risk	Environmental risks of the liability to third parties for the damage caused by the pollution and the liability to governments or third parties for the cost of removing pollutants plus severe punitive damage
	Social and employee risk	Failure to conform with laws and regulations about gender equality, supranational and international organizations and social dialogue
	Human rights risk	Risk of violations and discrimination in the workforce
	Corruption and bribery risk	Risk of offering, paying or receiving a bribe through an officer, employee, subsidiary, intermediary or any third party (individual or corporate) acting on behalf of the commercial organization

Source: our elaboration

Moreover, it should be underlined that the recent Decree 145/2018 has modified the information to disclose about risks: together with the exposition of the principal NF risks, it explicitly requires to disclose also how companies intend to manage and face the NF risks disclosed. In our research we thus examine NF sentences related not only to NF risk disclosure but also to NF risk management.

4.4 The Content Analysis

Content analysis is the most popular research tool examining qualitative disclosure, and it has been widely used to examine social and environmental information provided by companies, as they are submitted in narrative form, through annual reports (Guthrie and Petty 2000) or independent (voluntary) documents such as sustainability report of integrated report or intellectual capital statement (Dumay and Cai 2014a; b; Cinquini et al. 2012).

It was not until 1941 that the term 'content analysis' was first used to describe the 'systemic reading of a body of texts, images and symbolic matter, not necessarily from the author's or user's perspective' (Krippendorff 2004). Since then, content analysis has expanded beyond analysing religious texts and newspapers to all manner of texts and media, such as textbooks, comics, speeches, advertising,

Fig. 4.1 The content analysis. Source: based on Krippendorff (2013)

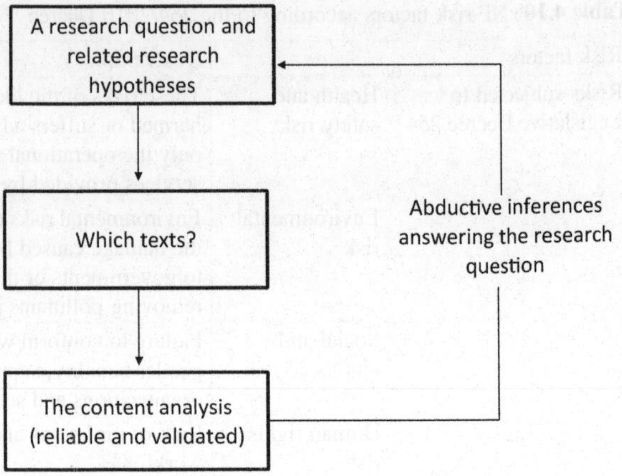

propaganda, letters, films and the World Wide Web (Krippendorff 2004; Krippendorff and Bock 2008).[1]

In 2013 Krippendorff defines content analysis as a research technique for making replicable and valid inferences from texts (or other meaningful matter) to the contexts of their use (Krippendorff 2013).

There are six phases that researchers have to follow to correctly implement a content analysis (Krippendorff 2013; Dumay and Cai 2015):

1. A body of text that a content analyst has available to begin the analytical effort
2. A research question that the analyst seeks to answer by examining the body of text
3. A context of the analyst's choice within which to make sense of the body of text
4. An analytical construct that operationalizes what the analyst knows about the context
5. Inferences that are intended to answer the research question, which constitute the basic accomplishment of the content analysis
6. Validating evidence, which is the ultimate justification of the content analysis[2]

Figure 4.1 illustrates graphically the steps that a researcher should follow for correctly content analysing texts.

[1]According to Krippendorff (2004), content analysis as a research methodology has its early origins in the 'inquisitional pursuits by the Church in the seventeenth century', when the Church became worried about the spread of non-religious printed matter after the invention of the printing press and thus began the pursuit of analysing texts to ensure they were in keeping with the doctrines of the Church (Dovring 2008). At the end of the nineteenth century, the proliferation of newspapers reignited interest in content analysis as methodology to analyse the social content of newspaper (Weber 2008) conducted content analysis research using newspapers as a source until such time as other forms of mass media, such as radio, became prominent (Krippendorff 2004).

[2]It is important here to make a distinction between the reliability and validity. According to Krippendorff (2008, p. 350), reliability 'is the extent to which data can be trusted to represent the phenomena of interest rather than spurious ones'. Validity, on the other hand, occurs when 'a measuring instrument … measures what it purports to measure' (Janis 2008, p. 359).

4.5 Form-Oriented Versus Meaning-Oriented Content Analysis

The content analysis method is widely used in disclosure studies, because it represents a means of categorizing items of text and can be used where a large amount of qualitative data needs to be analysed.

Researchers applying content analysis could follow two distinct approaches (Helfaya et al. 2019).

The first is known as *form-oriented mechanistic approach*, where textual analysis-based 'quantifications' of the contents are carried out. This approach captures and describes a proxy that is assumed to be closely associated with the intended goal (e.g. Campbell 2000; Wilmshurst and Frost 2000). In general, these studies focus on volume or frequency of disclosure.

The second approach is known as *meaning-oriented interpretive approach*. It was proposed by Smith and Taffler (2000) to contrast the form-oriented (mechanistic) approach. According to the authors, the mechanistic approach involves routine counting of words, sentences, lines, pages or items, whilst the meaning-oriented (interpretative) approach focuses on the meaning and nature of themes disclosed. Meaning-oriented has a greater level of interpretation of the content rather than just counting the disclosed items within a text.

Beck et al. (2010) stated that meaning-oriented content analyses have been widely adopted in the literature to analyse the textual content of reporting (e.g. Beattie et al. 2004; Diouf and Boiral 2017; Gray et al. 1995; Smith and Taffler 2000). This is due to the consideration that NFI disclosure for its qualitative nature and for the need to interpret certain aspects of content analysis could not answer. Furthermore, in a context of mandatory NFI such as that introduced in Italy with Decree 254/2016, where the way to report and disclose NFI is not specified, and thus the information to be evaluated is highly heterogeneous, a meaning-oriented content analysis is the right choice. In our research we thus used a meaning-oriented content analysis, to address the aim of our research better, that is, to investigate whether quality mandatory NF risk-related information affects the investors' decisions.

The choice to follow a meaning-oriented approach involves the content analysis obligatorily being performed manually, without the use of specific software, as the researcher has to focus on the meaning and nature of themes disclosed and has to interpret the text, and this is not achievable with a mechanistic approach, although recently accounting research has shifted towards an automated approach.

4.6 Content Analysis Studies on Risk Disclosure

Among the researchers who employed a manual content analysis to measure corporate risk disclosure, we can quote Beretta and Bozzolan (2004); Linsley and Shrives (2006); Abraham and Cox (2007); Miihkinen (2012); Ntim et al. (2013); Manes Rossi et al. (2017); Leopizzi et al. (2020); and De Luca and Phat (2019).

Beretta and Bozzolan (2004) propose a framework, comprising four dimensions, to analyse firms' risk disclosures, namely, quantity, density, depth and outlook profile. They find that the quantity of risk disclosure for their sample of Italian firms is mainly driven by firm size as opposed to industry type, but also that the influence of these two factors varies across the four dimensions.

Linsley and Shrives (2006) investigated risk disclosure by classifying each sentence related to risk into the following categories: financial/non-financial, monetary/non-monetary, good news/bad news and forward-looking/historic. The findings show that firm size and to a lesser extent environmental risk are statistically associated with risk disclosure, whereas gearing, asset cover and other measures of risk are not.

Abraham and Cox (2007), using data from the UK context, find that the number of executive directors and the number of independent non-executive directors, as well as lower institutional ownership and dual-listing (the UK/USA), are significantly positively related to higher levels of aggregated risk reporting and that these results are consistent across three of the four categories of risk disclosure identified, namely, total, business, and financial and not for internal control.

Miihkinen (2012), investigating both the quantity and quality for Finnish companies (measured with reference to semantic properties of risk, namely, depth and outlook), finds that both quantity and quality increase as a result of the implementation of this new Finnish standard.

Ntim et al. (2013), examining the risk disclosure for South African companies, find risk disclosure to be largely non-financial, historical, qualitative (non-monetary) in nature and consisting of good news. They also find corporate risk disclosure is negatively related to block ownership and institutional ownership and positively related to board diversity, board size and the number of independent non-executive directors.

The studies of Manes Rossi et al. (2017), Leopizzi et al. (2020) and De Luca and Phat (2019) are all focused on NF risk disclosure on the Italian context and carry out a manual content analysis. Manes Rossi et al. (2017) investigating NF risk disclosure in corporate integrated reporting in 2015 find that the majority of firms disclose non-monetary risk information, backward-looking information on risk and neutral news on risks. Leopizzi et al. (2020), who investigate 2017 mandatory NF declarations, find similar results. They find that the most disclosed NF risks are environmental, health and safety risks, that the majority of risk information is oriented to the past or the present and that the majority of companies disclose mostly neutral and positive information. Finally, De Luca and Phat (2019) find that companies provide risk-related information at different levels of specificity according to whether the information is risk description or risk management, whether the firms are operating in manufacturing or nonmanufacturing and the type of risk that the firms disclosed in their reports.

Among the studies employing an automated content analysis, we can quote the studies of Elshandidy et al. (2013); Neri and Russo (2013); Elshandidy et al. (2015); and Malafronte et al. (2016). No study focuses exclusively on NF risk disclosure.

Elshandidy et al. (2013) investigate the impact of corporate risk levels on voluntary, mandatory and aggregated (voluntary plus mandatory) risk disclosure in annual report narratives, where mandatory risk disclosure is identified according to a list of six mandatory requirements of the International Accounting Standards Board (IASB): contingencies, segment reporting, foreign exchange transactions, substance of transactions or investments, related-party disclosures and derivatives. The authors find that each risk disclosure type (mandatory and voluntary) has a different set of drivers.

Neri and Russo (2013) investigated risk disclosure in the Italian companies in the aftermath of the implementation of the Directive 51/2003/CE in Italy. The authors find that risk disclosure is determined not only by the new law requirements but also by other drivers such as company size.

Elshandidy et al. (2015) investigated whether firm and country characteristics influence variations in mandatory and voluntary disclosure. The authors find that variations in mandatory and voluntary risk reporting are influenced by systematic risk, the legal system and cultural values and that the latter two have high explanatory power for mandatory risk reporting variations over time.

Malafronte et al. (2016) investigated risk disclosure in insurance firms, finding that European insurers focus on quantity rather than quality of risk information. They also find that the amount of risk information provided in an annual report is associated with size, technical provision and country-level characteristics.

4.7 Going Beyond the Content Analysis: The Risk Disclosure Indexes

In order to qualify the information, relative scores were assigned to the nature of information disclosed. According to Guthrie and Parker (1990), the disclosure statement should be on both 'what was said and how it was said'. Therefore, many researchers had gone beyond only counting the number of disclosures made and have assigned scores to weight the information based on the nature of information disclosed (Beretta and Bozzolan 2004; Boesso and Kumar 2007).

Using scores to calibrate the information is theoretically justified, and numerous researchers have recommended such an approach. Among the studies that used this approach, we can quote Beretta and Bozzolan (2004); Linsley and Shrives (2006); Marshall and Weetman (2007); Deumes and Knechel (2008); Hill and Short (2009); Taylor et al. (2010); Miihkinen (2012); Elshandidy et al. (2013); Neri and Russo (2013); Ntim et al. (2013); Barakat and Hussainey (2013); and Al-Hadi et al. (2016).

Beretta and Bozzolan (2004) developed a synthetic risk measure on the basis of four dimensions, namely, quantity, density, depth and outlook profile. In other words, the raw quantity of disclosure (number of risk-reporting related phrases in the Management Discussion and Analysis report) is adjusted for two external factors to create a relative measure: (i) industry, and (ii) size.Density is defined as the ratio of the number of sentences in which risk information is provided to the total number of sentences included in the MD&A. In the authors' framework, depth is defined by two properties: (1) the sign of the economic impact (i.e. positive, negative, equal or not disclosed) of the risk-related disclosure and (2) the measures used to communicate the expected performance. Outlook profile refers to how management communicates the approach adopted to face the risks identified, thus distinguishing between those who simply identify risks and those who provide information about how management intends to mitigate them.

Linsley and Shrives (2006) calculated a risk disclosure index by classifying each risk disclosure sentence into the following categories: financial/non-financial, monetary/non-monetary, good news/bad news and forward-looking/historic.

Marshall and Weetman (2007) examine the risk information asymmetry gap by comparing UK and US non-financial firms external risk reporting against the managerial information set, determining the former by way of a disclosure index and the latter by way of a survey. The index is constructed around the themes covered by the survey. The authors show the information gap to be lower in the USA, where firms have higher levels of financial risk.

Deumes and Knechel (2008) employ a risk reporting disclosure index, based on six separately identifiable internal control factors, to investigate whether, and if so to what degree, the legal regulatory environment and the existence of agency conflicts incentivize the voluntary provision of risk information.

Hill and Short (2009) developed an index based upon seven categories, (1) internal risks; (2) external risks; (3) corporate development; (4) third-party risks; (5) information risks; (6) ongoing claims and disputes; and (7) 'boiler plate' disclosures, and five dimensions: (1) time orientation; (2) financial/non-financial; (3) quantitative/qualitative; (4) economic sign; and (5) risk management strategies. The authors used their index to assess the quality of risk disclosure over time (1991–2003). The authors find that firms tend to reveal a high proportion of forward-looking information, a low proportion of information on internal controls and risk management and also that managerial ownership is negatively associated with risk disclosure.

Taylor et al. (2010) developed for Australian firms an index comprising 27 financial risk management disclosure items, consisting of 13 mandatory items and

14 discretionary ones. The authors find that larger and highly leveraged firms tend to provide more risk information.

Miihkinen (2012) calculated a quality risk score using three dimensions, namely, the quantity of disclosure (number of words), the coverage of disclosure (concentration of disclosure topic among five types) and the semantic properties of the disclosure, proxied by two dimensions, depth (looking at both quantitative and qualitative effects of risk disclosure) and outlook (looking at action taken and/or programs planned to reduce risk).

Neri and Russo (2013) calculated an aggregate risk disclosure index, given by the sum of the four type of risks identified, namely. financial, legal, operational and business risks.

Elshandidy et al. (2013) calculated an aggregate risk disclosure index, given by the sum of the voluntary and mandatory risk disclosure.

Ntim et al. (2013) developed a quality risk disclosure index on the basis of four dimensions: non-financial/financial, historical/forward-looking, quantitative/qualitative and neutral/positive/negative. They find risk disclosure to be largely non-financial, historical, qualitative (non-monetary) in nature and consisting of good news.

Barakat and Hussaney (2013) used a self-constructed operational risk disclosure index composed of 14 main items, comprising 4 sub-items each, namely (i) qualitative information; (ii) quantitative information; (iii) forward-looking information; and (iv) graphical illustration or tabular presentation.

Among all indexes examined in the section, the majority belong to the level or disclosure index. Instead, the indexes developed by Beretta and Bozzolan (2004), Linsley and Shrives (2006), Hill and Short (2009), Miihkinen (2012), Ntim et al. (2013) and Barakat and Hussainey (2013) could be classified as quality indexes, that is, indexes aimed to qualify the risk-related information provided. An important step of our research is the calculation of a quality mandatory risk-related information disclosure index that we use as the interest variable to investigate the usefulness of such disclosure for the Italian investors. This means that we need to explain the concept of quality disclosure we accept in the book and to link it to the theoretical lens we used in the book before showing how we calculate our quality mandatory NF risk disclosure.

4.8 The Centrality of Quality of Mandatory Non-financial Disclosure

The EU Directive has been transposed into law for all EU Member States with the aim to rebuild trust with 'investors and consumers' (European Union 2014). The EU Directive is an act of policy to legitimize NFI disclosure based on two main theories, that a mandatory NFI disclosure improve the comparability of information and enhance corporate accountability (La Torre et al. 2018).

Issues in relation to the effect of mandatory NF disclosure in relation to accountability and improving transparency and stakeholders' trust are controversial (Hess 2007). A strand of literature argues that regulation could improve the quality of NF disclosures (La Torre et al. 2018), whilst another strand of research argues that regulation does not always improve the quality of NFI disclosures, just their quantity (Gulenko 2018).

The idea that regulation could improve the quality and comparability of non-financial reporting was initially confirmed in the literature (Deegan 2002) that argues that voluntary disclosure may be incomplete and lack accuracy, neutrality, objectivity and comparability with respect to mandatory disclosure (Adams 2004).

To this end, over the years, some European countries (Spain, France, Portugal, Finland, Denmark and Sweden) introduced mandatory reporting on environmental and social issues, with good result. For instance, a study comparing France, where regulation was in place, with the USA, with no regulation, highlights a higher quality of disclosure in France (Crawford and Williams 2010). The same results show two articles focused on mandatory disclosure in Italy after the EU Directive. The article of Caputo et al. (2020), starting from a notion of quality as adherence to the requirement of the law introducing the compulsoriness of NFI disclosure, argues that regulation improves the quality of NF disclosure. It is measured by an NF score given by a weighted sum of five different requirements: business model, sustainability policies, sustainability risks, NF key performance indicators and diversity. The article of Mion and Loza Adaui (2019) also provides evidence of the enhancement of the quality of sustainability reporting after implementation of the law on mandatory NFD. In this article, quality is a weighted index obtained summing 20 indicators belonging to 3 different areas: availability, credibility and strategic anchorage.

Both the articles of Mion and Loza Adaui (2019) and Caputo et al. (2020) investigate the quality mandatory NFI disclosure. Consistent with them, and also with Beretta and Bozzolan (2004) and Venturelli et al. 2017, we believe that only a quality NF disclosure is able to restore trust between companies and stakeholders, and we want to contribute to the lively debate in the literature investigating the usefulness of quality mandatory NF risk-related information disclosure in Italy. The next section explores the position of researchers as regards the quality of NF risk disclosures.

4.9 The Quality of Risk Disclosure in Empirical Studies

A good number of researchers who explored the existing status of mandatory and voluntary risk disclosure practices by companies highlighted that the current state is not satisfactory, that the existing forms of risk disclosure fail to fulfil the needs of the investors and other stakeholders and that the quality of these disclosure is questionable (Abraham and Shrives 2014; Mazumder and Hossain 2018).

Lajili and Zeghal (2005) conducted a content analysis of the annual reports of TSE300 Canadian companies. The authors concluded that financial risk is the most disclosed and that the description of the risk is superficial and only qualitative, characterized by lack of uniformity, clarity and quantification.

Linsley and Shrives (2005) find that though the public companies of the UK are disclosing on risk, these are minimal and incomplete in nature, mainly qualitative, and that firms disclose only financial risks.

Linsley et al. (2006) examined the risk disclosure practices of the UK and the Canadian banks. The authors found that the risk disclosures were qualitative and focused mainly on past issues rather than future risks.

Linsley and Lawrence (2007) focus on the readability of the risk disclosure in the annual reports of the UK companies. The authors find that the readability level of risk disclosure is mostly 'difficult' or 'very difficult'.

Konishi and Ali (2007), examining 100 companies listed in the Tokyo Stock Exchange, find that companies are mostly providing descriptive risk disclosure and that are reluctant to quantify the risk-related information.

Dobler et al. (2011) find that firms do not reveal quantitative and forward-looking attributes related to risk disclosure, but qualitative and retrospective information.

Oliveira et al. (2011) find that risk disclosure practices are likely to be categorized as generic, qualitative and backward-looking.

Berger (2012), analysing Indian companies in SENSEX, finds that the companies are not disclosing quantitative information; instead most of the disclosures are qualitative in nature.

Mokhtar and Mellett (2013) find a low level of risk disclosure. The authors found that companies are not even fulfilling the mandatory risk and these disclosures are mostly qualitative and not forward-looking.

Abraham and Shrives (2014), analysing the risk disclosure of four companies in the food production and processing industry, find that the risk disclosure is mostly 'symbolic' (rather than 'substantive') in nature.

Domínguez and Gámez (2014) in their study find that the Spanish divulge the basic characteristics of the financial risks involved. According to the authors, the risk reporting of Spanish companies is highly superficial and conservative in nature.

Zadeh et al. (2016) based on Malaysian-listed companies find that the level of risk disclosure is insufficient.

Table 4.11 summarizes the findings of studies in relation to the quality of risk disclosure.

In summary, according to the findings of the studies in Table 4.9, it can be said that, though companies around the world are becoming aware of risk disclosure and reporting on risks, the contents of these disclosures are not satisfactory: most of these reports are too generic and descriptive, and the lack of quality involves a lack of usefulness for the stakeholders of a company.

Table 4.11 Empirical articles on risk disclosure quality

Authors (year)/ Journal	Country	Sample	Risk disclosure quality
Lajili and Zeghal (2005) *CJAS*	Canada	300 firms in 1999	The description of the risk is superficial and only qualitative
Linsley and Shrives (2005) *JRF*	UK	79 FTSE 100 NF firms in 2001	Risk disclosure are minimal and incomplete, mainly qualitative
Linsley et al. (2006) *JBR*	UK	UK and Canadian banks	Risk disclosures are qualitative and focused mainly on past risks
Linsley and Lawrence (2007) *BAR*	UK	71 FTSE 100 non-financial firms in 2002	The readability level of risk disclosure is mostly difficult or very difficult
Konishi and Ali (2007) *JIAAPE*	Japan	100 companies listed in the Tokyo Stock Exchange	Companies are mostly providing descriptive risk disclosure
Dobler et al. (2011) *JIAR*	Canada, Germany, UK, USA	160 firm-year observations from 2005	Firms reveal qualitative and retrospective risk-related information
Oliveira et al. (2011) *MAJ*	Portugal	81 non-financial firms in 2005	Risk disclosure practices are generic, qualitative and backward-looking
Berger (2012)	India	Companies in SENSEX	Companies disclose qualitative risk-related information
Mokhtar and Mellett (2013) *MAJ*	Egypt	105 firms in 2007	Risk disclosures are mostly qualitative and not forward-looking
Abraham and Shrives (2014) *BAR*	UK	Four companies in the food production and processing industry	Risk disclosure is most symbolic rather than substantive in nature
Domínguez and Gámez (2014) *RC*	Spain	Largest Spanish companies	The risk reporting is highly superficial and conservative in nature
Zadeh et al. (2016) *IJEFI*	Malaysia	105 firms 2001 to 2011	The level of risk disclosure is insufficient

Source: our elaboration from Mazumder and Hossain (2018)

4.10 The Notion of Quality Shared in the Book

'Quality' is a key concept in many fields of research (Helfaya and Whittington 2019). The accounting reporting literature is aware of the complexity and subjective nature of this notion (Beattie et al. 2004; Ben-Amar and Chelli 2018; D'Amico et al. 2016; Kalu et al. 2016; Lee 2017; Lokuwaduge and Heenetigala 2017; Meng et al. 2014; Radu and Francoeur 2017).

Even in the NF reporting field, quality is a complex concept and has a multi-faceted and subjective nature (Beck et al. 2010; Hammond and Miles 2004; Helfaya and Whittington 2019). One of the most important limitations encountered in disclosure studies is the difficulty of measuring the extent of corporate disclosure (Healy and Palepu 2001).

The literature also argues that to acquire a rich understanding of reporting and disclosure quality, it is necessary to focus on several individual dimensions of quality (e.g. quantity, breadth, depth and time). Consequently, the amount of disclosure (the most frequent metric in the historic literature) is only one quality dimension. Indeed, some scholars note that it is often incorrectly assumed that the importance of a disclosure can meaningfully stand for the amount disclosed (Cho et al. 2010; D'Amico et al. 2016; Gray et al. 1995; Unerman 2000). For this reason, prior studies have advanced to include more dimensions to assess disclosure quality beyond quantity, based, for instance, on the characteristics of information disclosed, themes/topics covered, types of information and the language used in disclosure.

If we compare the two types of approach in measuring quality, we can argue that volumetric approaches, on the one hand, which count words, sentences or pages, are based upon the assumption that the volume of disclosure reflects its importance to the readers and so can be used as a measure of reporting quality (Helfaya et al. 2019). Even if researchers introduced improvement, such as the use of more than one measure of quantity to measure quality and even the use of unweighted disclosure indices, in the literature to assess the quality of corporate disclosure with quantity metrics is considered problematic and unweighted disclosure indices have been criticized for their fundamental assumption that all disclosed and measured items are equally important.

Meaning or interpretative approaches, on the other hand, such as weighted thematic content analysis have also been used to assess the quality of disclosure (Beck et al. 2010; Lee 2017). These approaches have mainly assessed what is disclosed and how it is disclosed by analysing the content using specific criteria and then weighting/scoring these criteria based on the perceived relative importance of each item. These weighted disclosure index studies include Toms (2002), Cormier et al. (2005), van Staden and Hooks (2007) and Meng et al. (2014). These weighted thematic content analysis studies seek to evaluate the content of specific disclosed topics, rather than merely counting them (Beck et al. 2010).

In most cases (i.e. about 80% of corporate environmental reporting research), the 'quality' is measured using a simple model including only one or two dimensions (Helfaya and Whittington 2019). We believe that, as quality is subjective and context-dependent, we need a comprehensive descriptive model (compound model) to assess quality.

In the NF disclosure literature, the most common approach in previous literature was based primarily on a checklist of themes/topics that capture the volume and variety of disclosure (Al-Tuwaijri et al. 2004; Cho et al. 2010; D'Amico et al. 2016; Hassan 2018; van Staden and Hooks 2007). Several authors accused the extant studies of not being able to fully assess the quality of disclosure (Beretta and Bozzolan 2008; Jizi 2017; Kalu et al. 2016; Patten and Zhao 2014; Radu and Francoeur 2017; Urquiza et al. 2009).

Accordingly, a number of disclosure studies have developed that take traditional content analysis approaches (e.g. volumetric and interpretative) and scoring methods (e.g. unweighted and weighted disclosure index) and then seek to improve how the variety and multidimensionality of informational themes are captured and assessed (Al-Tuwaijri et al. 2004; Beattie et al. 2004; Beretta and Bozzolan 2008; Helfaya et al. 2019; Helfaya and Kotb 2016; Meng et al. 2014; Michelon et al. 2015).

The different approaches of measuring the quality of disclosure could be divided into two groups: (a) unidimensional measures and (b) multidimensional measures (described below).

Helfaya and Whittington (2019), comparing unidimensional measures and compound measures, find that quantity is not enough to evaluate quality, as other dimensions should also be considered, and that one quality measure over another can affect significantly the findings of the analysis. Their findings highlight that the choice of measure of NFI disclosure is of key importance.

4.10.1 Unidimensional Measures

The unidimensional measures focus on the quantity of NFI and the scope (width) of items disclosed.

Quantity measure refers to the amount of information disclosed by companies, taking into account the number of words, sentences or unit pages with NFI information. Therefore, every word, sentence or proportion of page with NFI is considered. It is a simple measure in which quantity can be captured by:

1. Relative quantity (RQN): the percentage of NFI within the CSR report (e.g. total number of pages of NFI/total number of pages of NF report).
2. Standardized quantity index (SQNI): it captures and standardizes the absolute quantity of NFI information (pages) relative to the sample.

Regarding the *width* of environmental information disclosed, given a list of items, the value of a scope index (SCI) for a particular company is the result of dividing the number of NFI items disclosed by that company by the total number of NFI disclosure items that might be disclosed according to the list. The index is an unweighted index, so each item is assigned 0 point if there is no NFI of that item/

theme or 1 point if the information is provided, and the NFI could be narrative, physical or financial.

4.10.2 Multidimensional Measures

The multidimensional measures are computed in several steps to assess several dimensions, such as the volume, richness, credibility and/or presentation of the environmental information content (e.g. Al-Tuwaijri et al. 2004; Helfaya et al. 2019; Michelon et al. 2015; van Staden and Hooks 2007). Four are the most used compound measures in environmental disclosure: TQLI, ACHI, SHI and MQM (Helfaya and Whittington 2019).

TQLI was designed according to Beretta and Bozzolan (2008) and Urquiza et al. (2009) and empirically tested by Michelon et al. (2015). This index is given by the average sum of a quantity and a quality index claimed to capture both the quantity and quality of environmental information disclosed by companies. The quantity index is calculated with an SQNI. The quality index is a richness index, calculated as the average sum of the width dimension and the depth dimension. In turn, the width dimension is calculated as the average sum of coverage dimension and the dispersion dimension.[3]

ACHI is an index developed by Al-Tuwaijri et al. (2004), which combines the occurrence of the environmental items and the measures used to disclose it. Regarding the occurrence of environmental information, they score the environmental disclosure of each identified disclosure topic or item using a 'yes/no' or 1/0. Then, Al-Tuwaijri et al. (2004) assigned weights to the disclosure items based on the different measures used. Weights go from 0 (a company that does not disclose information) to 1 (general qualitative disclosure), 2 (detailed qualitative disclosure) or + 3 (quantitative disclosures). The environmental disclosure (ACHI) scores range from 0 to +3.

SHI is an index developed by van Staden and Hooks (2007), based on a 5-point scale as follows: Score 0 (no disclosure to this item); Score 1 (general narrative disclosure to this item); Score 2 (detailed narrative disclosure to this item); Score 3 (quantitative disclosure to this item); and Score 4 (benchmarking disclosure to this item).

MQM, developed by Helfaya et al. (2019), is the only score based on the findings of a questionnaire ascertaining the quality perceptions of 86 preparers and 177 users of corporate reporting. The MQM includes three overall quality dimensions: quality

[3]Coverage is the percentage of environmental topics (sub-items) disclosed by the company out of the total number of topics disclosed within the index. Dispersion measures the concentration of the items disclosed. Depth depends on the type of measures used to disclose the environmental information. These measures range from no disclosure (score = 0; minimum score) to general narrative disclosure (score = 1 score) to benchmarking disclosure (score = 4; maximum score) to reflect the usefulness of disclosed information.

of content (quantity, themes, measures of disclosure, types of information), credibility (adopting external reporting guidelines and inclusion of third-party insurance) and communication (using visual tools such as tables, graphs and images).

Of the four compound indices examined, three (TQLI, ACHI and SHI) belong to the objective quality indices; the fourth, MQM, belongs to the subjective indices. The next section illustrates the main differences between objective and subjective indices and relates them to the underlying theories.

4.11 Objective/Subjective Quality Indices and Theories Behind

On the basis of objectivity/subjectivity[4] of the measures that disclosure indices incorporate, they could fall into two main categories: subjective analyst indices (Beattie et al. 2004; Healy et al. 1999; Imhoff 1992; Sengupta 1998) and semi-objective indices (Comyns and Figge 2015; Diouf and Boiral 2017; Liesen et al. 2015; Michelon et al. 2015).

Subjective indices constitute corporate disclosure ratings assigned by a panel of leading analysts in each industry. The development of semi-objective indices requires a pre-determined list of items (topics of disclosure) which is then tested for its presence or absence. In an empirical sense, since they are not explicitly related to the inherent qualities of the disclosure itself and since such a list of items is derived from 'subjective' (or rather external) conceptualizations of 'standard disclosures', this approach is like a 'disclosure audit' against a pre-determined set of 'standard criteria'. Hence, assessment is based by certain set of externally imposed conceptual parameters, meaning that semi-objective indices pay attention to the inherent characteristics of the disclosed information (Comyns and Figge 2015; Diouf and Boiral 2017; Liesen et al. 2015).

Subjective indices find their theoretical underpinning in the agency theory. Agency theory assumes a privileged position for investors and the investment analysts in the decision-making processes, and the assessments are primarily driven towards the usefulness of information for investment decisions (Reverte 2009; Toms 2002). Accordingly, the conceptual parameters by and large emanate from the traditional financial reporting conceptual framework (e.g. decision usefulness, materiality, entity concept, timeliness, importance, etc.) which all nevertheless implicitly assume that 'investment' is the primary socio-economic and political decision/assessment towards which information needs to be provided (Reverte 2009). At its best, therefore, the implication is that non-financial information including

[4]The term objectivity refers to an empiricist notion of objectivity where judgemental criteria are derived from the inherent 'internal' qualities of the disclosure contents. Subjectivity, on the other hand, relates to the instances where the judgemental criteria emanating from an 'external' framework or theory are superimposed on the disclosure contents.

environmental reporting contents are to supplement the financial information contents so that the investor can make environmentally sensible investment decisions (see Michelon et al. 2015; Reverte 2009; Toms 2002). The theoretical underpinning of semi-objective indices is stakeholder and legitimacy theory. Stakeholder and legitimacy theory are not driven by a pre-determined conceptual framework of decision usefulness but by the inherent qualities of the actual information disclosed in the corporate reports; these models do not include a privileged user of such information. Instead, assumption seems to be that it is those inherent qualities that would ultimately determine the users of such information. From a producers' perspective, this also means that motivation for such disclosure is not necessarily to support a particular group of decision-makers but to meet the demands of legitimation emanating from emerging discourses and regimes of corporate reporting (e.g. Helfaya and Moussa 2017; Campbell 2000; Liesen et al. 2015; Michelon et al. 2015). Stakeholder and legitimacy theory are very similar, but whilst legitimacy theory considers the relationship between the organization and the society, considered as a unitary actor, stakeholder theory focuses primarily on the relationship between the organization and its stakeholders (Comyns 2016; Comyns and Figge 2015; Cho et al. 2015; Liesen et al. 2015). In a mandatory context, a new version of legitimacy theory, material legitimacy, could be the right theoretical lens (La Torre et al. 2018). The material legitimacy theory is a form of legitimacy that enables organizations to blend what is important (material) to the organization (strategic legitimacy) with the primary concerns of its major stakeholders (institutional legitimacy) (Dumay et al. 2015). Under this approach, thus, understanding how and what NFI is reported becomes more significant instead of analysing the motivations and drivers behind NFI disclosure (La Torre et al. 2018).

Beattie et al. (2004) noted that the majority of the corporate disclosure indices fall under the category of semi-objective indices, which are constructed through manual meaning-oriented interpretive content analysis. Also, our quality index belongs to this category. In detail, in the book we developed a semi-objective index, in the light of material legitimacy theory, through a meaning-oriented content analysis. The framework used to operationalize the analysis of the mandatory NF declaration is illustrated in the next section.

4.12 The Non-financial Quality Risk Disclosure Index[5]

According to the Decree, NF risk disclosure is qualitatively presented in annual report of the company (in the management commentary) or in separate reports such as Integrated and Sustainability Report. Content analysis has been chosen to analyse the risk and risk management disclosure. As our aim was to provide a quality NF risk

[5]The section is based on a work written with Francesco De Luca and Ho-Tan-Phat Phan (Veltri et al. 2020).

disclosure, and since quality is a complex concept, with a multi-faceted and subjective nature (Helfaya and Whittington 2019; Helfaya et al. 2019), we applied a meaning-oriented type of content analysis, focused on the nature of themes disclosed, with a greater level of interpretation of the content rather than just counting the disclosed items within a text. For this reason, the content analysis was performed manually (El-Haj et al. 2019).

Similar to Beretta and Bozzolan (2004) and Linsley and Shrives (2006), in the research we utilize the sentence as a basis of coding rather than other unit of coding that has been used in some prior research such Abraham and Cox (2007) and Li (2010). Seminal research (Bowman 1984; Milne and Adler 1999) is in favour of using the sentence rather than words owing to the reliability of the sentence compared with words which by itself could not indicate any thing. More importantly, using the sentence as a basis of coding is ideal to avoid the problem of double-counting; hence, the score is accomplished once the sentence contains at least one word that indicates risk.

Our self-constructed NF risk disclosure quality index is the outcome of subsequent phases. We first develop the coding scheme to guide the coders to put their observations into the correct data categories (identified in our paper by the five different NF risks and their content, based on Italian Decree No. 254/2016 and summarized in Table 4.1). In the second phase, we content analyse the NFDs, considering each sentence containing the word ‘risk’, choosing those about NF issues and checking (yes/not) which categories of NF risks of Table 4.1 were disclosed (Roberts et al. 2008) and if it was information related to a *risk description* or a *risk management policy description*.

In the third phase, we defined, on the basis of the related literature, the features considered to affect the quality of disclosure. The first feature in the literature hypothesized to be positively related with the quality of disclosure (Hope et al. 2016; Abraham and Shrives 2014) is the degree of specificity of information (e.g. information contains the names of persons, locations and organizations; quantifications of risk, such as values in percentages and money values in dollars; and chronological information, such as times and dates). The second feature supposed to be important in the literature for the quality of disclosure is the type of information, as the quantitative measures are hypothesized to be more informative for stakeholders than qualitative measures (Guthrie and Petty 2000; Beretta and Bozzolan 2004; Boesso and Kumar 2007). The third feature hypothesized to have an association with the quality of disclosure is the outlook orientation of information, meaning that forward-looking information is more informative than backward-looking information (Hooks et al. 2002; Lev and Zarowin 1999). Then we score these three features for each disclosed NF risk-related information, giving higher scores to company-specific information, forward-looking information and information disclosed both qualitatively and quantitatively.

At the end, in a similar way to Beretta and Bozzolan (2004) and Boesso and Kumar (2007), we approximate the quality of the NF risk information disclosed, for each risk category (Table 4.1), as a linear combination of aforementioned characters.

Formula (4.1) presents the index measuring the quality of the risk factor j of company i:

$$\mathrm{QUAL}^{ij} = \begin{cases} 0, \textit{if } \mathrm{DPT}^{ij}_{RD} = 0 \text{ and } \mathrm{DPT}^{ij}_{RM} = 0 \\ \mathrm{DPT}^{ij}_{RD} + \mathrm{DPT}^{ij}_{RM} + \mathrm{TO}^{ij} + \mathrm{TYP}^{ij}, \text{otherwise} \end{cases} \quad (4.1)$$

where $\mathrm{DPT}^{ij}_{RD} = 0$ if the *risk description* information is not disclosed, $\mathrm{DPT}^{ij}_{RD} = 1$ if the information is generally disclosed, $\mathrm{DPT}^{ij}_{RD} = 2$ if the information is industry-specific disclosed or $\mathrm{DPT}^{ij}_{RD} = 3$ if the information is company-specific disclosed. Similarly, $\mathrm{DPT}^{ij}_{RM} = 0$ if the information is not disclosed, $\mathrm{DPT}^{ij}_{RM} = 1$ if the *risk management policy* information is generally disclosed, $\mathrm{DPT}^{ij}_{RM} = 2$ if the information is industry-specific disclosed, or $\mathrm{DPT}^{ij}_{RM} = 3$ if the information is company-specific disclosed. $\mathrm{TO}^{ij} = 1$ if the disclosure includes piece of information projected into the future, and $\mathrm{TO}^{ij} = 0$ otherwise. $\mathrm{TYP}^{ij} = 3$ if the information is disclosed both qualitatively or quantitatively, or $\mathrm{TYP}^{ij} = 2$ if the information is disclosed quantitatively, or $\mathrm{TYP}^{ij} = 1$ if the information is disclosed qualitatively, or $\mathrm{TYP}^{ij} = 0$ if the information is not disclosed. It is worth noting here that in the case of both $\mathrm{DPT}^{i}_{RD} = 0$ and $\mathrm{DPT}^{i}_{RM} = 0$, we set $\mathrm{TO}^{i} = 0$ and $\mathrm{TYP}^{i} = 0$. The general quality index for each company is identified by Formula 4.2, and it is given by the linear combination of the quality index (identified in Formula 4.1) of each NF risk category as identified in Table 4.11:

$$LD254\_QUAL^{i} = \frac{1}{5}\sum_{j=1}^{5} QUAL^{ij} \quad (4.2)$$

To ensure the reliability of the data, this study conducted the reliability test of the coding results from two independent coders. This addressed the accuracy from the inter-observer standpoint. The reproducibility of the content analysis was assessed by calculating the Krippendorff's alpha after the two coders independently completed the entire coding. The alpha level for coding was 0.88, which showed a high degree of agreement among coders.

References

Abraham, S., & Cox, P. (2007). Analysing the determinants of narrative risk information in UK FTSE 100 annual reports. *The British Accounting Review, 39*(3), 227–248.

Abraham, S., & Shrives, P. J. (2014). Improving the relevance of risk factor disclosure in corporate annual reports. *The British Accounting Review, 46*(1), 91–107.

Adams, C. A. (2004). The ethical, social and environmental reporting-performance portrayal gap. *Accounting, Auditing & Accountability Journal, 17*(5), 731–757.

Al-Hadi, A., Hasan, M. M., & Habib, A. (2016). Risk committee, firm life cycle, and market risk disclosures. *Corporate Governance: An International Review, 24*(2), 145–170.

Al-Tuwaijri, S., Christensen, T., & Hughes, K. (2004). The relations among environmental disclosure, environmental performance, and economic performance: A simultaneous equations approach. *Accounting, Organizations and Society, 29*, 447–471.

ASX Corporate Governance Council (ASX CGC). (2014). *Corporate governance principles and recommendations* (3rd ed.). Sydney: ASX Corporate Governance Council.

Barakat, A., & Hussainey, K. (2013). Bank governance, regulation, supervision, and risk reporting: Evidence from operational risk disclosures in European banks. *International Review of Financial Analysis, 30*, 254–273.

Beattie, V., McInnes, B., & Fearnley, S. (2004). A methodology for analysing and evaluating narratives in annual reports: A comprehensive descriptive profile and metrics for disclosure quality attributes. *Accounting Forum, 28*(3), 205–236.

Beck, A., Campbell, D., & Shrives, P. (2010). Content analysis in environmental reporting research: Enrichment and rehearsal of the method in a British-German context. *The British Accounting Review, 42*, 207–222.

Ben-Amar, W., & Chelli. (2018). What drives voluntary corporate water disclosures? The effect of country-level institutions. *Business Strategy and the Environment, 27*(8), 1609–1622.

Beretta, S., & Bozzolan, S. (2004). A framework for the analysis of firm risk communication. *The International Journal of Accounting, 39*(3), 265–288.

Beretta, S., & Bozzolan, S. (2008). Quality versus quantity: The case of forward-looking disclosure. *Journal of Accounting, Auditing and Finance, 23*(3), 333–375.

Berger, T. (2012). Risk reporting practices of Indian companies in the SENSEX. *Asia Pacific Journal of Risk and Insurance, 6*(1), 1–14.

Boesso, G., & Kumar, K. (2007). Drivers of corporate voluntary disclosure: A framework and empirical evidence from Italy and the United States. *Accounting, Auditing & Accountability Journal, 20*(2), 269–296.

Bowman, E. H. (1984). Content analysis of annual reports for corporate strategy and risk. *Interfaces, 14*, 61–71.

Bravo, F. (2017). Are risk disclosures an effective tool to increase firm value? *Managerial and Decision Economics, 28*, 1116–1124.

Cabedo, J. D., & Tirado, J. M. (2004). The disclosure of risk in financial statements. *Accounting Forum, 28*(2), 181–200.

Campbell, D. (2000). Legitimacy theory or managerial reality construction? Corporate social disclosure in Marks and Spencer Plc corporate reports, 1969–1997. *Accounting Forum, 24*(1), 80–100.

Caputo, F., Leopizzi, R., Pizzi, S., & Milone, V. (2020). The non-financial reporting harmonization in Europe: Evolutionary pathways related to the transposition of the Directive 95/2014/EU within the Italian context. *Sustainability, 12*(1), 92.

Cho, C., Roberts, R., & Patten, D. (2010). The language of US corporate environmental disclosure. *Accounting, Organizations and Society, 35*, 431–443.

Cho, C. H., Laine, M., Roberts, R. W., & Rodrigue, M. (2015). Organized hypocrisy, organizational façades, and sustainability reporting. *Accounting, Organizations and Society, 40*, 78–94.

Cinquini, L., Passetti, E., Tenucci, A., & Frey, M. (2012). Analyzing intellectual capital information in sustainability reports: Some empirical evidence. *Journal of Intellectual Capital, 13*(4), 531–561.

Committee of Sponsoring Organizations of the Treadway Commission. (2018). *Enterprise risk management—Applying enterprise risk management to environmental, social and governance-related risks*. New York: The Committee of Sponsoring Organizations of the Treadway Commission.

Comyns, B. (2016). Determinants of GHG reporting: An analysis of global oil and gas companies. *Journal of Business Ethics 136*, 349–369.

Comyns, B., & Figge, F. (2015). Greenhouse gas reporting quality in the oil and gas industry: A longitudinal study using the typology of 'search', 'experience' and 'credence' information. *Accounting, Auditing & Accountability Journal, 28*(3), 403–433.

Cormier, D., Magnan, M., & Velthoven, B. V. (2005). Environmental disclosure quality in large German companies: Economic incentives, public pressures or institutional conditions? *The European Accounting Review, 14*(1), 3–39.
Crawford, E. P., & Williams, C. C. (2010). Should corporate social reporting be voluntary or mandatory? Evidence from the banking sector in France and the United States. *Corporate Governance, 10*, 512–526.
D'Amico, E., Coluccia, D., Fontana, S., & Solimene, S. (2016). Factors influencing corporate environmental disclosure. *Business Strategy and the Environment, 25*, 178–192.
De Luca, F., & Phat, H. (2019). Informativeness assessment of risk and risk-management disclosure in corporate reporting: An empirical analysis of Italian large listed firms. *Financial Reporting, 2*, 9–41.
Deegan, C. (2002). The legitimising effect of social and environmental disclosures – a theoretical foundation. *Accounting, Auditing & Accountability Journal, 15*(3), 282–311.
Deumes, R., & Knechel, W. R. (2008). Economic incentives for voluntary reporting on internal risk management and control systems. *Auditing: A Journal of Practice & Theory, 27*(1), 35–66.
Diouf, D., & Boiral, O. (2017). The quality of sustainability reports and impression management: A stakeholder perspective. *Accounting, Auditing & Accountability Journal, 30*(3), 643–667.
Dobler, M. (2008). Incentives for risk reporting –a discretionary disclosure and cheap talk approach. *The International Journal of Accounting, 43*, 184–206.
Dobler, M., Lajili, K., & Zéghal, D. (2011). Attributes of corporate risk disclosure: An international investigation in the manufacturing sector. *Journal of International Accounting Research, 10*(2), 1–22.
Domínguez, L. R., & Gámez, L. C. N. (2014). Corporate reporting on risks: Evidence from Spanish companies. *Revista de Contabilidad, 17*(2), 116–129.
Dovring, K. (2008). Quantitative semantics in 18th century Sweden. In K. Krippendorff & M. A. Bock (Eds.), *The content analysis reader* (pp. 4–8). Thousand Oaks, CA: Sage.
Dumay, J., & Cai, L. (2014a). A review and critique of content analysis as a methodology for inquiring into IC disclosure. *Journal of Intellectual Capital, 15*(2), 264–290.
Dumay, J., & Cai, L. (2014b). Using content analysis as a research methodology for investigating intellectual capital disclosure: A critique. *Journal of Intellectual Capital, 16*(1), 121–155.
Dumay, J., & Cai, L. (2015). Using content analysis as a research methodology for investigating intellectual capital disclosure: A critique. *Journal of Intellectual Capital, 16*(1), 121–155.
Dumay, J., & Hossain, M. D. A. (2019). Sustainability risk disclosure practices of listed companies in Australia. *Australian Accounting Review, 29*(2), 343–359.
Dumay, J., Frost, G., & Beck, C. (2015). Material legitimacy. *Journal of Accounting and Organizational Change, 11*(1), 2–23.
El-Haj, M., Rayson, P., Walker, M., Young, S., & Simaki, V. (2019). In search of meaning: Lessons, resources and next steps for computational analysis of financial discourse. *Journal of Business Finance & Accounting, 46*(3–4), 265–306.
Elshandidy, T., Fraser, I., & Hussainey, K. (2013). Aggregated, voluntary, and mandatory risk reporting incentives: Evidence from FTSE all-share. *International Review of Financial Analysis, 30*, 320–333.
Elshandidy, T., Fraser, I., & Hussainey, K. (2015). What drives mandatory and voluntary risk reporting variations across Germany, UK, and US? *The British Accounting Review, 47*(4), 376–394.
Elshandidy, T., Shrives, P. J., Bamber, M., & Abraham, S. (2018). Risk reporting: A review of the literature and implications for future research. *Journal of Accounting Literature, 40*, 54–82.
European Union. (2014). *Directive as regards disclosure of non-financial and diversity information by certain large undertakings and groups, 2014/95/EU*. Accessed March 25, 2019, from http://eur-lex.europa.eu/legalcontent/EN/TXT/PDF/?uri=CELEX:32014L0095&from=EN/
Global Reporting Initiative. (2013). *G4 guidelines–reporting principles and standard disclosures*. Accessed January 12, 2020, from www.globalreporting.org

Gray, R., Kouhy, R., & Lavers, S. (1995). Methodological themes: Constructing a research database of social and environmental reporting by UK companies. *Accounting, Auditing & Accountability Journal, 8*(2), 78–101.

Gulenko, M. (2018). Mandatory CSR reporting—Literature review and future developments in Germany. *Nachhaltigkeits Management Forum, 26*, 3–17.

Guthrie, J., & Petty, R. (2000). Intellectual capital: Australian annual reporting practices. *Journal of Intellectual Capital, 1*(3), 241–251.

Hammond, K., & Miles, S. (2004). Assessing quality assessment of corporate social reporting: UK perspectives. *Accounting Forum, 28*, 61–79.

Hassan, O. (2018). The impact of voluntary environmental disclosure on firm value: Does organizational visibility play a mediation role? *Business Strategy and the Environment, 27*, 1569–1582.

Healy, P., & Palepu, K. (2001). Information asymmetry, corporate disclosure, and the capital markets: A review of the empirical disclosure literature. *Journal of Accounting and Economics, 31*, 405–440.

Healy, P., Hutton, A., & Palepu, K. (1999). Stock performance and intermediation changes surrounding sustained increases in disclosures. *Contemporary Accounting Research, 16*(3), 485–520.

Helfaya, A., & Kotb, A. (2016). Environmental reporting quality: An analysis of global creditability initiatives. In M. Erdogdu, T. Arun, & I. Ahmad (Eds.), *Handbook of research on green economic development initiatives and strategies* (pp. 628–657). Hershey: IGI Global.

Helfaya, A., & Moussa, T. (2017). Do board's corporate social responsibility strategy and orientation influence environmental sustainability disclosure? UK evidence. *Business Strategy and the Environment, 26*(8), 1061–1077.

Helfaya, A., & Whittington, M. (2019). Does designing environmental sustainability disclosure quality measures make a difference? *Business Strategy and the Environment, 28*, 525–541.

Helfaya, A., Whittington, M., & Alawattage, C. (2019). Exploring the quality of corporate environmental reporting: Surveying preparers' and users' perceptions. *Accounting, Auditing & Accountability Journal, 32*(1), 163–193.

Hess, D. (2007). Social reporting and new governance regulation: The prospects of achieving corporate accountability through transparency. *Business Ethics Quarterly, 17*(3), 453–476.

Hill, P., & Short, H. (2009). Risk disclosures on the second-tier markets of the London Stock Exchange. *Accounting and Finance, 49*(4), 753–780.

Hooks, J., Coy, D., & Howard, D. (2002). The information gap in annual reports. *Accounting, Auditing & Accountability Journal, 4*, 501–522.

Hope, O.-K., Hu, D., & Lu, H. (2016). The benefits of specific risk-factor disclosures. *Review of Accounting Studies, 21*, 1005–1045.

ICAEW. (1997). *Financial reporting of risk: Proposals for a statement of business risk.* London: Institute of Chartered Accountants of England and Wales.

Imhoff, E. (1992). The relation between perceived accounting quality and economic characteristics of the firm. *Journal of Accounting and Public Policy, 11*(2), 97–118.

International Integrated Reporting Council (IIRC). (2013). *The International <IR> framework, London*. Retrieved from https://integratedreporting.org/resource/international-ir-framework/

Janis, I. (2008). The problem of validating content analysis. In K. Krippendorff & M. A. Bock (Eds.), *The content analysis reader* (pp. 358–366). Los Angeles: Sage.

Jizi, M. (2017). The influence of board composition on sustainable development disclosure. *Business Strategy and the Environment, 26*, 640–655.

Kalu, J., Buang, A., & Aliagha, G. (2016). Determinants of voluntary carbon disclosure in the corporate real estate sector of Malaysia. *Journal of Environmental Management, 182*, 519–524.

Konishi, N., & Ali, M. M. (2007). Risk reporting of Japanese companies and its association with corporate characteristics. *International Journal of Accounting, Auditing and Performance Evaluation, 4*(3), 263–285.

Krippendorff, K. (2004). *Content analysis: An introduction to its methodology* (2nd ed.). Thousand Oaks, CA: Sage.

Krippendorff, K., & Bock, M. A. (2008). *The content analysis reader*. Thousand Oaks, CA: Sage Limited.

Krippendorff, K. (2008). Testing the reliability of content analysis data. In K. Krippendorff & M. A. Bock (Eds.), *The content analysis reader* (pp. 350–357). Los Angeles, CA: Sage.

Krippendorff, K. (2013). *Content analysis: An introduction to its methodology*. Los Angeles, CA: Sage.

La Torre, M., Sabelfeld, S., Blomkvist, M., Tarquinio, L., & Dumay, J. (2018). Harmonising non-financial reporting regulation in Europe: Practical forces and projections for future research. *Meditari Accountancy Research, 26*(4), 598–621.

Lajili, K., & Zeghal, D. (2005). A content analysis of risk management disclosure in Canadian annual reports. *Canadian Journal of Administrative Sciences, 22*(2), 125–142.

Lee, K.-H. (2017). Does size matter? Evaluating corporate environmental disclosure in the Australian mining and metal industry: A combined approach of quantity and quality measurement. *Business Strategy and the Environment, 26*, 209–223.

Leopizzi, R., Iazzi, A., Venturelli, A., & Principale, S. (2020). Nonfinancial risk disclosure: The 'state of the art' of Italian companies. *Corporate Social Responsibility and Environmental Management, 27*(1), 358–368.

Lev, B., & Zarowin, P. (1999). The boundaries of the financial reporting and how to extend them. *Journal of Accounting Research, 2*, 353–385.

Li, F. (2010). The information content of forward-looking statements in corporate filings-A Naïve Bayesian machine learning approach. *Journal of Accounting Research, 48*(5), 1049–1102.

Liesen, A., Hoepner, A., Patten, D., & Figge, F. (2015). Does stakeholder pressure influence corporate GHG emissions reporting? Empirical evidence from Europe. *Accounting, Auditing & Accountability Journal, 28*(7), 1017–1074.

Linsley, P. M., & Lawrence, M. J. (2007). Risk reporting by the largest UK companies: Reliability and lack of obfuscation. *Accounting, Auditing & Accountability Journal, 20*(4), 620–627.

Linsley, P. M., & Shrives, P. J. (2005). Examining risk reporting in UK public companies. *The Journal of Risk Finance, 6*(4), 292–305.

Linsley, P., & Shrives, P. (2006). Risk reporting: A study of risk disclosure in the annual reports of UK companies. *The British Accounting Review, 38*(4), 387–404.

Linsley, P. M., Shrives, P. J., & Crumpton, M. (2006). Risk disclosure: An exploratory study of UK and Canadian banks. *Journal of Banking Regulation, 7*(3–4), 268–282.

Lokuwaduge, C. S. D. S., & Heenetigala, K. (2017). Integrating environmental, social and governance (ESG) disclosure for a sustainable development: An Australian study. *Business Strategy and the Environment, 26*, 438–450.

Malafronte, I., Porzio, C., & Starita, M. G. (2016). The nature and determinants of disclosure practices in the insurance industry: Evidence from European insurers. *International Review of Financial Analysis, 45*, 367–382.

Manes Rossi, F., Nicolò, G., & Levy Orelli, R. (2017). Reshaping risk disclosure through integrated reporting: Evidence from Italian early adopters. *International Journal of Business and Management, 12*(10), 11–23.

Marshall, A., & Weetman, P. (2007). Modelling transparency in disclosure: The case of foreign exchange risk management. *Journal of Business Finance & Accounting, 34*(5—6), 705–738.

Mazumder, M. M. M., & Hossain, D. M. (2018). Research on corporate risk reporting: Current trends and future avenues. *Journal of Asian Finance, Economics and Business, 5*(1), 29–41.

Meng, X., Zeng, S., Shi, J., Qi, G., & Zhang, Z. (2014). The relationship between corporate environmental performance and environmental disclosure: An empirical study in China. *Journal of Environmental Management, 145*, 357–367.

Michelon, G., Pilonato, S., & Ricceri, F. (2015). CSR reporting practices and the quality of disclosure: An empirical analysis. *Critical Perspectives on Accounting, 33*, 59–78.

Miihkinen, A. (2012). What drives the quality of firm risk disclosure? *The International Journal of Accounting, 47*(4), 437–468.

Milne, M., & Adler, R. (1999). Exploring the reliability of social and environmental disclosures content analysis. *Accounting, Auditing & Accountability Journal, 12*(2), 237–256.

Mion, G., & Loza Adaui, C. R. (2019). Mandatory nonfinancial disclosure and its consequences on the sustainability reporting quality of Italian and German companies. *Sustainability, 11*(17), 4612.

Mokhtar, E. S., & Mellett, H. (2013). Competition, corporate governance, ownership structure and risk reporting. *Managerial Auditing Journal, 28*(9), 838–865.

Neri, L., & Russo, A. (2013). Risk disclosures in the annual reports of Italian listed companies. *Financial Reporting, 3–4*, 141–168.

Ntim, C. G., Lindop, S., & Thomas, D. A. (2013). Corporate governance and risk reporting in South Africa: A study of corporate risk disclosures in the pre- and post-2007/2008 global financial crisis period. *International Review of Financial Analysis, 30*, 363–383.

Oliveira, J., Lima Rodrigues, L., & Craig, R. (2011). Risk-related disclosures by non-finance companies: Portuguese practices and disclosure characteristics. *Managerial Auditing Journal, 26*(9), 817–839.

Patten, D., & Zhao, N. (2014). Standalone CSR reporting by U.S. retail companies. *Accounting Forum, 38*(2), 132–144.

Radu, C., & Francoeur, C. (2017). Does innovation drive environmental disclosure? A new insight into sustainable development. *Business Strategy and the Environment, 26*, 893–911.

Reverte, C. (2009). Determinants of corporate social responsibility disclosure ratings by Spanish listed firms. *Journal of Business Ethics, 88*(2), 351–366.

Roberts, C., Weetman, P., & Gordon, P. (2008). *International financial reporting. A comparative approach* (3rd ed.). Essex: Pearson Education.

Sengupta, P. (1998). Corporate disclosure quality and the cost of debt. *The Accounting Review, 73* (4), 459–474.

Smith, M., & Taffler, R. (2000). The chairman's statement: A content analysis of discretionary narrative disclosures. *Accounting, Auditing & Accountability Journal, 13*(5), 624–646.

Taylor, G., Tower, G., & Neilson, J. (2010). Corporate communication of financial risk. *Accounting and Finance, 50*(2), 417–446.

Toms, J. (2002). Firm resources, quality signals, and the determinants of corporate environmental reputation: Some UK evidence. *The British Accounting Review, 34*, 257–282.

Truant, E., Corazza, L., & Scagnelli, D. S. (2017). Sustainability and risk disclosure: An exploratory study on sustainability reports. *Sustainability, 9*(636), 1–20.

Unerman, J. (2000). Methodological issues reflections on quantification in corporate social reporting content analysis. *Accounting, Auditing & Accountability Journal, 13*(5), 667–680.

Urquiza, F., Abed, M., & Trombetta, M. (2009). Disclosure indices design: Does it make a deference? *Spanish Accounting Review, 12*(2), 253–278.

van Staden, C., & Hooks, J. (2007). A comprehensive comparison of corporate environmental reporting and responsiveness. *The British Accounting Review, 39*, 197–210.

Veltri, S., De Luca, F., & Phat, H. (2020). Do investors value companies mandatory nonfinancial risk disclosure? An empirical analysis of the Italian context after the EU Directive. *Business Strategy and the Environment*. https://doi.org/10.1002/bse.2497.

Venturelli, A., Caputo, F., Cosma, S., Leopizzi, R., & Pizzi, S. (2017). Directive 2014/95/EU: Are Italian Companies Already Compliant? *Sustainability, 9*(8), 1385.

Weber, M. (2008). Towards a sociology of the press: An early proposal for content analysis. In K. Krippendorff & M. A. Bock (Eds.), *The content analysis reader* (pp. 9–11). Thousand Oaks, CA: Sage.

Wilmshurst, T., & Frost, G. (2000). Corporate environmental reporting: A test of legitimacy theory. *Accounting, Auditing & Accountability Journal, 13*(1), 10–26.

Zadeh, F. O., Rasid, S. Z. A., Basiruddin, R., Zamil, N. A. M., & Vakilbashi, A. (2016). Risk disclosure practices among Malaysian listed firms. *International Journal of Economics and Financial Issues, 6*(3), 1092–1096.

Part II
Testing the Usefulness of Non-Financial Risk Disclosure

Chapter 5
The Relationship Between Financial and Non-financial Risk

5.1 Introduction

In the chapter we introduce the first novelty element of our research. Different from the extant literature, which does not take into account the possibility that the financial and NF corporate risk disclosure could interact, we make a strong hypothesis in our research, namely, that the two typologies of risk disclosure are different yet interconnected and that financial risk disclosure affects the quality non-financial risk disclosure. In the chapter we illustrate the literature at the basis of our hypothesis, posit our research question and test our research hypothesis in the Italian context.

5.2 The Literature on the Relationship Between Financial and Non-financial Risk Disclosure

Stakeholders, researchers, practitioners and standard setters have become increasingly interested in the inclusion of NFI in annual reports. There is no common understanding and a general accepted definition of NFI (Haller et al. 2017; Doni et al. 2019), but there is a wide agreement in the literature that NFI refers to a broad range of themes and issues such as environmental and social policies, impacts and long-term risks related to these policies and allows stakeholders to draw a more comprehensive and realistic picture of a company (Manes Rossi et al. 2018).

In other words, firm survival can no longer be traced back only to an economic dimension of profit maximization, but it has to be included in a broader discourse encompassing the way in which the firm manages the risks arising from the social and environmental impacts of its activities in the medium and long term and demonstrates itself to be socially responsible (Milne and Gray 2007).

S. Veltri, *Mandatory Non-financial Risk-Related Disclosure*,
https://doi.org/10.1007/978-3-030-47921-3_5

Companies are growingly disclosing a wider range of dimensions of company performance, activities, risks undertaken and outcomes, related to environmental and social issues answering to these new and urgent stakeholders' information needs (Hitt et al. 2017).

Among NFI, risk disclosures are among the most important type of NFI valued by investors (Bozzolan and Miihkinen 2019).

Examining risk reporting is a relatively new stream of literature; it is enough to think that Linley and Shrives, in their 2005 article, affirm that 'no prior empirical studies of the risk information content of annual reports has been undertaken' (Linsley and Shrives 2005, p. 1). The authors in their article find that UK companies disclose only financial risks. Also, Lajili and Zeghal (2005), analysing 300 Canadian firms, find that financial risk is the most disclosed type of risk. Dobler et al., in 2011, carried out the first multi-country investigation of comprehensive corporate risk disclosure, based on a detailed content analysis of 160 annual reports in the US, Canadian, the UK, and German settings (Dobler et al. 2011). The authors find that risk disclosure is most prevalent in management reports, concentrates on financial risk categories and comprises little quantitative and forward-looking disclosure across sample countries.

The prevalence of financial risk disclosure is also testified by two recent articles on risk disclosure, the Tahat et al.'s (2019) review and the Elshandidy et al.'s (2018) review. The review of Tahat et al. (2019) highlights that the literature on risk reporting is largely dominated by the accounting standards for financial instruments issued by the FASB and the IASB. The literature review on risk reporting by Elshandidy et al. (2018) also shows that the majority of empirical studies included in the review focus on financial risk. It is worth underlining that the dichotomy and relationships between financial and NF risk are not an argument on which Elshandidy et al. (2018) focus their attention, preferring instead to discuss the distinctions between, and implications of, research on (1) mandatory versus voluntary disclosures, emphasizing difference between the incentives for, and informativeness of, risk reporting; (2) quantitative versus qualitative disclosures; and (3) risk reporting in the US versus international settings.

If we reconsider the studies included in Table 4.2 (Chap. 4), we can make some considerations: (1) all authors examining corporate risk clearly identify the category of financial risk (except Truant et al. 2017); (2) all authors identifying financial risks agree on the content of this risk category; (3) none of the authors (except for Leopizzi et al. 2020) clearly identifies the category of NF risks; and (4) the content of the 'NF' risk categories is not the same, even if the authors use the same labels.

The probable reason for the similar content in the financial risks category relies on a more general accepted definition and content of a type of risk that is more easily measurable compared with the NF risks, for which there is not a general acceptation of the definition in the literature and the items that should be comprised within it. It is a type of risk more difficult to measure with respect to the financial risks, as it is forward-looking and not disciplined by accounting principles (Hoogervorst 2019).

Table 5.1 classifies the financial and NF risk categories in several empirical studies on risk disclosure.

Table 5.1 Content of financial and NF risk categories

Author(s), journal, year	Financial risks	NF risks
Cabedo and Tirado *Accounting Forum* (2004)	Market Operational Credit Liquidity	Business Strategic
Linley and Shrives *The Journal of Risk Finance* (2005)	Interest rate Exchange rate Commodity Liquidity Credit	Operational Empowerment Information processing and technology integrity risk Strategic risk
Linley and Shrives *BAR* (2006)	Interest rate Exchange rate Commodity Liquidity Credit	Operational Empowerment Information processing and technology integrity risk Strategic risk
Neri and Russo *Financial Reporting* (2013)	Market Interest Credit Liquidity	Legal Operational Business
Truant et al. *Sustainability* (2017)	Strategic (including financial)	External Operational Social Environmental Business ethics responsibility Reputational
Manes Rossi et al. *IJBM* (2017)	Interest rate Exchange rate Commodity Liquidity Credit	Operational Empowerment Information processing and technology integrity Strategic
Bravo *MDE* (2017)	Liquidity Credit Results Market	Operation Business Strategy Regulation
Leopizzi et al. *CSREM* (2020)	–	Compliance Strategic Operational Environmental, health and safety General
De Luca and Phat *Financial Reporting* (2019)	Credit Market . Interest rate - Exchange rate . Market prices Liquidity	Strategic Reputation Operation Compliance Reporting
Dumay and Hossain *AAR* (2019)	Economic	Environmental Social

Source: our elaboration

None of the studies included in Table 5.1 and, as far as we are aware, no study in risk disclosure literature take into consideration the relationships existing between these two typologies of risk.

In the next section, on the basis of the existing literature, we posit the first hypothesis of our research.

5.3 The First Research Hypothesis

Company reporting is progressively incorporating NF risk disclosure. Therefore, it is worth asking to what extent the latter is related and consistent with the already standardized financial information (IIRC 2013) and provides useful information to stakeholders.

In this section we analyse the risk disclosure literature on the existence of a possible association and interaction between financial risk disclosure and NFI.

Usefulness and materiality are key issues that relate to both financial and non-financial information and constitute the common elements to the two typologies of risk.

Nevertheless, financial information has a different nature (the result of past events and measurable in terms of financial consequences and impacts) with respect to NFI (more forward-looking and less measurable). This dichotomy leads to a more difficult judgment about the *materiality* grade of information and, as a consequence, to a not foreseeable perception from users of that information (Van Der Lugt and Malan 2012).

As for the principles behind these two kinds of information, financial information relies on the concept of *recognition* and on the related probability that any future economic benefit associated with the assessed item will flow to or from the entity with a reliably measurable value. NFI, instead, the EU Directive and the Italian Decree 254/2016 that implemented it refer to the *relevance* of the NFI to be provided.

This means that, whilst it is not so easy to understand how to address the requirement of relevance in a context of limited availability of metrics, the measurement of financial risk, for large European companies, should refer to the International Accounting Standards (IAS).

Moreover, the financial information is a backward-looking, historic information, not able to explain the long-term strategy of a company. NFI, instead, which is a forward-looking information, is able to explain the company long-term strategy.

In the literature there are two competing positions. A first strand of literature supports a substitutive effect between financial and NF information, arguing that financial risk disclosure has a negative effect on NF risk disclosure (Ewert and Wagenhofer 2016). The theorists of this position argue that more forward-looking accounting information acts in the sense of reducing the information content of financial reports, as a forward-looking accounting information affects the smoothness of reported earnings, which can conflict with the manager's smoothing incentive and the willingness to incorporate private information in the financial report. These conflicting aims cause a decline in the capital market's ability to infer the financial and non-financial information in reported earnings.

A second strand of the literature, instead, posits that NF risk disclosure could not substitute (or be substituted by) the financial risk disclosure, because the two types of disclosure provide different information to investors (Hoogervorst 2019). Whilst, in fact, financial risk information is backward-looking and measurable in terms of financial consequences and impacts, NF risk-related information is more forward-looking and less measurable, and it is often presented in a narrative form. This stream of the literature, therefore, believes that the narrative information about the NF risks borne by the firm, together with the financial risks provided in the annual accounts, are necessary to give the investors a comprehensive risk profile of the firm and thus the relationship between financial and NF risks is a complementary relationship.

Consistent with the last literature stream examined, we do not believe that NF risk disclosure could substitute (or be substituted by) the financial risk disclosure, because the two types of risk disclosure provide different information. Instead, we believe that the two kinds of risk disclosure are related by a complementary relationship, mimicking that found by Rajgopal (1999) with reference to the various formats providing risk information and that found by Einhorn (2005) and Bagnoli and Watts (2007) with reference to the link between voluntary and mandatory disclosure. Both financial and NF risk disclosure are necessary to provide a complete framework of the risk profile of the company.

No study, to the best of our knowledge, has previously investigated the relationship between financial and NF risk disclosure. We address the dynamics of the relationship between financial and NF risk disclosure postulating that financial risk affects NF risk disclosure.

As there is not enough empirical evidence supporting substitutive or complementary effect, we expect that financial risks affect NF risks, but we have no expectations on the sign.

Therefore, we explicit the first research hypothesis as follows:

H1 *Financial risk disclosure affects the quality of NF risk disclosure.*

5.4 Measuring the Financial Risk

Financial risk is a type of financial information, and, as with any other corporate financial information, it should respect accounting principles to be included within the annual report. For financial risk-related information, the main principle is the recognition principle, and the related probability that any future economic benefit associated with the assessed item will flow to or from the entity with a reliably measurable value.

Therefore, with reference to the financial risk information, EU companies have to follow IAS 37—Provisions, Contingent Liabilities and Contingent Assets for risks and uncertainties requirements. This accounting standard pursued the aim to avoid the opportunistic and earnings manipulation behaviours of companies possibly related to making provisions for future costs that were not present obligations.

According to the International Accounting Standard 37 (IAS 37) *Provisions, Contingent Liabilities and Contingent Assets*, a provision is a liability of an uncertain timing and/or amount. It should be underlined that IAS 37 gives considerable discretion to the management of both the timing of recognition and the measurement of provisions of a firm (Baboukardos 2018; Schneider et al. 2017).

We choose to measure financial risk disclosure with IAS 37 provisions, as one of the aims of our research is to evaluate the usefulness of financial and non-financial corporate risk disclosure for the stakeholders of a company and previous studies on bank loan loss provisions have shown that the recognition of provisions can be interpreted by investors as a signal of management's private information about the future financial performance of a firm (Beaver et al. 1989; Wahlen 1994).

At present, IAS 37 restricts provisions to items meeting the definition of a liability as provided for in the 2010 version of the Conceptual Framework. The IASB is also carrying on a research to decide whether to start a project to develop proposals to amend aspects of IAS 37 and, if so, which aspects of IAS 37 to amend. In fact, stakeholders have identified problems with some aspects of IAS 37 deriving from (IASB 2020):

1. The existence of two different principles in IAS 37 for identifying liabilities that appear contradictory and have resulted in inconsistent and sometimes unsatisfactory requirements. IFRIC 21 Levies, an interpretation of IAS 37, has been criticized for resulting in information that is not useful to investors.
2. The diversity in practice because IAS 37 does not specify whether a provision for an obligation to deliver goods or services should comprise only the incremental costs of fulfilling the obligation or also include an allocation of directly related overheads or whether the carrying amount of the provision should be reduced by the risk of non-performance by the entity (sometimes called 'own credit risk').

5.5 Analysing the Relationship Between Financial and Non-financial Risk in the Italian Context

In this section we test the research hypothesis, that is, that financial risk disclosure affects quality NF risk disclosure in the sample identified in Chap. 3, that is, the 51 larger listed companies obliged to disclose their NF information in the Italian context.

The data related to financial risk disclosure have been taken from the annual report of the company. The data related to NF risk disclosure have been taken from the NF disclosure of the company reported in a specific section of the Management Report or, alternatively, in independent documents. In detail, if the NFI is integrated into the management report, it can be included as a special section of management

Table 5.2 Description of variables

Variable	Description
PROV	Natural logarithm of provision for risks and uncertainties
LD254_QUAL	Quality of risk disclosure subject to the Legislative Decree 254

Source: our elaboration

report required under article 2428 of the Italian Civil Code, or the information can also be spread out across a number of sections rather than in one specific section; if so, a specific section must indicate the appropriate references. If the NFI is provided with autonomous documents such as the sustainability report or the integrated report, the management report must indicate where NFI disclosure can be found.

The year considered is the 2017 alone, as the first year of implementation in Italy of the EU Directive. For this reason, to test our first research hypothesis, we employed an ordinary least squares (OLS) regression model.

Once the quality NF risk disclosure index was calculated (see Chap. 4, Sect. 4.12) and the financial risk measured with the provisions included in annual accounts according to the IAS 37, we defined the OLS equation regression (5.1), where the *i* subscript indicates the firms, going from 1 to 51.

$$\begin{aligned} LD254_{QUALi} &= \pi_0 + \pi_1\ PROV_i + \varepsilon_i \mathrm{LD254}_{QUAL} \\ &= \varphi_0 + \varphi_1 \mathrm{PROV} + \varphi_2 \mathrm{EPS} + \varphi_3 \mathrm{BVPS} + \varphi_4 \mathrm{LEV} + \varphi_5 \mathrm{IND} \end{aligned} \quad (5.1)$$

In Eq. (5.1) PROV is the proxy we used to measure financial risks (with the 'Provision for risks and uncertainties' under IAS 37), whilst $\mathrm{LD254}_{qual}$ is the proxy for the quality measurement of NF risk (our self-constructed quality index). Consistent with Hassan (2018) and Leopizzi et al. (2020), a log transformation of the continuous variable PROV was used when appropriate, to reduce the impact of outliers on the current analysis.

Table 5.2 summarizes the variables included in Eq. (5.1).

The focus of Eq. 5.1 is on coefficient φ_1, which reflects the relationship between financial and NF risks. If the coefficient φ_1 is found to be significantly different from zero, it can be postulated that financial risk affects NF risks. In detail, a positive and statistically significant coefficient indicates that financial risks positively affect NF risks, that is, that large PIEs, used to disclose detailed information on financial risks, also disclose quality NF risk-related information, supporting a complementary effect of the two kinds of corporate risk. Instead, a negative and statistically significant coefficient supports a substitutive effect among financial and NF risks.

Table 5.3 provides details on the descriptive statistics of the disclosure quality index in each type of NF risk (QUALj), on the basis of the scheme provided by the 254/2016 Decree.

Environmental risk obtains the highest mean (6.67) among the risk factors, followed by health and safety risk (6.51), corruption and bribery risk (5.31), social and employee risk (5.16) and human rights risk (4.29). The minimum of QUAL indexes of environmental risk and health and safety risk are 2.00 and 3.00,

Table 5.3 Descriptive Statistics on QUALj

$QUAL_j$	N	Minimum	Maximum	Mean	Std. deviation
Health and safety risk	51	3.00	10.00	6.51	1.49
Environmental risk	51	2.00	9.00	6.67	1.60
Social and employee risk	51	0.00	10.00	5.16	2.57
Human rights risk	51	0.00	10.00	4.29	2.63
Corruption and bribery risk	51	0.00	10.00	5.31	2.35
LD254_QUAL	51	1.80	8.40	5.59	1.28

Source: our elaboration

Table 5.4 The relationship between the financial and NF risks

	Equation 5.1	
	Est.	S.E.
LD254_QUAL		
Intercept	4.557***	0.333
PROV	−0.267***	0.075
R^2	*0.204*	
Adj. R^2	*0.188*	
F	*12.550*	
df	*49*	

Significance codes: ***0.001; **0.01; *0.05

Source: our elaboration

respectively, whilst the other three factors obtain the minimum QUAL which equals zero. Standard deviations of health and safety risk and environmental risk are generally lower than corruption and bribery, social and employee risk and human rights risk. These results illustrate the general disclosure practice of Italian firms about NF risks 1 year after the Legislative Decree 254. In general, Italian companies in the sample disclose the information about health and safety risk and environmental risk better than corruption and bribery, social and employee risk and human rights risk. Table 5.4 provides evidence of the relationship between the financial and NF risks.

The results of Eq. (5.1) provide evidence of a negative (substituting effect) significant association between financial and NF risks, consistent with a substituting effect hypothesis.

Equation (5.1) regression results are statistically significant at small p-values (<0.001), thus providing sufficient evidence to conclude that the model as a whole has statistically significant predictive capability.

References

Baboukardos, G. (2018). The valuation relevance of environmental performance revisited: The moderating role of environmental provisions. *The British Accounting Review, 50*(1), 32–47.

Bagnoli, M., & Watts, S. (2007). Financial reporting and supplemental voluntary disclosures. *Journal of Accounting Research, 45*(5), 885–913.

Beaver, W., Eger, C., Ryan, S., & Wolfson, M. (1989). Financial reporting, supplemental disclosures, and bank share prices. *Journal of Accounting Research, 27*(2), 157–178.

Bozzolan, S., & Miihkinen, A. (2019). *The quality of mandatory non-financial (risk) disclosures: The moderating role of audit firm and partner characteristics*. SSRN. Accessed January 10, 2020, from https://ssrn.com/abstract=3342703

Bravo, F. (2017). Are risk disclosures an effective tool to increase firm value? *Managerial and Decision Economics, 28*, 1116–1124.

Cabedo, J. D., & Tirado, J. M. (2004). The disclosure of risk in financial statements. *Accounting Forum, 28*(2), 181–200.

De Luca, F., & Phat, H. (2019). Informativeness assessment of risk and risk-management disclosure in corporate reporting: An empirical analysis of Italian large listed firms. *Financial Reporting, 2*, 9–41.

Dobler, M., Lajili, K., & Zéghal, D. (2011). Attributes of corporate risk disclosure: An international investigation in the manufacturing sector. *Journal of International Accounting Research, 10*(2), 1–22.

Doni, F., Bianchi Martini, S., Corvino, A., & Mazzoni, M. (2019). Voluntary versus mandatory non-financial disclosure: EU Directive 95/2014 and sustainability reporting practices based on empirical evidence from Italy. *Meditari Accountancy Research*. https://doi.org/10.1108/medar-12-2018-0423.

Dumay, J., & Hossain, M. D. A. (2019). Sustainability risk disclosure practices of listed companies in Australia. *Australian Accounting Review, 29*(2), 343–359.

Einhorn, E. (2005). The nature of the interaction between mandatory and voluntary disclosures. *Journal of Accounting Research, 43*(4), 593–621.

Elshandidy, T., Shrives, P. J., Bamber, M., & Abraham, S. (2018). Risk reporting: A review of the literature and implications for future research. *Journal of Accounting Literature, 40*, 54–82.

Ewert, R., & Wagenhofer, A. (2016). Why more forward-looking accounting standards can reduce financial reporting quality. *The European Accounting Review, 25*(3), 487–513. https://doi.org/10.1080/09638180.2015.1043927.

Haller, A., Link, M., & Groß, T. (2017). The term 'non-financial conformation' – A semantic analysis of a key feature of current and future corporate reporting. *Accounting in Europe, 9480*, 1–23.

Hassan, O. A. G. (2018). The impact of voluntary environmental disclosure on firm value: Does organizational visibility play a mediation role? *Business Strategy and the Environment, 27*(8), 1569–1582.

Hitt, M. A., Jackson, S. E., Carmona, S., Bierman, L., Shalley, C. E., & Wright, M. (2017). *The Oxford handbook of strategy implementation*. New York: Oxford University Press.

Hoogervorst, H. (2019, December 19). *Speech of the Chair of the International Accounting Standards Board Hans Hoogervorstat at the 9th Symposium on Accounting Research hosted by the Autorité des Normes Comptables (ANC)*, Paris. Accessed January 10, 2020, from https://www.ifrs.org/news-and-events/2019/12/accounting-standards-and-the-long-term/

IASB. (2020). *Provisions-targeted improvements*. Accessed March 2020, Available at https://www.ifrs.org/projects/work-plan/provisions/#about

International Integrated Reporting Council (IIRC). (2013). *The International <IR> framework, London*. Retrieved from https://integratedreporting.org/resource/international-ir-framework/

Lajili, K., & Zeghal, D. (2005). A content analysis of risk management disclosure in Canadian annual reports. *Canadian Journal of Administrative Sciences, 22*(2), 125–142.

Leopizzi, R., Iazzi, A., Venturelli, A., & Principale, S. (2020). Nonfinancial risk disclosure: The 'state of the art' of Italian companies. *Corporate Social Responsibility and Environmental Management, 27*(1), 358–368.

Linsley, P. M., & Shrives, P. J. (2005). Examining risk reporting in UK public companies. *The Journal of Risk Finance, 6*(4), 292–305.

Linsley, P., & Shrives, P. (2006). Risk reporting: A study of risk disclosure in the annual reports of UK companies. *The British Accounting Review, 38*(4), 387–404.

Manes Rossi, F., Nicolò, G., & Levy Orelli, R. (2017). Reshaping risk disclosure through integrated reporting: Evidence from Italian early adopters. *International Journal of Business and Management, 12*(10), 11–23.

Manes Rossi, F., Tiron-Tudor, A., Nicolò, G., & Zanellato, G. (2018). Ensuring more sustainable reporting in Europe using non-financial disclosure—De Facto and De Jure evidence. *Sustainability, 10*(1162), 1–20.

Milne, M. J., & Gray, R. (2007). Future prospects for corporate sustainability reporting. *Sustainability Accounting and Accountability, 1*, 184–207.

Neri, L., & Russo, A. (2013). Risk disclosures in the annual reports of Italian listed companies. *Financial Reporting, 3–4*, 141–168.

Rajgopal, S. (1999). Early evidence on the informativeness of the SEC's market risk disclosure: The case of commodity price risk exposure of oil and gas producers. *The Accounting Review, 74*(3), 251–280.

Schneider, T., Michelon, G., & Maier, M. (2017). Environmental liabilities and diversity in practice under international financial reporting standards. *Accounting, Auditing and Accountability Journal, 30*(2), 378–403.

Tahat, Y., Dunne, T., Fifield, S., & Power, D. (2019). Risk related disclosure: A review of the literature and an agenda for future research. *Accounting Forum, 43*(2), 193–219.

Truant, E., Corazza, L., & Scagnelli, D. S. (2017). Sustainability and risk disclosure: An exploratory study on sustainability reports. *Sustainability, 9*(636), 1–20.

Van Der Lugt, C., & Malan, D. (2012). *Making investment grade: The future of corporate reporting. New trends in capturing and communicating strategic value*. Cape Town: Published by United Nations Environment Programme.

Wahlen, J. M. (1994). The nature of information in commercial bank loan loss disclosures. *Accounting Review, 69*(3), 455–478.

Chapter 6
The Value Relevance Analysis

6.1 Introduction

In the chapter we illustrate the other theoretical framework at the basis of our research, that is, the semi-strong market efficiency theory, according to which, on average, the market reflects all the publicly available information. This theory is the necessary prerequisite to make the value relevance theory work, a theory that focuses on the shareholders' perspective and investigates the variables that investors consider value relevant, to which they attach an autonomous value importance in effecting their investment decisions and the market value of the firms. The most famous model in value relevance analysis is the Ohlson model (OM) (1995) that we employed in the research. In the chapter we describe the three main assumptions of the model which lead to the baseline OM (1995), the criticisms of these assumptions, the simplified OM (1995) used in the empirical literature review, the main studies addressed to investigate the relationship between accounting fundamentals and the market value of the firm, the other information variable and the modified OM used in the research.

6.2 The Semi-strong Market Efficiency Theory

In Chap. 3 we declared that, regarding the theoretical foundations of the study, our paper is embedded within the material legitimacy theory, meaning that, in a context of mandatory reporting, the coercive force of the law prevails; companies disclose because they must and disclose risk information relevant (material) both for the company and for the stakeholders (Dumay et al. 2015).

Nevertheless, as one of the aims of our research is the usefulness of risk information for investors, i.e. if the corporate risk disclosure is a substantive or

S. Veltri, *Mandatory Non-financial Risk-Related Disclosure*,
https://doi.org/10.1007/978-3-030-47921-3_6

symbolic practice, we need to refer to another theory to complement the material legitimacy one, as the legitimacy theory makes no assumption of the rational, wealth-maximizing individual behaviour operating in markets.

Our study relies on the semi-strong market efficiency theory, according to which, on average, the market reflects all the publicly available information (Beaver 1981; Fama 1970, 1991; Fama et al. 1969) and makes uses of the value relevance methodology to investigate whether risk disclosure is reflected in the stock price at a specific time. Theoretically speaking, in fact, under the 'semi-strong' theory of market efficiency, information is defined as value relevant if it has a predicted association with equity market values (Ball and Brown 1968).

Value-relevant information directly influences the market value of a firm. Hence, value relevance association studies examine the association between the provided information and equity market values by assuming that these values reflect the investors' aggregated beliefs (Barth et al. 2001).

In our research, therefore, semi-strong market efficiency theory supports the (material) legitimacy theory and posits that risk disclosures affect the market value of the firm.

6.3 The Value Relevance Analysis (VRA) and the Ohlson Model (OM) (1995)

The value relevance analysis (VRA) is a traditional current of accounting studies, positing that the value of the firm is the accounting book value plus the present value of expected future residual income (RI) (Burgstahler and Dichev 1997; Cheng and McNamara 2000).

The main objective of this strand of literature is that of estimating the relevance of an accounting value in the determination of market value (Courteau 2008).

Within value relevance research, two perspectives can be identified: the measurement perspective and the informational perspectives. The measurement perspective requires the specification of a value relevance regression equation derived from a valuation model that expresses firm value as a function of accounting variables, whereas the informational approach considers only whether accounting data are useful for investors (i.e. if they affect share processes) without any link to an underlying valuation model (van Cauwenberge and de Beelde 2010).

Most studies within value relevance research follow an informational perspective, thus employing ad hoc regressions instead of linking to valuation models, but the researchers employing a measurement perspective have had their main reference in the Ohlson (1995) model (thereafter OM (1995)).

The Ohlson model (OM) (1995) is the main point of reference in market-based accounting research (Giñer and Iníguez 2006b; Pope 2010). The success of OM (1995) among accounting scholars is due to development, by this author, of a rigorous theory for firm evaluation in terms of accounting. In this model, market evaluation is a function of both the fundamental accounting variables and the 'other information' variable (ν), which contains all the information affecting future firm profitability and thus market forecasts.

Although the model underwent several empirical tests, particularly in the USA, much has yet to be learned on the market value/accounting values ratio in other geographical contexts, as well as in environments characterized by different forms of accounting regulation like Italy, which presents different characteristics in terms of both size (number of quoted firms) and orientation towards the market or towards banks (Courteau 2008; Mazzotta and Veltri 2014, 2016; Veltri and Ferraro 2018; Jaggi et al. 2016).

OM (1995) is the best known of the models of value relevance aimed at formalizing the relationship between accounting values and firm value. This model constitutes a solid theoretical framework for market evaluation based on fundamental accounting variables (capital and income), as well as on other kinds of information which may be relevant in predicting firm value.

OM (1995) focused on three main assumptions (Dechow et al. 1999). The first considers firm value as the actualization of expected dividends (dividend discounted model—DDM). The second assumption, known as clean surplus relation (CSR), establishes that all modifications to the value of net firm assets are classified as income or as dividends. The third assumption, known as linear information dynamics (LID), shows that the residual earnings in time (X_t^a) are determined in part by the residual earnings of the previous year (X_{t+1}^a) and partly by a series of other pieces of information, known to the market at time t, but not yet incorporated in the accounting system and, thus, excluded from the calculation (ν_t). This assumption confers originality on the model and leads to its formulation in the way considered in the present study.

6.4 OM (1995): From the Three Main Assumptions to the Market Value of the Firm

OM (1995) relates the MV of a firm to basic accounting data and other kinds of information. The model relies on three basic assumptions.

The first assumption is that the value of the equity of a firm is equal to the present value of expected dividends (PVED):

$$V_t = B_t + \alpha_1 X_t^a + \alpha_2 \nu_t \text{ (PVED)}$$

where V_t is the intrinsic value of the firm's equity at time t; d is net dividends paid at time t; r is the discount rate or the cost-of-equity capital, assumed to be risk-free; and $E_t[\ ]$ is the expected value operator conditioned on date t information. This assumption derives from the dividend discounted model (DDM), the traditional model for firm valuation (Miller and Modigliani 1961) which approaches the problem of the evaluation of the firm from the shareholder perspective and hence with the economic no-arbitrage conditions that are standard in theoretical finance (Rubinstein 1976).

The second assumption is referred to as the clean surplus relation (CSR). According to CSR, all the changes to book value are reported as either income or dividends thus ascribed exclusively to financial accounts, unless they are transactions between the firm and its shareholders (Feltham and Ohlson 1995):

$$b_t = b_{t-1} + x_t - d_t \text{ (CSR)}$$

where b_t and x_t are the book value of equity and the net income at time *t*, respectively.

Ohlson introduced the CSR identity to express the equity value of the firm in terms of accounting fundamentals (future earnings and book value), rather than dividends, thus shifting the emphasis in valuation from wealth distributions (measured by dividends) to the wealth generating capacity of firms (measured by accounting fundamentals).

Combining PVED equation and CSR equation, *V* can be rewritten as follows:

$$V_t = b_t + \sum_{\tau=1}^{\infty} \frac{E_t[b_{t+\tau-1} + x_{t+\tau} - b_{t+\tau}]}{(1+r)^{\tau}} \tag{6.1}$$

Simple algebraic manipulations allow Eq. (6.3) to be rewritten as follows:

$$V_t = b_t + \sum_{\tau=1}^{\infty} \frac{E_t[x_{t+\tau} - rb_{t+\tau-1}]}{(1+r)^{\tau}} - \frac{E_t[b_{t+\infty}]}{(1+r)^{\infty}} \tag{6.2}$$

The final term in Eq. (6.2) is assumed to be zero, whilst the expression in brackets [ ] is known as RI or abnormal earnings. Book value at date *t*–1 multiplied by the capital cost is considered 'normal earnings' of the firm; thus, earnings for the period t minus 'normal earnings' can be defined 'abnormal earnings' (Ota 2002).

$$X_t^a = x_t - rb_{t-1} \tag{6.3}$$

Equation (6.2) can be rewritten as follows:

$$V_t = b_t + \sum_{\tau=1}^{\infty} \frac{E_t\left[x_{t+\tau}^a\right]}{(1+r)^{\tau}} \text{ (RI)}$$

The above question is the RI version of DMM. The RI model implies that the value of a firm equals its book value of equity and the present value of anticipated abnormal earnings (RI).

The third assumption, originally proposed in Ohlson (1995) and Feltham and Ohlson (1995), is that abnormal earnings and information other than current residual income (ν) evolve according to a first-order autoregressive (AR 1) process, implying a linear information dynamics (LID):

$$\nu_t^a = \gamma \nu_t + \varepsilon_{2t+1}$$

$$b_{t+1}^a = \omega x_t^a + \nu_t + \varepsilon_{1t+1} \text{ (LID)}$$

where ν is information other than abnormal earnings and ω and γ are fixed persistence parameters that are non-negative and less than one and ε_1 and ε_2 represent the stochastic errors assumed to have normal distribution and mean zero uncorrelated with other variables in the model. The original empirical applications of OM (Ohlson 1995; Lundholm 1995; Dechow et al. 1999) depend on the third assumption, since Ohlson solved the problem related to the difficult task of observing future expectations. This produces a closed valuation formula, in which value depends solely on known accounting information plus the 'other information' variable.

Combining the RI and LID equations, the resulting valuation equation is linear in book equity value, abnormal earnings and other information variable:

$$V_t = b_t + \alpha_1 X_t^a + \alpha_2 \nu_t \text{ (OM)}$$

where

$$\alpha_1 = \frac{\varphi}{(r - \varphi)}$$

$$\alpha_2 = \frac{\varphi}{(r - \varphi)(r - \gamma)}$$

6.5 Critically Considering the Three OM (1995) Assumptions

Ohlson's (1995) valuation model (OM) is the most widely diffused accounting-based valuation model among empirical researchers (see, among others, Burgstahler and Dichev 1997; Nwaeze 1998; Francis and Schipper 1999; Collins et al. 1999; Barth et al. 1999; McCrae and Nilsson 2001; Ota 2002; Giñer and Iníguez 2006a,b; Wang 2013) because, by relating accounting numbers to security prices in a rigorous yet parsimonious way, it gives a general framework for a market-based accounting research and it is easy to implement empirically (Callen and Morel 2001).

The three assumptions the model is based on are expressive of its attractive properties. Its first assumption, i.e. that the price of a share is equal to the present value of the expected dividends (PVED), demonstrates that OM displays economic properties consistent with finance theory.

Its second assumption (the clean surplus relation—CSR), i.e. all modifications to the value of net firm assets are reported as income or as dividends, demonstrates how certain accounting system attributes can be linked to the valuation of the firm.

Finally, its third assumption (the linear information dynamics—LID), i.e. a linear autoregressive model for abnormal earnings and other information variable, allows for a direct analysis of the relevance of dividend policy in valuation (Pope 2010).

Compared with other competing valuation models, OM (1995) and its variants explain stock prices better than discounted cash flow models over truncated, finite horizons (Bernard 1995; Jiang and Lee 2005), as the use of accrual accounting numbers provides a correction to discounted cash flow valuation, reducing valuation errors. Moreover, by replacing dividends with (abnormal) earnings, the model allows for estimating the firm value of non-dividend paying firms (Frankel and Lee 1998; Callen and Morel 2005), providing evidence that earnings are a better predictor of future firm returns than are cash flows (Lee et al. 2013).

Among the few studies testing the empirical validity of OM, the majority of them respected the three assumptions at the basis of OM (1995), above all, the PVED assumption, as it is consistent with rational, no-arbitrage pricing, and the CSR assumption, as it is an accounting identity allowing the substitution of dividends with accounting numbers in the valuation equation, whilst the LID assumption, being an original assumption of Ohlson (1995), has been more criticized. The study of Dechow et al. (1999) relaxed the assumption of market efficiency that is considered a prerequisite to make OM (1995) work.

Some studies, rejecting the dividend displacement assumption,[1] allow a separate autonomous value relevance to the components of net shareholder cash flow (NSCF), namely, dividends (DIV), share buybacks (SBB) and net of capital contribution (CC).

Some other studies intervened on the clean surplus relation (Stark 1997; Rees 1997; Akbar and Stark 2003a). As regards dividends, these articles provided evidence of a positive relationship with market value, mainly for their signalling properties, as dividends carry information about future earnings and their persistence (Hand and Landsman 2005; Goncharov and Veenman 2014). Moreover, the studies of Pope and Wang (2005) and Clubb 2013) provide evidence that dividends attract a more positive coefficient when accounting is conservative. Other studies found similar results, also considering capital contributions (CC) (Dedman et al. 2009; Shah et al. 2009), whilst no studies considered SBB except Dedman et al. (2014) and Dedman et al. (2012).

Several studies, instead, criticized the LID, as it is an original Ohlson hypothesis (Burgstahler and Dichev 1997; Zhang 2000; Biddle et al. 2001; Tippett and Yilmaz

[1]Dividend displacement means that dividends reduce market value on a one-to-one basis (an additional euro of dividend payments reduces the total market value of the firm by one euro) (Miller and Modigliani 1961; Dedman et al. 2014). As a consequence, shareholders' wealth is unchanged by the increase in dividends. The key assumptions of M&M's theory are that corporate distributions have no information content, there are no agency problems and there are no tax advantages or disadvantages associated with corporate distributions (Dedman et al. 2012).

2002; Barth et al. 2005; Ashton et al. 2003; Beneish and Harvey 1998) and, in detail, pointed out that the equity valuation coefficients of OM are composed of parameters that are non-linearly related (Myers 1999; Callen and Morel 2001; Morel 2003). However, no study has so far succeeded in providing evidence that the OM modified to include a non-linear dynamic of parameters improves upon the original OM in predicting security prices. Among these studies, we can quote the recent study of Leccadito and Veltri (2015) that uses an alternative assumption to LID and test whether this improves the accuracy of the model in forecasting security prices. In detail, the authors modified the OM (1995) assuming that abnormal earnings and other information variables follow a regime switching (RS) dynamic, as RS models are a simple yet effective way to capture non-linear relationships between variables. After having applied the OM modified to the companies listed in the USA stock market during the period 1980–2011, the authors find that the RS Ohlson model offers a very limited improvement over the AR (1) OM in terms of predictive ability.

6.6 OM (1995): The Simplified Model Used in Empirical Studies

In order to use OM (1995) within a regression model addressed to prove a causal relation between accounting variables and the MV of the firm, researchers modified the OM equation to include the intercept and the error term and substituted the intrinsic value of firm (V), not observable, with the market value of equity (MV).

The resulting valuation equation is:

$$\mathrm{MV}_t = \beta_0 + \beta_1 b_t + \beta_2 X_t^a + \beta_3 \nu_t + \varepsilon_t \tag{6.4}$$

where MV_t is the MV of the equity of the firm at time t. Equation (6.4) shows how the value of a firm at any moment t is affected by three terms: its current net assets (B_t), which depend on the current residual earnings (X_t^a), and a term which depends on the information available through extra-accounting sources at time t (ν_t). The intercept term (β_0) and a residual term (ε) have been added with the function to catch the variations of share prices not explained by the right side equation variables; a β_1 coefficient has been added to the b_t variable, and the α_1 and α_2 coefficients have been substituted by the β_2 and β_3 coefficients; the attention of researchers is focused on β_1, β_2 and β_3 coefficients.

In searching to provide evidence of the existence of a relationship between the accounting variable and the MV of the firm, researchers further simplified Eq. (6.4) by substituting the abnormal earnings, hard to estimate, with net income (x_t) to reduce valuation errors deriving from the estimate of the cost of capital necessary to calculate the residual income. Many empirical studies also omitted the 'other information' variable, normally unobservable, or assumed that it enters the empirical estimation process as a component of the intercept term. They also use data scaled on a per-share basis, which provides the natural starting point.

After these further simplifications, Eq. (6.4) became the following:

$$P_t = \beta_0 + \beta_1 \text{BVPS}_t + \beta_2 \text{EPS}_t + \varepsilon_t \tag{6.5}$$

where P is the share price, BVPS is the book value per share and EPS is the earnings per share. The above equation is the one most widely used by scholars in empirical research (Aboody 1996; Amir and Lev 1996; Barth et al. 1999). Most of the literature refers to the USA (Bauman 1999; Myers 1999; Dechow et al. 1999; Callen and Morel 2001), even if later on several researches have been conducted in European countries. Among these we can quote the studies of McCrae and Nilsson (2001), Ota (2002), Giñer and Iníguez (2006a) and Cormier et al. (2000), which consider the Swedish, Japanese, Spanish and Swiss markets, respectively. As regards studies conducted on the Italian context applying OM (1995), we can quote Ferraro and Veltri (2011), Veltri and Silvestri (2011), Silvestri and Veltri (2012), Cardamone et al. (2012), and Veltri and Ferraro (2018). Some studies have also been carried out in the European context (Agostino et al. 2011; Carnevale et al. 2014; Carnevale and Mazzuca 2014). Examining in detail empirical value relevance studies is out of the scope of the section; anyway, we can say that, generally speaking, the majority of studies which employed OM (1995) to test the value relevance of the 'other information variable' hypothesized to affect firm's market value provided evidence of the existence of an association between the accounting fundamentals (book equity and earnings) with the firm's market value.

6.7 OM (1995): Examining the Deflators

To mitigate heteroscedasticity, all variables are deflated for a scale factor, and then the deflated variables are substituted for the undeflated variables in the valuation model. By and large, the most used deflator in value relevance regressions is the number of shares that are selected, which is one of the possible deflators that a researcher could use.

The choice of the best deflator is a debated argument in the literature, and there are different opinions as to the best possible deflator (Akbar and Stark 2003a; Akbar and Stark 2003b; Dedman et al. 2009; Shen and Stark 2013).

In 2009, Barth and Clinch (2009) supported the choice of number of shares as deflator. In their paper, the authors contest the criticism moved to the number of shares as deflator by a previous article (Easton 1998), underlining that the Easton (1998) results do not demonstrate that deflating by book value produces superior results; instead they underline that part of the estimation problem is made up of the omission of size-related variables from the simple regression of market value on earnings and book value and that this problem can be faced by adding in net shareholder cash flows (i.e. dividends' less capital contributions) to the valuation model (as suggested by Ohlson 1999).

Moreover, the articles of Akbar and Stark (2003a, b), examining the influence of large firms in valuation model regressions in the UK, by comparing five different deflators (opening market value, market value, book value, sales and number of shares) provide evidence that any of the deflators tested as proxies for scale appear superior in ameliorating the influence of large firms, as in our sample.

In addition, the recent article of Shen and Stark (2013), comparing the performances of the basic Ohlson (1995) model, where market value is regressed on book value and earnings, against the extended valuation models, where corporate value is modelled as a linear function of accounting variables hypothesized to be associated with company value (in detail: book value, earnings, dividends, capital contributions and capital expenditures), provides evidence that extended models generally provide less bias and a more accurate valuation model compared to the basic model.

6.8 OM (1995): Focusing on the 'ν' Variable

The real contribution of OM (1995) comes from its modelling of the LID (Dechow et al. 1999; Lo and Lys 2000). The difficulty concerning the empirical tests of OM lies in identifying 'ν', which denotes information other than abnormal earnings that has yet to be captured in current financial statement but affects future abnormal earnings. Some authors omitted 'ν' from the regression equation when they tested OM or assumed it to be a constant because it is unobservable, but this is not a solution, since, as a result, the 'ν' variable is absorbed in the error term, causing positive serial correlation, so violating one of the Gauss-Markov assumptions of the multiple regression model (Ota 2002). In other words, omitting 'ν' from empirical specification of the OM may yield highly biased inferences on the coefficients of the regression (Ohlson 1995; Hand and Landsman 1998). From a theoretical point of view, setting 'ν' to zero assumes that current information on book value and net income are completely sufficient for equity valuation or, that is the same, the only accounting information present in the regression function captures value-relevant information with no lag. Ohlson, in his 1995 article, defines 'ν' as a scale variable, but he does not concretely establish the analytical content of the 'other information' variable. The lack of definition of the 'ν' variable caused many researchers to neglect its use in testing the model. Hand (2001) highlights that up to 1998, almost all empirical researches on OMs disdained the informational content of 'ν' because of the difficulties entailed in its identification (Hand 2001; Hand and Landsman 1998). Few researchers took this variable into consideration, each following intuition, chose an intuitive path instead of a deriving it from a formal rational process (among others, Amir and Lev 1996; Myers 1999; Dechow et al. 1999; Barth et al. 1999). For instance, Amir and Lev developed a proxy for 'ν', using various items of non-financial information in the wireless communication industry; Myers chose as proxy of 'ν', among others, new patents, approval of laws for a new medicament in pharmaceutical companies and long-term contracts. Dechow et al. (1999) view in the lack of specification of the 'ν' variable as a major limitation of the OM.

Ohlson intervened in the debate on the 'ν' variable suggesting researchers can use analysts' earnings expectations combined with current accounting data to infer the variable that relates to other information. He intervened again in 2001 making clear that ignoring 'ν' reduces the empirical content of the model and that there are no reasons to eliminate 'ν' from the model since the variable can be based on observable data, such as forecasts of analysts, even if Ohlson referred to the variable 'other information' as a 'mysterious' variable (Ohlson 2001).

Since the value relevance is a transversal methodology, the value relevance literature reviews are as many as the other variable information (ν) on which researchers focused their attention. Briefly speaking, value relevance methodology has been employed to test the usefulness for investors of both accounting variables other than fundamental accounting variables, such as the IFRS adoption (Agostino et al. 2011), the other comprehensive income (Veltri and Ferraro 2018; Mechelli and Cimini 2014; Devalle et al. 2010; Tsalavoutas et al. 2012), the research and development expenditures (Callen and Morel 2005; Sha et al. 2008; Dedman et al. 2009) and non-accounting variables, such as corporate social responsibility disclosure (Carnevale et al. 2014; Carnevale and Mazzuca 2014), environmental disclosure (Clarkson et al. 2013; Plumlee et al. 2015) and intellectual capital disclosure (Veltri and Silvestri 2011; Silvestri and Veltri 2012). The analysis of value relevance studies focused on an accounting other information variable is out of the scope of the book, whilst the analysis of the main value relevance studies focused on a non-accounting other information variable will be carried out in the next chapters.

6.9 OM (1995): Simplifying Assumptions and Further Models

OM (1995) has become the main reference model in market-based accounting research. Its main contribution is that it provides a solid theoretical framework for stock valuation based on fundamental accounting variables, earnings and book value, and, in addition, it allows for any other information which could be relevant to predict these figures and hence the value of the firm. Nevertheless, OM (1995) is a simple model. It assumes that investors are risk-neutral, accounting is unbiased, clean surplus always holds, there is no role for detail in accounting, there are no information asymmetries, tax rates faced by shareholders are irrelevant, real options are not explicitly taken into account and abnormal earnings and 'ν' evolve in an autoregressive manner.

To overcome limitations deriving from these simplifications, Ohlson himself, with other authors, intervened in the debate on the base model expressed by Eq. (6.1) (Ohlson 1995, 2001; Feltham and Ohlson 1995). After his best known (1995) OM, Ohlson himself issued articles for taking into account the crucial interactions of key variables left outside the baseline models like the interactions between growth and conservative accounting (Feltham and Ohlson 1995, 1996; Gode and Ohlson 2005). Furthermore, subsequent papers of Ohlson introduced a new strict earnings-focused approach (Ohlson 2005). Other authors focused on the question of firm-specific risk (Gebhardt et al. 2001), information asymmetry (Hand and Landsman 1999), taxes (Collins and Kempsley 2000; Harris and Kemsley 1999), real options (Yee 2000) the time-series properties of abnormal earnings (Dechow et al. 1999) and the linearity of function (Yee 2000)

6.10 The Modified OM (1995) Employed in the Research

To test whether the mandatory reporting of NF risk in Italy (and the financial risk disclosure) has a decision usefulness for investors, it was decided to employ a value regression model belonging to the measurement perspective (van Cauwenberge and de Beelde 2010). This choice is justified considering that in the empirical test the intention was to use a model directly linked to a rigorous and tested valuation model, which is appropriate for the measurement approach. Using an incremental value relevance approach allows the testing of the decision usefulness of an additional metric beyond the accounting information included in the traditional accounting-based valuation models, which have their main reference in the OM (1995).

Then we had to choose the better specification of our model and the right estimation approach for our empirical accounting-based estimation OM (1995) (Shen and Stark 2013). From an empirical point of view, the question was to use the baseline OM (1995) modified to include the risk disclosure or a further model inspired to OM (1995) but including some improvements. In other words, the question is under what circumstances a model that takes care of all these improvements fits the data significantly better than does the OM (1995) (Hand 2001).

In the case in hand, we decided to use the baseline version of the OM (1995). We based our decision on the empirical study of Giñer and Iníguez (2006a,b), which shows that models based on the original version are able to explain market values with greater accuracy and fewer distortions of the real data than more complex models, such as that of Feltham and Ohlson (1995).

Our model allows the substitutions of abnormal earning with net income, but requires the inclusion of the other variable (ν) term. Coherently with the literature stream that believes ignoring 'ν' severely reduces the empirical content of the model (Ohlson 2001; Hand 2001; Dechow et al. 1999), our research focuses on capturing 'ν', the expression of expected future accounting data, with the disclosure of corporate risks.

As regards the choice of the deflator of total values, consistent with Barth and Clinch (2009) and Shen and Stark (2013), we decided to use the OM (1995) scaled by the number of shares.

Again, researchers using OM (1995) could use price and return regression models. In other words, value relevance could thus be measured in terms of the levels of equity prices (i.e. price-levels models) or in terms of changes in share prices (i.e. returns models). The objective when using a return approach is to evaluate what is reflected in share price changes during a particular period, whereas the objective when using a price-levels approach is to evaluate what is reflected in stock price at a specific time (Barth 2006). Both types of value relevance studies inform us of the value relevance of information, although the research question when using share returns instead of share prices may also be related to the information timeliness (Barth 2006; Reverte 2016).

Kothari and Zimmerman (1995), in their article comparing level (price) and change (return) regression models, emphasize that the slope coefficients are less biased in price models than in the returns model. For this reason, we decided to use level models to obtain more economically sensible and less biased coefficients, and it was decided to manage the specification problems ascribed to level models by using standard error estimates that are robust to heteroscedasticity problems (Devalle et al. 2010; van Cauwenberge and de Beelde 2010).

References

Aboody, D. (1996). Market valuation of employee stock options. *Journal of Accounting and Economics, 22*, 357–391.

Agostino, M., Drago, D., & Silipo, D. B. (2011). The value relevance of IFRS in the European banking industry. *Review of Quantitative Finance and Accounting, 3*, 437–457.

Akbar, S., & Stark, A. W. (2003a). Deflators net shareholder cash flows, dividends, capital contributions and estimated models of corporate valuation. *Journal of Business Finance and Accounting, 9–10*, 1211–1233.

Akbar, S., & Stark, A. W. (2003b). Discussion of scale and the scale effect in market-based accounting research. *Journal of Business Finance and Accounting, 30*(1–2), 57–72.

Amir, E., & Lev, B. (1996). Value-relevance of non-financial information: The wireless communication industry. *Journal of Accounting and Economics, 22*(1–3), 3–30.

Ashton, D., Cooke, T., & Tippet, M. (2003). An aggregation theorem for the valuation of equity under linear information dynamics. *Journal of Business and Financial Accounting, 30*(3–4), 413–440.

Ball, R., & Brown, P. (1968). An empirical evaluation of accounting income numbers. *Journal of Accounting Research, 6*(2), 159–178.

Barth, M. E. (2006). Research, standard setting, and global financial reporting. *Foundations and Trends ® in Accounting, 1*(2), 71–165.

Barth, M. E., & Clinch, G. (2009). Scale effects in capital markets-based accounting research. *Journal of Business Finance and Accounting, 36*(3–4), 253–288.

Barth, M. E., Beaver, W. H., Hand, J. M. R., & Landsman, W. R. (1999). Accruals, cash flows and equity values. *Review of Accounting Studies, 4*(3–4), 205–229.

Barth, M. E., Beaver, W. H., & Landsman, W. R. (2001). The relevance of the value relevance literature for financial accounting standard setting: Another view. *Journal of Accounting and Economics, 31*(1–3), 77–104.

Barth, M. E., Beaver, W. H., Hand, J. M. R., & Landsman, W. R. (2005). Accruals, accounting-based valuation models and the prediction of equity values. *Journal of Accounting Auditing and Finance, 20*(4), 311–345.

Bauman, M. P. (1999). An empirical investigation of conservatism in book value measurement. *Managerial Finance, 25*(12), 42–54.

Beaver, W. H. (1981). Market efficiency. *The Accounting Review, 56*(1), 23–37.

Beneish, M. D., & Harvey, C. R. (1998). Measurement error and non-linearity in the earnings-returns relation. *Review of Quantitative Finance and Accounting, 11*, 219–247.

Bernard, V. L. (1995). The Feltham-Ohlson framework: Implications for empiricists. *Contemporary Accounting Research, 11*(2), 733–747.

Biddle, G. C., Chen, P., & Zhang, G. (2001). When capital follows profitability: Non-linear residual income dynamics. *Review of Accounting Studies, 6*(2/3), 229–265.

Burgstahler, D., & Dichev, I. (1997). Earnings, adaptation and equity value. *Accounting Review, 22* (2), 187–216.

Callen, J. L., & Morel, M. (2001). Linear accounting valuation when abnormal earnings are AR(2). *Review of Quantitative Finance and Accounting, 16*(3), 191–203.

Callen, J. L., & Morel, M. (2005). The valuation relevance of R&D expenditures: Time series evidence. *International Review of Financial Analysis, 14*(3), 304–325.

Cardamone, P., Carnevale, C., & Giunta, F. (2012). The value relevance of social reporting: Evidence from listed Italian companies. *Journal of Applied Accounting Research, 13*(3), 255–269.

Carnevale, C., & Mazzuca, M. (2014). Sustainability report and bank valuation: Evidence from European stock markets. *Journal of Applied Accounting Research, 23*(1), 69–90.

Carnevale, C., Mazzuca, M., & Venturini, S. (2014). Corporate social reporting in european banks: The effects on a firm's market value. *Corporate Social Responsibility and Environmental Management, 19*(3), 159–177.

Cheng, C. S. A., & McNamara, R. (2000). The valuation accuracy of the price-earnings and price book benchmark valuation methods. *Review of Quantitative Finance and Accounting, 15*, 349–370.

Clarkson, P. M., Fang, X., Li, Y., & Richardson, G. (2013). The relevance of environmental disclosures: Are such disclosures incrementally informative? *Journal of Accounting and Public Policy, 32*(5), 410–431.

Clubb, C. (2013). Information dynamics, dividend displacement, conservatism and earnings measurement: A development of the Ohlson (1995) valuation framework. *Review of Accounting Studies, 18*, 360–385.

Collins, J. H., & Kempsley, D. (2000). Capital gains and dividend taxes in firm valuation: Evidence of triple taxation. *Accounting Review, 75*(4), 405–427.

Collins, D., Pincus, M., & Xie, H. (1999). Equity valuation and negative earnings: The role of book value of equity. *Accounting Review, 74*(1), 29–61.

Cormier, D., Magnan, M., & Morard, B. (2000). The contractual and value relevance of reported earnings in a dividend focused environment. *The European Accounting Review, 3*, 387–417.

Courteau, L. (2008). *Valore d'impresa e valori di bilancio*. Milan: FrancoAngeli.

Dechow, P., Hutton, A., & Sloan, R. (1999). An empirical assessment of the residual income valuation model. *Journal of Accounting and Economics, 26*, 1–34.

Dedman, E., Mouselli, S., Shen, Y., & Stark, A. W. (2009). Accounting, intangible assets, stock market activity and measurement and disclosure policy –views from the UK. *Abacus, 3*, 312–341.

Dedman, E., Kungwal, T., & Stark, A. W. (2012). *Omitted variables and tests of dividend displacement*. Available at SSRN: http://ssrn.com/abstract=2028444

Dedman, E., Kungwal, T., & Stark, A. W. (2014). *The information content of regular dividends and share buybacks for market value and future earnings in the UK*. Accessed February 2020, Available at SSRN: https://ssrn.com/abstract=2518480 or doi: https://doi.org/10.2139/ssrn.2518480.

Devalle, A., Onali, E., & Magarini, R. (2010). Assessing the value relevance of accounting data after the introduction of IFRS in Europe. *Journal of International Financial Management and Accounting, 21*, 85–119.

Dumay, J., Frost, G., & Beck, C. (2015). Material legitimacy. *Journal of Accounting & Organizational Change, 11*(1), 2–23.

Easton, P. D. (1998). Discussion of revalued financial, tangible, and intangible assets: Association with share prices and non-market-based value estimates. *Journal of Accounting Research, 56*, 235–247.

Fama, E. F. (1970). Efficient capital markets: A review of theory and empirical work. *Journal of Finance, 25*(2), 383–417.

Fama, E. F. (1991). Efficient capital markets: II. *Journal of Finance, XLVI*(5), 1575–1617.

Fama, E. F., Fisher, L., Jensen, M. C., & Roll, R. (1969). The adjustment of stock prices to new information. *International Economic Review, 10*(1), 1–21.

Feltham, G. A., & Ohlson, J. A. (1995). Valuation and clean surplus accounting for operating and financial activities. *Contemporary Accounting Research, 11*, 689–731.

Feltham, G. A., & Ohlson, J. A. (1996). Uncertainty resolution and the theory of depreciation measurement. *Journal of Accounting Research, 34*(2), 209–234.

Ferraro, O., & Veltri, S. (2011). The value relevance of intellectual capital on the firm's market value: An empirical survey on the Italian listed firms. *International Journal of Knowledge-Based Development, 2*(1), 66–84.

Francis, J., & Schipper, K. (1999). Have financial statements lost their relevance? *Journal of Accounting Research, 37*(2), 319–352.

Frankel, R., & Lee, C. M. C. (1998). Accounting valuation market expectation and cross-sectional stock returns. *Journal of Accounting Economics, 25*(3), 283–319.

Gebhardt, W. R., Lee, C. M., & Swaminathan, B. (2001). Toward an implied cost of capital. *Journal of Accounting Research, 39*(1), 135–176.

Giñer, B., & Iníguez, R. (2006a). La capacidad de los modelos Feltham-Ohlson para predecir el resultado anormal: Una application empirica. *Revista Espanola de Financiacion y Contabilitad, 8*, 56–93.

Giñer, B., & Iníguez, R. (2006b). An empirical assessment of the Feltham-Ohlson models considering the sign of abnormal earnings. *Accounting and Business Research, 36*(3), 169–190.

Gode, D., & Ohlson, J. A. (2005). *A unified valuation framework for dividends, free cash flows, residual income, and earnings growth-based models*. Working paper.

Goncharov, I., & Veenman, D. (2014). Stale and scale effects in markets-based accounting research: Evidence from the valuation of dividends. *European Accounting Review, 23*, 25–55.

Hand, J. R. (2001). Discussion of earnings, books value, and dividends in equity valuation: An empirical perspective. *Contemporary Accounting Research, 18*(1), 121–130.

Hand, J., & Landsman, W. (1998). *Testing the Ohlson model: v or not v, that is the question*. Working paper, University of North Carolina.

Hand, J., & Landsman, W. (1999). *The pricing of dividends in equity evaluation*. Working paper, University of North Carolina.

Hand, J. R. M., & Landsman, W. R. (2005). The pricing of dividends in equity valuation. *Journal of Business Finance and Accounting, 32*, 435–469.

Harris, T. S., & Kemsley, D. (1999). Dividend taxation in firm valuation: New evidence. *Journal of Accounting Research, 37*(2), 275–292.

Jaggi, B., Allini, A., Manes Rossi, F., & Caldarelli, A. (2016). Impact of accounting traditions, ownership and governance structures on financial reporting by Italian firms. *Review of Pacific Basin Financial Markets and Policies, 19*(1), 1–29.

Jiang, J., & Lee, B. S. (2005). An empirical test of the accounting-based residual income model and the traditional present value of dividend model. *Journal of Business Research, 78*(4), 1465–1504.

Kothari, S., & Zimmerman, J. (1995). Price and return models. *Journal of Accounting and Economics, 20*, 155–192.

Leccadito, A., & Veltri, S. (2015). A regime switching Ohlson model. *Quality & Quantity, 49*(5), 2015–2035.

Lee, S.-C., Lin, C.-T., & Yu, M.-T. (2013). A fractional cointegration approach to testing the Ohlson accounting based valuation model. *Review of Quantitative Financial Accounting, 41*(3), 535–547.

Lo, K., & Lys, T. (2000). The Ohlson model contribution to valuation theory limitations and empirical applications. *Journal of Accounting Auditing and Finance, 15*, 337–367.

Lundholm, R. J. (1995). A tutorial on the Ohlson and Feltham/Ohlson model: Answers to some frequently asked questions. *Contemporary Accounting Research, 11*(2), 749–761.

Mazzotta, R., & Veltri, S. (2014). The relationship between corporate governance and the cost of equity capital. Evidence from the Italian stock exchange. *Journal of Management and Governance, 18*, 419–448.

Mazzotta, R., & Veltri, S. (2016). Does board composition affect intellectual capital efficiency? Evidence from the Italian context. *European Journal of Economics, Finance and Administrative Sciences, 86*, 30–46.

McCrae, M., & Nilsson, H. (2001). The explanatory and predictive power of different specifications of the Ohlson (1995) valuation models. *The European Accounting Review, 10*(2), 315–341.

Mechelli, A., & Cimini, R. (2014). Is comprehensive income value relevant and does location matter? A European study. *Accounting in Europe, 11*(1), 59–87.

Miller, M., & Modigliani, F. (1961). Dividend policy, growth and the valuation of share. *Journal of Business, 34*, 411–433.

Morel, M. (2003). Endogenous parameter time series estimation of the Ohlson model: Linear and nonlinear analyses. *Journal of Business and Financial Accounting, 30*(9–10), 1341–1362.

Myers, J. (1999). Implementing residual income valuation with linear information dynamics. *Accounting Review, 74*, 1–28.

Nwaeze, E. T. (1998). Regulation and the valuation relevance of book value and earnings: Evidence from the United States. *Contemporary Accounting Research, 15*(4), 547–573.

Ohlson, J. A. (1995). Earnings, book values, and dividends in equity valuation. *Contemporary Accounting Research, 11*(2), 661–687.

Ohlson, J. A. (1999). On transitory earnings. *Review of Accounting Studies, 4*, 145–162.

Ohlson, J. (2001). Earnings, books value, and dividends in equity valuation: An empirical perspective. *Contemporary Accounting Research, 18*(1), 107–120.

Ohlson, J. A. (2005). On accounting-based valuation formulae. *Review of Accounting Studies, 10* (2–3), 323–347.

Ota, J. (2002). A test for the Ohlson (1995) model: Empirical evidence from Japan. *The International Journal of Accounting, 37*, 157–182.

Plumlee, M., Brown, D., Hayes, R. M., & Marshall, R. S. (2015). Voluntary environmental disclosure quality and firm value: Further evidence. *Journal of Accounting and Public Policy, 34*(4), 336–361.

Pope, P. (2010). Bridging the gap between accounting and finance. *The British Accounting Review, 42*(2), 88–102.

Pope, P., & Wang, P. (2005). Earnings components, accounting bias and equity valuation. *Review of Accounting Studies, 10*(4), 387–407.

Rees, W. P. (1997). The impact of dividends, debt and investment on valuation models. *Journal of Business Finance and Accounting, 24*(7), 1111–1140.

Reverte, C. (2016). Corporate social responsibility disclosure and market valuation: Evidence from Spanish listed firms. *Review of Managerial Science, 10*, 411–435.

Rubinstein, M. E. (1976). The valuation of uncertain income streams and the pricing of options. *The Bell Journal of Economics, 7*(2), 407–425.

Sha, S. Z. A., Stark, A., & Akbar, S. (2008). Firm size, sector and market valuation of R&D expenditures. *Applied Financial Economics Letters, 4*(2), 87–91.

Shah, S. Z., Stark, A. W., & Akbar, S. (2009). The value relevance of major media advertising expenditure: Some UK evidence. *International Journal of Accounting, 2*, 187–206.

Shen, Y., & Stark, A. W. (2013). Evaluating the effectiveness of model specifications and estimation approaches for empirical accounting-based valuation models. *Accounting and Business Research, 6*, 660–682.

Silvestri, A., & Veltri, S. (2012). A test of the Ohlson model on the Italian stock exchange. *Accounting & Taxation, 4*(1), 83–94.

Stark, A. W. (1997). Linear information dynamics, dividend irrelevance: Corporate valuation and the clean surplus relationship. *Accounting and Business Research, 3*, 219–228.
Tippett, M., & Yilmaz, F. (2002). Residual income, reversibility, and the valuation of equity. *The British Accounting Review, 34*(2), 141–165.
Tsalavoutas, I., André, P., & Evans, L. (2012). The transition to IFRS and the value relevance of financial statements in Greece. *The British Accounting Review, 44*, 262–277.
van Cauwenberge, P., & de Beelde, I. (2010). A critical note on empirical comprehensive income research. *Betriebswirftschaftliche Forschung Und Praxis, 62*, 82–101.
Veltri, S., & Ferraro, O. (2018). Does other comprehensive income matter in credit-oriented systems? Analyzing the Italian context. *Journal of International Accounting, Auditing and Taxation, 30*, 18–31.
Veltri, S., & Silvestri, A. (2011). Direct and indirect effects of human capital on firm value: Evidence from Italian companies. *Journal of Human Resource Costing and Accounting, 15* (3), 232–254.
Wang, M.-C. (2013). Value relevance on intellectual capital valuation methods: The role of corporate governance. *Quality & Quantity, 47*, 1213–1223.
Yee, K. K. (2000). Opportunities knocking: Residual income valuation of an adaptive firm. *Journal of Accounting Auditing and Finance, 15*(3), 225–266.
Zhang, G. (2000). Accounting information, capital investment decisions, and equity valuation: Theory and empirical implications. *Journal of Accounting Research, 38*(2), 271–295.

Chapter 7
The Value Relevance of Financial Risk

7.1 Introduction

In this chapter we investigate the value relevance of financial risk-related information disclosure, that is, the usefulness of financial risk information for investors. In the chapter, we present the main empirical studies addressed to test the usefulness of financial risk information for investors' investment decisions. On the basis of the literature, we posit our second research hypothesis, which we test on the sample identified in Chap. 3, after having modelled this research hypothesis with an Ohlson model-based value relevance regression equation.

7.2 The Risk Informativeness Literature

To the risk informativeness literature belong the empirical studies focused on providing evidence of the usefulness of corporate risk-related information for shareholders, that is, whether the risk information is relevant for investors to make their decisions.

It should be underlined that there is a difference between the terms 'informativeness' and 'value relevance'. Both relate to the usefulness of risk information for the shareholders, but under an informativeness approach, the usefulness could be operationalized in different ways (such as prediction or future volatility of trading revenues, information asymmetry, etc.), whilst under a value relevance approach, the aim is to investigate whether (risk) information is value relevant for investors, that is, that investors value risk-related information in their investing decisions in the equity value of the company. Therefore, under a value relevance approach, the usefulness is operationalized as the market value of the company, which could be proxied in the empirical researches with the total equity market value of a firm or scaling this term

S. Veltri, *Mandatory Non-financial Risk-Related Disclosure*,
https://doi.org/10.1007/978-3-030-47921-3_7

using several variables as deflators, such as the number of shares (and in this case the market value is the share price), the book value, the sales (Akbar and Stark 2003a, b).

Historically, the informativeness literature focused on the financial risk disclosure usefulness (Dobler et al. 2011; Elshandidy et al. 2018). This section is devoted to illustrating the main empirical studies focused on financial risk-related usefulness for investors.[1]

It has to be underlined that the majority of the studies related to the informativeness of financial risk disclosure is based on the US context. The reason is that the heavily regulated risk reporting environment in the USA has encouraged researchers to investigate the informativeness of the mandated risk disclosures in this context. Elshandidy et al. (2018) first had the intuition to divide the EU/AUS and US risk reporting literature. In their review, the authors provide evidence of their intuition that in a mandatory environment like the USA, research focused on the informativeness question, whilst in contexts like the European Union and Australia, where disclosure of risk has traditionally been voluntary, researchers have broadly focused on the incentives question (Elshandidy et al. 2018).

Nevertheless, the informativeness issue has started to be addressed in the EU/AUS context (e.g. Elshandidy and Neri 2015; Elshandidy and Shrives 2016; Miihkinen 2013) and also in emerging countries (Moumen et al. 2015). Among the two likely reasons that led to a growth in value relevance research in contexts other than the USA, there are the increased pressure from professional bodies (e.g. ICAEW 2011) and the availability of data and more sophisticated content analysis techniques (Elshandidy et al. 2018).

As the US context is a strongly regulated environment, the empirical papers focused mainly on the impact of risk regulations on market indicators. Therefore, since the US-based research is wide, we decided to divide the empirical papers into early US-based research and late US-based research. Early US-based research focused on the informativeness of FFR no. 48, whilst late US-based research focused on the informativeness of item 1A, Risk Factors, of the 10-K filing, mandated in 2005.[2]

Among the studies belong to the early US-based research, we can quote the studies of Rajgopal (1999), Jorion (2002), and Pérignon and Smith (2010).

---

[1]The risk value relevance literature focused on the NF risk disclosure usefulness will be analysed in the next chapter.

[2]The Financial Reporting Release (FFR) no. 48 from the Securities and Exchange Commission (SEC) requires companies to disclose both quantitative and qualitative information about potential losses arising from the use of financial instruments and covers interest rates, commodity prices, foreign currency rates and equity investments. Companies have the choice of disclosure formats, that is, tabular format, sensitivity analysis and Value at Risk (VaR), as well as three measurement bases: cash flows, earnings and fair values. In turn, in tabular format, risk is not explicitly quantified. Rather, a table lists the attributes of market-sensitive assets and liabilities are provided. Sensitivities are measures of the potential losses arising from hypothetical changes in market rates, whilst VaR identifies the maximum loss, with a certain degree of probability (i.e. 90%, 95% and 99%) that is expected specific to a certain item (or items) (e.g. revenues, assets) over the next period (e.g. day, month and year) (Jorion 2006).

Table 7.1 Main informativeness early US-based empirical studies

Authors/ journal (year)	Country	Sample	Research focus	Main results
Rajgopal *TAR* (1999)	USA	149 oil and gas firm-years from 1993 to 1996	To investigate the association between the FRR No.48 disclosures and the equity return sensitivity to oil and gas price changes	The author provides evidence of the association investigated
Jorion *TAR* (2002)	USA	Eight banks from 1995 to 1999	To investigate the association between the FRR No.48 VaR risk disclosures and the variability of banks' unexpected trading revenues	The author provides evidence of the association investigated
Pérignon and Smith *JEP* (2010)	USA	The largest 10 US banks from 1996 to 2005	To investigate the association between the FRR No.48 VaR risk disclosures and the future volatility of trading revenues	The authors do not provide evidence of the association investigated

Source: Our elaboration

Rajgopal (1999), investigating the US oil and gas firms, finds that market voluntary risk disclosure is positively associated with equity return sensitivity to oil and gas price changes, thus suggesting that risk disclosure is informative for investors.

Jorion (2002), investigating the relation between mandatory VaR disclosures and the subsequent variability of banks' unexpected trading revenues for a sample of eight banks, finds VaR disclosures useful for investors in predicting them.

Pérignon and Smith (2010), investigating the relation between both mandatory and voluntary (aggregate) VaR disclosures and the future volatility of trading revenues for a sample of ten largest banks, find that VaR disclosures are not useful for investors in predicting it.

Table 7.1 summarizes the main empirical informativeness early US-based studies highlighting authors, journal, year, sample, research focus and main results.

The late US-based empirical papers all present some common features, such as that they make use of much larger datasets, of structured filings (i.e. 10-Ks) that are publicly available, and rely on more sophisticated, generally automated content analysis techniques to analyse narrative risk disclosure contained in the 10 K filing (mandated in 2005). Among these studies, we can quote Kravet and Muslu (2013), Bao and Datta (2014), Campbell et al. (2014), Filzen (2015), Hope et al. (2016), Bravo (2017) and Campbell et al. (2019).

Kravet and Muslu (2013) investigate, on a sample of 28,110 firm-year observations from 1994 to 2007, whether and how changes in mandatory risk disclosures are related to changes in investor and analyst activities before and after 10-K filings. The authors find that annual increases in risk disclosures are associated with increased stock return volatility and trading volume around and after the filings.

Bao and Datta (2014) examine, for 7679 firm-year observations from 2006 to 2010, the impact of each type of voluntary risk disclosure identified (30) on the volatility of the stock return. They find that 22 types of risk disclosure are uninformative, 3 types of risk disclosure (funding, macroeconomic cyclical industry and credit risks) are positively related to investor perceived risk and the other 5 types of risk disclosure (human resources, regulation changes, infrastructure, operation disruption and debt risks) are negatively related to it.

Campbell et al. (2014) examine, for 9076 US firm-year observations from 2005 to 2008, whether mandatory risk information (articulated into financial, systematic, idiosyncratic, legal and regulatory tax) is associated with firm value. The authors find that changes in (unexpected) risk disclosure influence investors' assessments of firm risk and value. The authors provide evidence of a positive and significant association between risk disclosure and stock return volatility and a negative and significant association between risk disclosure and abnormal returns.

Filzen (2015) investigates the association between mandatory risk factor updates in 10 Q filings with negative abnormal returns at the time the updates were disclosed and whether quarterly updates are followed by negative earnings shocks using a sample of US 13,165 firms' quarterly reports. The author finds that firms which update their risk factors section have significantly lower future unexpected earnings and are more likely to experience future extreme negative earnings shocks.

Hope et al. (2016) first establish a new measure (*specificity*) to quantify the level of specificity of the qualitative aggregate risk factor disclosures of firms, and then they examine the association between specificity and market indicators (short-term price reactions and trading volumes). The authors find that the market reaction to the 10-K filing is positively and significantly associated with *specificity*.[3]

Bravo (2017) investigates the association between voluntary and mandatory risk disclosure and firm value proxied by the market-to-book ratio and Tobin's Q in a sample of 95 companies included in Standard and Poor's 500 index belonging to the manufacturing industry. Bao and Datta (2014) examine, in a sample, the impact of 30 types of voluntarily disclosed risk, on the investors perceived risk, roxied with the volatility of the stock returns. The authors find that 22 types of risk disclosed are uninformative, 3 (funding, macroeconomic cyclical industry, and credit risks) are positively related to investor perceived risk, and the other 5 (human resources, regulation changes, infrastructure, operation disruption, and debt risks) are negatively related to investor perceived risk, calculated following the framework of Dobler et al. (2011), Cabedo and Tirado (2004) and Linsley and Shrives (2006) and obtained by dividing the number of information categories disclosed by a company by the total number of categories that a company may disclose. The author provides evidence of a positive association between risk disclosure and firm value.

Campbell et al. (2019) investigate the association between Form 10-K tax-related risk factor disclosures and future cash flow levels and stock returns on 5813 US

[3]For example, a firm will have a higher specificity score if its risk factor disclosures include the names of persons, locations and organizations; quantifications of risk, such as values in percentages and money values in dollars; and chronological information, such as times and dates.

firm-year observations for 2005–2013. The authors find that investors incorporate this relation into stock prices.

Table 7.2 summarizes the main empirical informativeness late US-based studies highlighting authors, journal, year, sample, research focus and main results.

As for the informativeness empirical studies conducted in other than the US context, we can quote the studies of Miihkinen (2013), Abdullah et al. (2015), Elbannan and Elbannan (2015), Elshandidy and Neri (2015), Moumen et al. (2015), dos Santos and Coelho (2018), Kamaruzaman et al. (2019) and Li et al. (2019).

In the Finnish context, Miihkinen (2013) investigates the association between mandatory risk disclosure and information asymmetry, providing evidence that quality risk disclosure negatively affects information asymmetry.

Abdullah et al. (2015) investigate the association between voluntary risk management disclosure and firm value, proxied with market capitalization, Tobin's Q and market to book value of the equity ratio on a sample of 395 firms listed on the main market of Bursa Malaysia in 2011. The authors find that risk disclosure has a positive and significant relationship with firm value.

Moumen et al. (2015) investigate whether voluntary risk disclosure in the annual report contains value-relevant information for investors to predict future earnings in 12 Middle Eastern and North African (MENA) countries. The authors provide evidence of this association, finding a positive relationship between voluntary risk information and the market's ability to anticipate 2-year ahead future earnings change.

Elbannan and Elbannan (2015) examine whether bank risk disclosures are associated with operating performance and market valuation proxied by Tobin's Q within the Egyptian context. The authors find risk disclosure to be positively associated with operating performance and Tobin's Q.

Elshandidy and Neri (2015) study a sample of non-financial firms in the UK and Italy and examine first how corporate governance influences firms' decisions to reveal risk information mandatorily and/or voluntarily and then study the impact of observed risk reporting on market liquidity, providing evidence of a positive association between risk disclosure and market liquidity.

In the Brazilian context, dos Santos and Coelho (2018) investigate whether the disclosure in accounting reports of information on risk and its management affects, at the margin, firm valuations in the Brazilian capital market. Their findings confirmed that risk disclosure is value relevant for investors, providing evidence of a negative association between risk disclosure and firm value.

Kamaruzaman et al. (2019) investigate the association between risk disclosure and firm value in the Malaysian context, providing evidence of a negative association between risk disclosure and firm value.

Li et al. (2019) investigate the effect of risk disclosure on corporate investment efficiency, providing evidence of a positive and significant association between risk disclosure and corporate investment efficiency.

Table 7.3 summarizes the main empirical informativeness non-US-based studies highlighting authors, journal, year, sample, research focus and main results.

Table 7.2 Main informativeness late US-based empirical studies

Authors/ journal (year)	Country	Sample	Research focus	Main results
Kraveat and Muslu *RAST* (2013)	USA	28,110 firm-year observations from 1994 to 2007	To investigate whether and how changes in mandatory risk disclosures are related to changes in investor and analyst activities before and after 10-K filings	The authors provide evidence of the association investigated
Bao and Datta *MS* (2014)	USA	7679 firm-year observations 2006–2010	To investigate the impact of each type of voluntary risk disclosure identified (30) on the volatility of the stock return	The authors do not provide evidence of the association investigated for 22/30 risks and provided evidence for 8/30 risks
Campbell et al. *RAST* (2014)	USA	9076 firm-year observations from 2005 to 2008	To investigate whether risk information is associated with stock returns volatility and abnormal returns	The authors provide evidence of the association investigated
Filzen *AH* (2015)	USA	13,165 firm-year observations from 2006 to 2010	To investigate the association between mandatory risk factor updates in 10 Q filings with abnormal returns and earnings shocks	The author provides evidence of the association investigated
Hope et al. *RAST* (2016)	USA	14,865 firm-year observations from 2006 to 2011	To investigate the association between specificity (a self-constructed measure) and short-term price reactions and trading volume change	The authors provided evidence of the association investigated
Bravo *MDE* (2017)	USA	95 manufacturing companies included in the S&P 500 index in 2009	To investigate the association between two disclosure measures (RD_level and RD_coverage) and two firm value measures: market-to-book ratio and Tobin's Q	The author provides evidence of the association investigated
Campbell et al. *RAST* (2019)	USA	5813 US firm-year observations for the 2005–2013 period	To investigate the association between Form 10-K tax-related risk factor disclosures and future cash flow levels and stock returns	The authors provided evidence of the association investigated

Source: Our elaboration

Table 7.3 Main informativeness non-US-based empirical studies

Authors/ journal (year)	Country	Sample	Research focus	Main results
Miihkinen *AA* (2013)	Finland	386 firm-year observations 2006–2009	To investigate the association between the quality risk disclosure and the information asymmetry	The author provides evidence of the association investigated
Abdullah et al. *JAAR* (2015)	Malaysia	7395 firms from the year 2011	To investigate the association between voluntary risk management disclosure and firm value (Tobin's Q; market to book value of equity ratio)	The authors provide evidence of the association investigated
Moumen et al. *RIBF* (2015)	12 Middle Eastern and North African (MENA) countries	809 firm-year observations for non-financial firms during 2007–2009	To examine whether voluntary risk disclosure in the annual report contains value-relevant information for investors to predict future earnings	The authors provide evidence of the association investigated
Elbannan and Elbannan *JAAF* (2015)	Egypt	283 firm-year observations 2002–2011 of financial firms	To examine whether bank risk disclosures are associated with market valuation (Tobin's Q)	The authors provide evidence of the association investigated
Elshandidy and Neri *CGIR* (2015)	UK, Italy	Non-financial firms from June 2005 to June 2010	To investigate the impact of observed risk reporting on market liquidity	The authors provide evidence of the association investigated
dos Santos and Coelho *RCF* (2018)	Brazil	100 Brazilian companies from 2012 to 2014	To investigate whether the disclosure in accounting reports of information on risk and its management affects, at the margin, firm valuations	The authors provide evidence of the association between risk disclosure and firm value
Kamaruzaman et al. *IJMFA* (2019)	Malaysia	5813 US firm-year observations for the 2005–2013 period	To investigate the association between risk disclosure and firm value	The authors provided evidence of the association investigated
Li et al. *IREF* (2019)	China	18,651 firm-year observations for the 2007–2014 period	To investigate the effect of risk disclosure on corporate investment efficiency	The authors provided evidence of the association investigated

Source: Our elaboration

7.3 The Second Research Hypothesis

Analysing the studies illustrated in the previous section, we can divide them into three main streams. The first one, named by Kravet and Muslu (2013) the *null hypothesis*, predicts that the risk-related disclosures information is uninformative, as it is boiler-plate, and too general to make a difference for investors. This argument is theoretically supported by Abraham and Shrives (2014) according to which risk disclosure is overly generalized and managers disclose symbolic rather than substantive risk-related information. Two empirical studies can be included in this first argument, and they are the studies of Pérignon and Smith (2010), which find that VaR disclosures are not useful for investors in predicting the future volatility of trading revenues, and partially the study of Bao and Datta, which finds that 22 types of risk disclosure out of 30 identified are uninformative in relation to the investors' perceived risks.

The majority of studies included in the previous section thus support the idea that any information regarding the risk of a firm is useful for investors but with two opposite effects. The second hypothesis is that risk disclosures resolve the known risk factors and contingencies of a company, thereby reducing users' risk perceptions (the *convergence* argument) and thus increasing firm value indicators. The third hypothesis is that risk disclosures reveal unknown risk factors and contingencies, thereby increasing users' risk perceptions (the *divergence* argument) and thus decreasing firm value indicators (Kravet and Muslu 2013).

7.3.1 *The Convergence Hypothesis*

The convergence hypothesis assumes that there is little heterogeneity of risk information. Firms have high information transparency and investors have low risk perception. After risk reporting quality is improved, information transparency rises (Roulstone 1999), and market indicators increase by lowering information asymmetry and the agency problem. In other words, the convergence hypothesis considers the homogeneity of risk information compared to the other information provided by the company. Therefore, providing overall risk information, interpreting known risk factors and unexpected events and revealing previously unknown specific risk factors, companies obtain to reduce investors' risk perception and thus to increase firm value (Hope et al. 2016). The hold of the convergence hypothesis is based on some assumptions (Li et al. 2019). First, disclosed risks update corporate risk condition revealing unknown risk factors, thus increasing the public information supply and also indicating to investors, who enhance in this way their understanding of the company, and the managers' confidence in managing the risks. Second, more risk disclosure reflects the prudence attitude by management. When considering the environment of high risks and uncertainty, managers will prefer a superior project over an inferior and be encouraged to make an optimal investment decision, which effectively moderates the agency problem between controlling shareholders and minority shareholders. Third, risk disclosure is helpful for investors to achieve a future volatility of earnings; therefore, it could reduce their required compensation for risks and result in more precise pricing. Finally, high-quality information disclosure can reduce the external cost of capital and demand for excess capital resulting from temporary mispricing, assisting superior firms in obtaining an optimal amount of capital, depressing overinvestment and mitigating underinvestment, which increase investment efficiency (Healy and Palepu 2001; Biddle and Gilles 2006).

Under a convergence perspective, the increased transparency of firms as regards corporate risks rises information transparency, lowering information asymmetry Miihkinen 2013), and this causes a lower volatility of stock returns (Bao and Datta 2014) and enhances market liquidity (Elshandidy and Neri (2015); firm value (Elbannan and Elbannan 2015; Bravo 2017), cash flow levels and stock returns [Campbell et al. (2019); and investment efficiency (Li et al. 2019)].[4]

Table 7.4 summarizes the main informativeness empirical studies supporting convergence hypothesis in chronological order.

7.3.2 The Divergence Hypothesis

In the divergence argument, a strong heterogeneity of risk information (Li et al. 2019) is hypothesized. Firms have low information transparency and investors have high-risk perception. The difficulty of quantifying risk information triggers market participants' fear of unknown risks in that it increases their risk perception (Kravet and Muslu 2013). Information asymmetry between investors and firms is intensified resulting from an uncertainty of the information environment and increasing difficulty of understanding of risk disclosure (Campbell et al. 2014), because investors cannot judge the real situation of a firm.

When a firm discloses significant risk information, investors may perceive that the firm is facing huge risks and require compensation to avoid unknown risks or even withdraw their ownership of the shares.

Summarizing, under the divergence hypothesis, the revelation by companies of previous unknown risk factors and unexpected events raises investors' risk perception and thus decreases firm value (Li 2006; Kravet and Muslu 2013; Campbell et al. 2014).

The divergence argument considers that risk disclosure improves investors' risk perception; thus, starting from a situation of high perception of the risk, this causes higher equity return sensitivity to price changes (Rajgopal 1999); higher return

[4]The studies of Moumen et al. (2015) and Hope et al. (2016) have not been classified under a divergence or convergence approach, as, in the context of risk factor disclosure, they were interested only in the magnitude (if the risk information is relevant) and not in the direction of the investors' expectation changes. They focused on unsigned market reaction.

Table 7.4 Main informativeness empirical studies supporting convergence

Authors/ journal (year)	Country	Research focus	Main results	Sign of the association
Miihkinen *AA* (2013)	Finland	To investigate the association between the quality risk disclosure and the information asymmetry	The author provides evidence of the association investigated	Negative
Bao and Datta *MS* (2014)	USA	To investigate the impact of each type of voluntary risk disclosure identified (30) on the volatility of the stock return	The authors provide evidence of the association investigated for 8/30 risks	Negative (for 5 risks on 30 identified)
Abdullah et al. *JAAR* (2015)	Malaysia	To investigate the association between voluntary risk management disclosure and firm value (Tobin's Q; market to book value of equity ratio)	The authors provide evidence of the association investigated	Positive
Elbannan and Elbannan *JAAF* (2015)	Egypt	To examine whether bank risk disclosures are associated with market valuation (Tobin's Q)	The authors provide evidence of the association investigated	Positive
Elshandidy and Neri *CGIR* (2015)	UK, Italy	To investigate the impact of observed risk reporting on market liquidity	The authors provide evidence of the association investigated	Positive
Bravo *MDE* (2017)	USA	To investigate the association between two disclosure measures (RD_level and RD_coverage) and two firm value measures: market-to-book ratio and Tobin's Q	The author provides evidence of the association investigated	Positive
Campbell et al. *RAST* (2019)	USA	To investigate the association between Form 10-K tax-related risk factor disclosures and future cash flow levels and stock returns	The authors provided evidence of the association investigated	Positive
Li et al. *IREF* (2019)	China	To investigate the effect of risk disclosure on corporate investment efficiency	The authors provided evidence of the association investigated	Positive

Source: Our elaboration

volatility (Jorion 2002; Bao and Datta 2014; Kravet and Muslu 2013; Campbell et al. 2014; Hope et al. 2016); lower future expected earnings (and future negative earnings shock) (Filzen 2015); higher abnormal returns (Campbell et al. 2014); higher abnormal trading volume around the 10-K filing date (Kravet and Muslu 2013; Hope et al. 2016); higher 2-year ahead future earnings change (Moumen et al.

Table 7.5 Main informativeness empirical studies supporting convergence

Authors/ journal (year)	Country	Research focus	Main results	Sign of the association
Rajgopal *TAR* (1999)	USA	To investigate the association between the FRR No.48 disclosures and the equity return sensitivity to oil and gas price changes	The author provides evidence of the association investigated	Positive
Jorion *TAR* (2002)	USA	To investigate the association between the FRR No.48 VaR risk disclosures and the variability of banks' unexpected trading revenues	The author provides evidence of the association investigated	Positive
Kravet and Muslu *RAST* (2013)	USA	To investigate whether and how changes in mandatory risk disclosures are related to changes in investor and analyst activities before and after 10-K filings	The authors provide evidence of the association investigated	Positive
Bao and Datta *MS* (2014)	USA	To investigate the impact of each type of voluntary risk disclosure identified (30) on the volatility of the stock return	The authors provide evidence of the association investigated for 8/30 risks	Positive (for 3 risks on 30 identified)
Campbell et al. *RAST* (2014)	USA	To investigate whether risk information is associated with stock returns volatility and abnormal returns	The authors provide evidence of the association investigated	Positive with volatility Negative with abnormal returns
Filzen *AH* (2015)	USA	To investigates the association between mandatory risk factor updates in 10 Q filings with abnormal returns and earnings shocks	The author provides evidence of the association investigated	Negative
dos Santos and Coelho *RCF* (2018)	Brazil	To investigate whether information on risk and its management affects, at the margin, firm valuations	The authors provide evidence of the association investigated	Negative
Kamaruzaman et al. *IJMFA* (2019)	Malaysia	To investigate the association between risk disclosure and firm value	The authors provided evidence of the association investigated	Negative

Source: Our elaboration

2015); and lower market value of the firm (dos Santos and Coelho 2018; Kamaruzaman et al. 2019).

Table 7.5 summarizes the main informativeness empirical studies supporting divergence hypothesis in chronological order.

From the analysis, it emerges that it is not clear whether the convergence or divergence hypothesis is more consistent in describing the impact of the risk disclosure on firm market value.

For this reason, we stated the second research hypothesis as follows:

H2 Financial risks disclosure affects market firm value.

7.4 Analysing the Value Relevance of Financial Risk in the Italian Context

In this section we test the research hypothesis, which is that financial risk disclosure is value relevant for investors, in the sample identified in Chap. 3, that is, the 51 Italian largest listed companies disclosing their financial risk-related information in the Italian context.

As the value relevance studies rely on the basic assumption of stock market efficiency, i.e. that stock prices pick up the effects of all relevant information, their inferences may be misleading if the stock market under analysis is not efficient. In this respect, the study by Kristoufek and Vosvrda (2014) compares the efficiency of 41 stock indices worldwide based on the correlation structure of the returns (long-term and short-term memory) and local herding behaviour (fractal dimension). Their results show that Italy attains 11th place out of the 41 indices in the efficiency index.

The data related to financial risk disclosure have been taken from the company's annual report. We measured the financial risk with the provisions included in annual accounts according to the IAS 37, Provisions for risks and uncertainties.

The year considered is 2017 alone, as the first year of implementation in Italy of the EU Directive. For this reason, we employed an ordinary least squares (OLS) regression model to test our first research hypothesis.

The equation regression we used to formalize the relationship is a modified Ohlson model (1995) (OM), in which the other variable information (ν) is proxied with the financial risk-related information disclosure.

To mitigate heteroscedasticity, all variables were deflated for a scale factor, and then the deflated variables were substituted for the undeflated variables in the valuation model. In the main model, as deflator the number of shares was selected, which is by and large the most used deflator in CI/OCI value relevance regressions and also because it was supported by Barth and Clinch (2009). In addition, the recent article of Shen and Stark (2013), comparing the performances of the basic Ohlson (1995) model, where market value is regressed on book value and earnings, against the extended valuation models, where corporate value is modelled as a linear function of accounting variables hypothesized to be associated with company value, has provided evidence that the extended model generally provides less bias and a more accurate valuation model compared to the basic model. Therefore, consistent with Barth and Clinch (2009) and Shen and Stark (2013), we decided to use an extended model scaled by the number of shares.

Consistent with Kothari and Zimmerman, who in their 1995 article emphasized that the slope coefficients are less biased in price models than in returns model (Kothari and Zimmerman 1995), it was decided to use level models to obtain more economically sensible and less biased coefficients, and it was decided to manage the specification problems ascribed to level models by using standard error estimates that are robust to heteroscedasticity problems.

Equation (7.1) defines the modified OM we use to test H2:

$$P_i = \sigma_0 + \sigma_1 \text{ EPS}_i + \sigma_2 \text{ BVPS}_i + \sigma_3 \text{ PROV}_i + \sigma_4 \text{ LEV}_i + \sigma_5 \text{ IND}_i + \kappa_i \quad (7.1)$$

In Eq. (7.1), P is the share price (market value divided by the number of shares), and PROV is the proxy we use to measure financial risks (with the 'Provision for risks and uncertainties' under IAS 37), whilst LEV and IND are the control variables of Eq. (7.1).[5] As for the control variables, we selected them after a careful review of the literature (De Villiers and Marques 2016; Hassan 2018; De Villiers et al. 2019; García-Sánchez et al. 2019). As control variables we include the financial leverage (LEV) of the firms, and the industry to which the sampled firms (IND) belong, as firms with less debt belonging to some more sensitive industries like oil and gas, industrial and basic material sectors (Chan and Welford 2005) are more likely to disclose risks to their stakeholders. In the first step, we also included SIZE, measured with the natural logarithm of total assets, as the control variable. When executing the regression model, we realized that variable SIZE has quite high VIF (about 4) as compared to other variables. Moreover, by Pearson's product-moment correlation test, we found that SIZE and PROV are highly correlated. Hence, we dropped SIZE off the models, also considering that BV is also a firm size measure (Hassan 2018) and that the model used is a share price specification, able to mitigate the scale effect (Barth and Clinch 2009).

Consistent with Hassan (2018) and Landau et al. (2020), a log transformation of all continuous variables was used when appropriate, to reduce the impact of outliers on the current analysis.

Table 7.6 summarizes all variables included in Eq. (7.1).

The focus of Eq. 7.1 is on coefficient σ_3, which reflects the association between financial risks and share price. If the coefficient σ_3 is found to be significantly different from zero, it can be postulated that financial risk affects the market value of the firm.

In detail, a positive and statistically significant coefficient indicates that financial risks information disclosed by firms are considered value relevant by investors. Companies enhance their transparency, improving their risk reporting level and quality. This lowers information asymmetry and investors transfer this in the share prices, which increase (*convergence* hypothesis).

[5]Control variables could be defined as the variables hypothesized in the literature to affect the dependent variable that, if ignored, could cause biased coefficients and thus distortions in the interpretation of the results of the regression.

Table 7.6 Description of variables

Variables	Description
P	Natural logarithm of value share price (market value/number of shares)
BVPS	Natural logarithm of book value per share
EPS	Natural logarithm of earnings per share
PROV	Natural logarithm of provision for risks and uncertainties
LEV	Natural logarithm of LEVERAGE
IND	IND = 1 if the company is incorporated in manufacturing industry; IND = 0, otherwise

Source: Our elaboration

Table 7.7 The results of Eq. (7.1)

	Equation 7.0		Equation 7.1	
	Est.	S.E.	Est.	S.E.
Intercept	−0.695*	0.290	−0.530	0.383
EPS	2.209***	0.359	1.827***	0.385
BVPS	0.578***	0.092	0.578***	0.088
PROV			−0.090*	0.024
IND	0.638.	0.334	0.031	0.174
LEV	−0.678	0.345	−0.182	0.175
R^2	*0.787*		*0.816*	
Adj. R^2	*0.778*		*0.795*	

Significance codes: '***' 0.001 '**' 0.01 '*' 0.05 '.' 0.1

Equation 7.0: Basic Ohlson model without other information variable

Equation 7.1: Modified Ohlson model with additional information of PROV

Source: Our elaboration

Instead, if the σ_3 coefficient is negative and statistically significant, it means that financial risk information disclosed by firms is also considered value relevant by investors and they incorporate this information in the share prices, but the share prices lower because investors perceive that the firm is facing huge risks (*divergence* hypothesis).

Table 7.7 presents the results of regression Eq. (7.1).

Equation (7.1) regression results are statistically significant at small *p*-values (<0.001), thus providing sufficient evidence to conclude that the model as a whole has statistically significant predictive capability.

The results of Eq. (7.1) provide evidence of a negative significant association between financial risks and firm market value, consistent with a divergence hypothesis, coherently with Rajgopal (1999); Jorion (2002); Bao and Datta (2014); Kravet and Muslu (2013); Campbell et al. (2014); Filzen, (2015); Moumen et al. (2015); Hope et al. (2016); dos Santos and Coelho (2018); and Kamaruzaman et al. (2019).

About the goodness of fit, Eq. 7.1 which includes the financial risks as another information variable, enhances the R-squared, meaning that the variation in the share price is explained by the traditional accounting variables EPS and BVPS and the disclosed information of financial risks.

As far as we are aware, it is the first value relevance study on financial risks within the Italian context. As for the comparison with the other empirical studies, it should be underlined that only two empirical studies, that of Moumen et al. (2015) and that of dos Santos and Coelho (2018), used a modified Ohlson model (1995) to investigate the association between financial risks and the market value of a firm.

References

Abdullah, M., Shukor, Z. A., Mohamed, Z. M., & Ahmad, A. (2015). Risk management disclosure: A study on the effect of voluntary risk management disclosure toward firm value. *Journal of Applied Accounting Research, 16*(3), 400–432.

Abraham, S., & Shrives, P. J. (2014b). Improving the relevance of risk factor disclosure in corporate annual reports. *The British Accounting Review, 46*(1), 91–107.

Akbar, S., & Stark, A. W. (2003a). Deflators net shareholder cash flows, dividends, capital contributions and estimated models of corporate valuation. *Journal of Business Finance and Accounting, 9–10*, 1211–1233.

Akbar, S., & Stark, A. W. (2003b). Discussion of scale and the scale effect in market-based accounting research. *Journal of Business Finance and Accounting, 30*(1–2), 57–72.

Bao, Y., & Datta, A. (2014). Simultaneously discovering and quantifying risk types from textual risk disclosures. *Management Science, 60*(6), 1371–1391.

Barth, M. E., & Clinch, G. (2009). Scale effects in capital markets-based accounting research. *Journal of Business Finance and Accounting, 36*(3–4), 253–288.

Biddle, G., & Gilles, H. (2006). Accounting quality and firm-level capital investment. *The Accounting Review, 81*(5), 963–982.

Bravo, F. (2017). Are risk disclosures an effective tool to increase firm value? *Managerial Decision Economics, 28*, 1116–1124.

Cabedo, J. D., & Tirado, J. M. (2004). The disclosure of risk in financial statements. *Accounting Forum, 28*(2), 181–200.

Campbell, J. L., Chen, H., Dhaliwal, D. S., Lu, H., & Steele, L. B. (2014). The information content of mandatory risk factor disclosure in corporate filings. *Review of Accounting Studies, 19*(1), 396–455.

Campbell, J. L., Cecchini, M., Cianci, A. M., Ehinger, A. C., & Werner, E. M. (2019). Tax-related mandatory risk factor disclosures, future profitability, and stock returns. *Review of Accounting Studies, 24*(1), 264–308.

Chan, J. C., & Welford, R. (2005). Assessing corporate environmental risk in China: An evaluation of reporting activities of Hong Kong listed enterprises. *Corporate Social Responsibility and Environmental Management, 12*(2), 88–104.

De Villiers, C., & Marques, A. (2016). Corporate social responsibility, country-level predispositions, and the consequences of choosing a level of disclosure. *Accounting and Business Research, 46*(2), 167–195.

De Villiers, C., Ma, D., & Marques, A. (2019). CSR disclosure, dividend pay-outs and firm value: Relations and mediating effects. *Third conference on CSR, economic and financial markets*, 10–11 October, Dusseldorf. Retrieved January 25, 2019, from https://cdn.whu.edu/.

Dobler, M., Lajili, K., & Zéghal, D. (2011). Attributes of corporate risk disclosure: An international investigation in the manufacturing sector. *Journal of International Accounting Research, 10*(2), 1–22.

dos Santos, J. G. C., & Coelho, A. C. (2018). Value-relevance of disclosure: Risk factors and risk management in Brazilian firms. *Revista Contabilidade & Finanças, 29*(78), 1–19.

Elbannan, M. A., & Elbannan, M. A. (2015). Economic consequences of bank disclosure in the financial statements before and during the financial crisis: Evidence from Egypt. *Journal of Accounting, Auditing & Finance, 30*(2), 181–217.

Elshandidy, T., & Neri, L. (2015). Corporate governance, risk reporting practices, and market liquidity: Comparative evidence from the UK and Italy. *Corporate Governance: An International Review, 23*(4), 331–356.

Elshandidy, T., & Shrives, P. J. (2016). Environmental incentives for and usefulness of textual risk reporting: Evidence from Germany. *The International Journal of Accounting, 51*(4), 464–486.

Elshandidy, T., Shrives, P. J., Bamber, M., & Abraham, S. (2018). Risk reporting: A review of the literature and implications for future research. *Journal of Accounting Literature., 40*, 54–82.

Filzen, J. J. (2015). The information content of risk factor disclosures in quarterly reports. *Accounting Horizons, 29*(4), 887–916.

García-Sánchez, I.-M., Hussain, N., Martínez-Ferrero, J., & Ruiz-Barbadillo, E. (2019). Impact of disclosure and assurance quality of corporate sustainability reports on access to finance. *Corporate Social Responsibility and Environmental Management, 26*(4), 832–848.

Hassan, O. (2018). The impact of voluntary environmental disclosure on firm value: Does organizational visibility play a mediation role? *Business Strategy and the Environment, 27*, 1569–1582.

Healy, P., & Palepu, K. (2001). Information asymmetry, corporate disclosure, and the capital markets, a review of the empirical disclosure literature. *Journal of Accounting and Economics, 31*, 405–440.

Hope, O.-K., Hu, D., & Lu, H. (2016). The benefits of specific risk-factor disclosures. *Review of Accounting Studies, 21*, 1005–1045.

ICAEW. (2011). *Reporting business risks: Meeting expectations*. London: Institute of Chartered Accountants of England and Wales.

Jorion, P. (2002). How informative are value at risk disclosures? *The Accounting Review, 77*(4), 911–931.

Jorion, P. (2006). *Value-at-Risk* (3rd ed.). New York: McGraw-Hill.

Kamaruzaman, S. A., Ali, M. M., Ghani, E. K., & Gunardi, A. (2019). Ownership structure, corporate risk disclosure and firm value: A Malaysian perspective. *International Journal of Managerial and Financial Accounting, 11*(2), 113–131.

Kothari, S., & Zimmerman, J. (1995). Price and return models. *Journal of Accounting and Economics, 20*, 155–192.

Kravet, T., & Muslu, V. (2013). Textual risk disclosures and investors' risk perceptions. *Review of Accounting Studies, 18*(4), 1088–1122.

Kristoufek, L., & Vosvrda, M. (2014). Measuring capital market efficiency: Long-term memory, fractal dimension and approximate entropy. *The European Physical Journal B, 87*(162), 1–9.

Landau, A., Rochell, J., Klein, C., & Zwergel, B. (2020). Integrated reporting of environmental, social, and governance and financial data: Does the market value integrated reports? *Business Strategy and the Environment, 29*, 1750. https://doi.org/10.1002/bse.2467.

Li, F. (2006). *Do stock market investors understand the risk sentiment of corporate annual reports*? (Working paper). University of Michigan.

Li, Y., He, J., & Xiao, M. (2019). Risk disclosure in annual reports and corporate investment efficiency. *International Review of Economics and Finance, 63*, 138–151.

Linsley, P., & Shrives, P. (2006). Risk reporting: A study of risk disclosure in the annual reports of UK companies. *The British Accounting Review, 38*(4), 387–404.

Miihkinen, A. (2013). The usefulness of firm risk disclosures under different firm riskiness, investor-interest, and market conditions: New evidence from Finland. *Advances in Accounting, 29*(2), 312–331.

Moumen, N., Ben Othman, H., & Hussainey, K. (2015). The value-relevance of risk disclosure in annual reports: Evidence from MENA emerging markets. *Research in International Business and Finance, 34*, 177–204.

Ohlson, J. A. (1995). Earnings, book values, and dividends in equity valuation. *Contemporary Accounting Research, 11*(2), 661–687.

Pérignon, C., & Smith, D. R. (2010). The level and quality of value-at-risk disclosure by commercial banks. *Journal of Banking & Finance, 34*(2), 362–377.

Rajgopal, S. (1999). Early evidence on the informativeness of the SEC's market risk disclosure: The case of commodity price risk exposure of oil and gas producers. *The Accounting Review, 74*(3), 251–280.

Roulstone, D. T. (1999). Effect of SEC financial reporting release no. 48 on derivative and market risk disclosures. *Accounting Horizons, 13*(4), 343–363.

Shen, Y., & Stark, A. W. (2013). Evaluating the effectiveness of model specifications and estimation approaches for empirical accounting-based valuation models. *Accounting and Business Research, 6*, 660–682.

Chapter 8
The Value Relevance of Non-financial Risk

8.1 Introduction

In this chapter we investigate the value relevance of the NF risk-related information disclosure, that is, the usefulness of NF risk information for investors. In the chapter, we present the main empirical studies that address to test the usefulness of NF risk information for investors' investment decision. On the basis of the literature, we posit our second research hypothesis, that we test on the sample identified in Chap. 3, after having modelled this research hypothesis with an Ohlson-model-based value relevance regression equation.

8.2 The Non-financial Risk Informativeness Literature

Different from the financial risks, there is no literature focused on the informativeness of NF risk-related information. The lack of NF risk disclosure regulation has driven researchers to focus on voluntary reporting, and also the very recent research after the Legislative Decree which made NF risk-related information disclosure mandatory are still focused on the reasons for disclosure (Truant et al. 2017), or on the state of the art of the NF risk disclosure in the Italian context (Manes Rossi et al. 2017; De Luca and Phat 2019; Leopizzi et al. 2020), without investigating whether this information is useful for investors.

Nevertheless, we can make reference to the empirical studies focused on the value relevance of NFI in general terms.

In the literature, researchers agree on the difficulty of correctly defining the term NFI, which is an ambiguous term including diverse kinds of information (Doni et al. 2019). We can make reference to the definition of Yeldar (2012), which is sufficiently wide to include every kind of NFI. In his research, Yeldar defines NFI as:

S. Veltri, *Mandatory Non-financial Risk-Related Disclosure*,
https://doi.org/10.1007/978-3-030-47921-3_8

'Information incorporating a wide range of issues which are likely to have a short-, medium- and long-term effect on business performance. Typically, there are extra-financial issues beyond the traditional range of financial variables that are considered as part of the investment decision-making processes. Extra-financial factors include, but are not limited to, corporate governance, intellectual capital management, human rights, occupational health and safety and human capital practices, innovation, research and development (RD), customer satisfaction, climate change and natural resource management, consumer and public health, reputation risk, and the broader environmental and social impacts of corporate activity such as biodiversity impacts and community impacts'.

Following the first paper on the value relevance of nonfinancial information (Anderson and Frankle 1980; Amir and Lev 1996), several empirical studies have examined the value relevance of corporate NFI. Specifically, the research on the NFI value relevance focused on three groups of NFI, that is, environmental, social and governance (ESG) ones, with a predominance of environmental value relevance studies (Reverte 2016).

This section cannot provide an exhaustive literature of the value relevance studies of NFI. We just present some studies focused on the association between CSR/environmental disclosure and firm value indicators, underlining that NFI value relevance studies provided mixed results.[1]

8.3 The CSR Value Relevance Literature

As for the value relevance CSR studies, we can quote the studies of Richardson and Welker (2001), Schadéwitz and Niskala (2010), El Ghoul et al. (2011), Dhaliwal et al. (2011, 2012), Berthelot et al. (2012), Cardamone et al. (2012), Carnevale et al. (2012), De Klerk and De Villiers (2012), Gietl et al. (2012), Servaes and Tamayo (2013), Cho et al. (2013), Gregory et al. (2014), Carnevale and Mazzuca (2014), De Klerk et al. (2015), De Villiers and Marques (2016), Bowerman and Sharma (2016), Kaspereit and Lopatta (2016), Cahan et al. (2016), Reverte (2016), Miralles-Quiros et al. (2017), Rossi and Harjoto (2019) and Aureli et al. (2020).

Richardson and Welker (2001) test the hypothesis that there is an inverse association between social disclosure and the cost of capital. The authors find instead a significant positive association between the two variables.

Schadéwitz and Niskala (2010) studied the value relevance of Finnish GRI-compliant reporters in the period 2002–2005. The results obtained show that GRI standards represent an important explanatory factor for the market value of firms.

---

[1]We excluded from the section all the studies focused on the association between NFI and firm performance measured in economic terms (e.g. ROA, ROE, etc.). Also, have also been excluded the studies focused on environmental/CSR performance and not on environmental/CSR disclosure.

El Ghoul et al. (2011) examine the effect of CSR disclosures (measured with KLD data) on the cost of equity capital for a large sample of US firms. The authors find that firms with better CSR scores exhibit a lower cost of equity capital.

Dhaliwal et al. (2011) find that firms with superior CSR performance that publish a stand-alone CSR report experience a reduction in the lagged cost of equity capital.

Dhaliwal et al. (2012) find that CSR disclosure through a stand-alone CSR report improves analyst forecast accuracy.

Berthelot et al. (2012) investigate whether capital markets take the disclosures of CSR reports into account, drawing on a sample of Canadian companies listed on the Toronto Stock Exchange. Their results suggest that investors positively value CSR report.

Cardamone et al. (2012) analysed the value relevance of social reports on a sample of 178 Italian companies listed on the Milan Stock Exchange from 2002 to 2008. Their findings show a significant negative correlation between the market value of firms and social report publication.

Gietl et al. (2012) investigated the impact of sustainability reporting under the global reporting initiative (GRI) on the firm value of non-financial EUROSTOXX 600 firms. Their findings show that the highest level of GRI-aligned reporting has a negative and significant influence on the firm value of smaller or less profitable firms (while no significant impact is detected for larger and more profitable firms).

Carnevale et al. (2012), for a sample of European listed banks for the 2002–2008 period, found no significant correlation between stock prices and social reporting. Moving to a cross-country analysis, some countries have switched to a positive association; for others the association remains negative.

De Klerk and De Villiers (2012) used a modified Ohlson model to examine the role of corporate social responsibility reporting in providing information value relevant for company shareholders for 100 South African companies. The authors find a positive association between share prices and CSR disclosures.

Servaes and Tamayo (2013) investigate the association between CSR disclosures for US firms, as measured with the KLD data over the period 1991–2005, and firm value. The authors find that CSR disclosures and firm value are positively related only for firms with high customer awareness, (proxied by advertising expenditures); for firms with low customer awareness, the relation is either negative or insignificant.

Cho et al. (2013) investigate the association between CSR disclosures (data drawn from KLD) and information asymmetry. The authors find that the disclosure of CSR concerns about firms are much more impactful in reducing information asymmetry and improving firm transparency than disclosures regarding the positive CSR strengths of firms.

Gregory et al. (2014) investigated the association between CSR disclosures (data drawn from KLD) and firm value, finding that, in general, CSR strengths disclosures are positively valued and CSR concerns disclosures are negatively valued.

Carnevale and Mazzuca (2014), for a sample of European banks, provide evidence that publishing a sustainability report produces a positive effect on stock prices.

De Klerk et al. (2015) used a modified Ohlson (1995) model to examine the relationship between CSR disclosure and share prices among the 100 largest UK companies. They find that higher levels of CSR disclosure are associated with higher share prices.

Jain et al. (2016) examine whether short sellers, as informed investors, take into consideration ESG disclosure in making investment decisions. The authors find that firms' market value and future financial performance (measured by price per share, return on equity, and return on assets) are lower, whereas operating risk is higher for firms with low composite ESG scores.

Bowerman and Sharma (2016) studied the usefulness for investors of CSR disclosures in the UK and Japan markets, finding out that only UK investors consider CSR disclosure value relevant for their investment decision-making.

Kaspereit and Lopatta (2016) examined whether relative corporate sustainability (as measured by the Sustainable Asset Management ranking, at the basis of membership in the Dow Jones Sustainability Index, DJSI) and sustainability reporting (in terms of GRI application levels) are associated with a higher market valuation for a sample of the 600 largest European companies over the period 2001–2011. They provide evidence of a positive association among CSR disclosures and firm value, stronger when they use DJSI.

De Villiers and Marques (2016) investigate the association of different levels of CSR disclosure with share prices for the largest European firms. Their results indicate that a high level of CSR disclosure is associated with higher share prices (and low level of CSR disclosure with lower share prices).

Cahan et al. (2016) examine the association between unexpected CSR disclosure and firm value measured by Tobin's Q, using proprietary data that rate corporate social responsibility (CSR) disclosures of firms in 21 countries. The authors provide evidence of a positive association between the two variables.

Using a sample of listed Spanish companies pertaining to the IBEX35 index for 2007–2011, Reverte (2016) examines whether firms with higher CSR disclosure ratings are more valued by market participants. By using a modified Ohlson model, the author finds that CSR disclosure does have both a positive direct and indirect effect (by modifying the value relevance of earnings and book value of equity on stock prices).

Miralles-Quiros et al. (2017) examined whether GRI-compliant CSR disclosure provides relevant information and incremental value to investors on the European stock markets of Denmark, Finland, France, Germany, Italy, the Netherlands, Norway, Spain, Sweden and the UK over the period 2001–2013. The overall results reveal that European investors as a whole valued this type of information, especially in the years before the international financial crisis, even if there are differences among markets.

Rossi and Harijoto (2019) examine the association between corporate NF disclosure ratings in the Italian context for 2001–2018 (so including the period after the enactment of the Legislative Decree 254/2016), measured utilizing the Standard Ethics Rating (SER) and the performance of firms (measured with total shareholder return, economic value added (EVA) and Tobin's Q). The authors find SER ratings are positively related to firm value.

For the 500 largest European firms for 2007–2013, De Villiers et al. (2019) investigated the association between unexpected (i.e. the portion of CSR disclosure that comes as a surprise to capital markets) CSR disclosure and firm value and whether this association is mediated by dividend pay-outs (dividends divided by net income). The authors find that dividend pay-outs fully mediate the positive association between unexpected CSR disclosure and the share price of firms, providing evidence of an indirect association.

Aureli et al. (2020) investigate the impact of the ESG disclosures on the security returns analysing 33 different event windows on a sample of 170 report disclosures from 55 listed companies from all over the world from 2009 to 2016. Their results show two significant event windows and an increasing level of significance in the reports released after 2013.

Generally speaking, the majority of investigated studies provide evidence in support of a positive relationship between CSR disclosure and share prices, even if some studies (Gietl et al. 2012) report a negative correlation with market values. The studies on the value relevance of ESG information share the tendency to focus on the largest companies (e.g. De Klerk et al. 2015) and use GRI for assessing ESG disclosure (e.g. Schadéwitz and Niskala (2010), on a single country (e.g. Berthelot et al. 2012) and on a single industry (e. g. Cardamone et al. 2012). With respect to the studies on the value relevance of accounting and financial information, they are more recent and make use of adequate tools to investigate the value relevance of disclosed NFI, such as models based on the modified Ohlson model (De Klerk and De Villiers 2012; De Klerk et al. 2015) whilst few studies used event study methodology (Jain et al. 2016; Aureli et al. 2020). Furthermore, few studies condition the association between CSR disclosure and firm value to another variable (Servaes and Tamayo 2013) or distinguish between good and bad disclosure news (Gregory et al. 2014). Table 8.1 presents the main CSR disclosure value relevance studies in chronological order.

8.4 The Environmental Value Relevance Literature

As for the environmental studies, it should be underlined that they are the majority of value relevance studies focused on NFI value relevance (De Villiers and Marques 2016; Cahan et al. 2016; Reverte 2016).

Among these studies, we should quote Li and McConomy (1999), Blacconiere and Patten (1994), Blacconiere and Northcutt (1997), Al-Tuwaijri et al. (2004), Freedman and Patten (2004), Hassel et al. (2005), Bewley (2005), Cormier and Magnan (2007), Sinkin et al. (2008), Aerts et al. (2008), Moneva and Cuellar (2009), Déjean and Martinez (2009), Griffin and Sun (2012), Clarkson et al. (2013), Matsumura et al. (2014), Plumlee et al. (2015) and Hassan (2018).

Table 8.1 The main CSR disclosure value relevance literature

Authors/journal (year)	Country	Research focus	Main results	Sign of the association
Richardson and Welker *AOS* (2001)	Canada	To test the hypothesis of an inverse association between social disclosure and the cost of capital	The authors do not provide evidence of the hypothesis tested	Positive
Schadéwitz and Niskala *CSREM* (2010)	Finland	To investigate the association between the GRI compliant disclosures and the firm's market value	The authors provide evidence of the association investigated	Positive
El Ghoul et al. *JBF* (2011)	USA	To investigate the effect of CSR disclosures (measured with KLD data) on the cost of equity capital	The authors provide evidence of the association investigated	Negative
Dhaliwal et al. *AR* (2011)	USA	To investigate the association between the ESG disclosures through a stand-alone CSR report and the cost of the equity capital	The authors provide evidence of the association investigated	Negative
Dhaliwal et al. *AR* (2012)	USA	To investigate the association between the ESG disclosures through a stand-alone CSR report and the analyst forecast accuracy	The authors provide evidence of the association investigated	Positive
Berthelot et al. *CSREM* (2012)	Canada	To investigate the association between the CSR disclosures and the company market value	The authors provide evidence of the association investigated	Positive
Carnevale et al. *CSREM* (2012)	Sample of European listed banks	To investigate the association between the publication of a CSR report and the banks' share price	The authors provide evidence of the association investigated	Negative
Gietl *FAeJ* (2012)	Non-financial EUROSTOKK firms	To investigate the impact of GRI-compliant sustainability reporting on firm value	The author provides evidence of the association investigated	Negative
De Klerk and De Villiers	South Africa	To investigate the association between the CSR disclosures and	The authors provide evidence of the association investigated	Positive

(continued)

Table 8.1 (continued)

Authors/ journal (year)	Country	Research focus	Main results	Sign of the association
MEDAR (2012)		the company share prices		
Servaes and Tamayo *MS* (2013)	USA	To investigate the association between the CSR disclosures and the firm value	The authors provide evidence of the association investigated only for firms with high customer awareness	Positive
Cho et al. *JAPP* (2013)	USA	To investigate the association between the CSR disclosures (concerns and strengths) and information asymmetry	The authors provide evidence of the association investigated for CSR concerns disclosures	Negative
Gregory et al. *JBE* (2014)	USA	To investigate the association between the CSR disclosures (1 concerns and 2 strengths) and firm value	The authors provide evidence of the associations investigated	1. Negative 2. Positive
De Klerk et al. *PAR* (2015)	UK	To investigate the association between the CSR disclosures and the company share prices	The authors provide evidence of the association investigated	Positive
Carnevale and Mazzuca *BEQ* (2014)	Sample of European listed banks	To investigate the association between the publication of a CSR report and the banks' share price	The authors provide evidence of the association investigated	Positive
Jain et al. *JMAR* (2016)	USA	To investigate the association between the ESG disclosures and firms' market value	The authors provide evidence of the association investigated	Positive
Bowerman and Sharma *COC* (2016)	UK and Japan	To investigate the usefulness of CSR disclosures for investment decision-making	The authors provide evidence of the association investigated for UK	Positive
Kaspereit and Lopatta *BE* (2016)	600 largest European companies	To investigate the association between the CSR disclosures and the firm's market valuation	The authors provide evidence of the association investigated	Positive
De Villiers and Marques *ABR* (2016)	Largest European firms	To investigate the association of different levels of CSR disclosure with share prices	The authors provide evidence of the association investigated	Positive

(continued)

Table 8.1 (continued)

Authors/ journal (year)	Country	Research focus	Main results	Sign of the association
Cahan et al. *EAR* (2016)	21 countries	To examine the association between unexpected CSR disclosure and firm value	The authors provide evidence of the association investigated	Positive
Reverte *RMS* (2016)	Spain	To investigate the association between the CSR disclosures and the company share prices	The authors provide evidence of the association investigated	Positive
Miralles-Quiros et al. *CSREM* (2017)	European stock markets	To examine whether GRI-compliant CSR disclosure provides relevant information to investors	The authors provide evidence of the association investigated	Positive
Rossi and Harjoto *RMS* (2019)	Italy	To examine the association between corporate NF disclosure ratings and the firm's performance	The authors provide evidence of the association investigated	Positive
De Villiers et al. *EAA conference* (2019)	The 500 largest European firms	To investigate the association between unexpected CSR disclosure and firm value	The association investigated is verified indirectly through the dividend pay-outs	Positive
Aureli et al. *CSREM* (2020)	International sample of listed companies	To examine the impact of the ESG disclosures on the security returns	The authors provide evidence of the association investigated	Positive

Source: Our elaboration

Li and McConomy (1999) on a sample of Canadian natural resource companies listed on the Toronto Stock Exchange investigate the relationship between the disclosure of future removal and site restoration costs that firms are obliged to disclose according the Canadian accounting standard of 1990 and firm value, employing a modified Ohlson model. The authors find a negative and significant association between these environmental provisions and the firms' market value.

Blacconiere and Patten (1994) examine the association between environmental disclosures and stock price reaction for firms not involved in Union Carbide's chemical Bhopal leak (1984). Their evidence indicates that firms with more extensive environmental disclosures in their financial report *prior* to the chemical leak experienced a less negative reaction than firms with less extensive disclosures.

Blacconiere and Northcutt (1997) examine the relation between stock price reactions to the Superfund Amendments and Reauthorization Act (SARA) of 1986 and environmental information. The authors find that chemical firms with more extensive environmental disclosures included in their 10-K reports had a less negative reaction to SARA, while firms with greater exposure to Superfund costs had a more negative market reaction.

Al-Tuwaijri et al. (2004), for a sample of 198 US environmentally exposed firms, examine the interrelations between environmental disclosure, environmental performance and economic performance, as measured by stock price through a three-stage least squares (3SLS) simultaneous equation model. The authors find that environmental performance is significantly and positively associated with environmental disclosure, and that "good" environmental performance is significantly associated with "good" economic performance.

Freedman and Patten (2004) study market reaction to the Toxic Release Inventory information and 10-K report environmental disclosures employing a cross-sectional analysis for a sample of 112 US firms. Their results show a positive market reaction to environmental disclosure.

Hassel et al. (2005) investigate how environmental information is reflected in the market value of listed Swedish companies, using a modified Ohlson model in which environmental performance, calculated on the basis of the environmental disclosures of firms and other private and public information concerning environmental issues, is included as a proxy for other value-relevant information. The authors find that environmental performance has a negative influence on the market value of firms.

Bewley (2005) employs a sample of the US and Canadian firms during the period from 1984 to 1997 and a residual-income valuation model based on the Ohlson (1995) framework to investigate the role of financial reporting regulation on the association between reported environmental liabilities and market valuation. The author provides evidence of a negative association between reported environmental liability and market valuation and that this association was changed in some cases by the regulation factor.

Cormier and Magnan (2007) investigate the impact of environmental reporting on the relationship between the earnings of a firm and its stock market value. To assess how country-specific contexts may affect the impact of environmental reporting, they focus on three countries that employ different reporting and governance regimes such as Canada, France and Germany. Results suggest that decisions to report environmental information have a moderating impact on the stock market valuation in the German context, whilst they do not significantly influence the stock market valuation of Canadian and French firms' earnings.

Aerts et al. (2008) investigate interrelations between corporate environmental disclosure, financial markets (as proxied by financial analysts' earnings forecasts) and public pressures (as proxied by the media exposure of a firm). The authors find that enhanced environmental disclosure translates into more precise earnings forecasts by analysts.

Sinkin et al. (2008) study the relationship between the adoption of an eco-efficient business strategy, signalled by the issuance of corporate environmental reports, and the firm value using a modified Ohlson model. The authors find that that implementation of eco-efficient business strategies is associated with higher firm value.

Moneva and Cuellar (2009), on a sample of listed Spanish companies and using a modified Ohlson model, investigate the association between environmental reporting and financial performance, distinguishing between financial and non-financial environmental disclosure. The authors find a positive and significant association between financial environmental disclosure and share price, no evidence of an association for non-financial environmental information and share prices. Furthermore, their evidence corroborates the increase of the value relevance of compulsory environmental information with respect to the voluntary one and for companies belonging to environmentally sensitive industries more than companies operating in other industries.

Déjean and Martinez (2009) investigate the relationship between voluntary environmental disclosure and the cost of capital in the French context, finding a positive association between the two variables.

Griffin and Sun (2012) investigate the association between voluntary environmental disclosure and firm market value in the US context. The authors find that voluntary disclosure involving greenhouse gas emissions produces positive returns to shareholders and that this response is stronger for smaller companies with limited public information availability.

Clarkson et al. (2013) examine the association between voluntary environmental disclosures and (1) firm value and (2) cost of equity capital for public US companies from five pollution industries for 2003 and 2006 using a modified Ohlson model. Their findings show that there is a positive association between environmental disclosures and share prices, but there is no association between environmental disclosures and the cost of capital.

Matsumura et al. (2014) examine the effects on firm value of voluntarily disclosing carbon emissions for the S&P 500 belonging to the Carbon Disclosure Project for the to-year period 2006–2008. The authors find that firm value is negatively affected by carbon emissions disclosures but also that the median value of disclosing firms is higher than that of comparable non-disclosing firms.

Plumlee et al. (2015) on a sample of US firms from both sensitive and non-sensitive industries over the period from 2000 to 2005, examine the relationship between the quality of the voluntary GRI compliant environmental disclosures of a firm and (1) firm value in terms of share price and future expected cash flows and (2) cost of equity capital using a modified Ohlson model. The authors document (1) a positive association between voluntary environmental disclosure quality and firm value and (2) both a negative and positive association between voluntary environmental disclosure quality and the cost of equity capital, according to the type and nature of this disclosure.

Hassan (2018) investigates (1) whether corporate environmental disclosure affects firm value measured with the market value of equity of a firm and (2) whether organizational visibility (i.e. the extent to which analysts follow, and institutions hold, a firm's stock) proxied with analyst coverage (NOA) and institutional ownership (INST) mediates this association. The authors utilize a sample of S&P Global 1200 companies from 2010 to 2015, and a modified Ohlson model, shaping the complex interrelationships between the variables of interest through a structural equation modelling. The author finds that that prior environmental disclosure positively and significantly affects firm value consistent with results from prior studies and that organizational visibility, measured by NOA, plays a full mediation role on the relationship between prior environmental disclosure and firm value, but the results are not significant when INST is used as proxy for organizational visibility.

Summarizing, we can say that research on the value relevance of the environmental disclosure provides inconsistent results, reporting a negative correlation (Hassel et al. 2005), no correlation disclosure (Moneva and Cuellar 2009) or a positive correlation between environmental disclosure and firm value (Plumlee et al. 2015; Clarkson et al. 2013). Table 8.2 presents the main environmental disclosure value relevant studies in chronological order.

8.5 The Third Research Hypothesis

In the sustainability and environmental literature, there are two contrasting theoretical perspectives for investigating the impact of environmental and cSR disclosure on the earnings of a firm and its stock market value (Cormier and Magnan 2007; Reverte 2016).

On the one hand, environmental and CSR disclosures comprise mostly information with a positive attitude ('good news'), such as costs, investment and strategies related to ESG issues, whose disclosure is likely to take out much uncertainty from the reported net earnings of a firm, thus enhancing its credibility and, ultimately, its stock market valuation.

On the other hand, the content and meaning of certain aspects of environmental and CSR reporting have a negative attitude ('bad news'), often already known to the stakeholders, for example through the media. For instance, the disclosure of high levels of pollutant emissions, which explicitly signal to investors that some costly environmental obligations are not explicitly recognized in the liabilities of a firm (Hughes 2000; Clarkson et al. 2004), could be interpreted as a signal that management should improve its transparency as it would gain support among its various stakeholders, allowing them to derive more precise estimates of its future earnings.

Hence, even a 'negative' disclosure, such as the communication to shareholders of NF risks, enhances the relationship between the earnings of a firm and its stock market valuation.

Coherent with Cormier and Magnan (2007), we therefore believe that, irrespective of the nature or sign of the information being reported about, the NFI disclosure enhances the stock market valuation of a firm.

For this reason, we stated the third research hypothesis as follows:

H3 Non-financial risks disclosure positively affects firm market value.

Table 8.2 The main environmental disclosure value relevance literature

Authors/ journal (year)	Country	Research focus	Main results	Sign of the association
Li and McConomy *JAAF* (1999)	CANADA	To investigate the relationship between the disclosure of future removal and site restoration costs and the firm value	The authors provide evidence of the association investigated	Negative
Blacconiere and Patten *JAE* (1994)	INDIA	To examine the association between environmental disclosures and stock price reaction	The authors provide evidence of the association investigated	Weaker negative reaction
Blacconiere and Northcutt *JAAF* (1997)	USA	To examine the association between environmental disclosures and stock price reaction	The authors provide evidence of the association investigated	Weaker negative reaction
Al-Tuwaijri et al. *AOS* (2004)	USA	To examine the interrelations between environmental disclosure, environmental performance and economic performance	The authors provide evidence of the (indirect) association investigated	Positive
Freedman and Patten *AF* (2004)	USA	To study market reaction to the Toxic Release Inventory information and 10-K report environmental disclosures	The authors provide evidence of the association investigated	Positive
Hassel et al. *EAR* (2005)	SWEDEN	To investigate how environmental information is reflected in the market value	The authors provide evidence of the association investigated	Negative
Bewley *JIFMA* (2005)	USA and CANADA	To investigate the role of financial reporting regulation on the association between reported environmental liabilities and market value	The authors provide evidence of the association investigated	Negative
Cormier and Magnan *EE* (2007)	Multi country (Canada, France and Germany)	To investigate the impact of environmental reporting on the relationship between a firm's earnings and its stock market value	The authors provide partial evidence of the association investigated (only for Germany)	Positive
Aerts et al. *EE* (2008)	Multi country	To investigate relations between corporate environmental disclosure, financial markets and public pressures	The authors provide evidence of the association investigated	Positive

(continued)

Table 8.2 (continued)

Authors/ journal (year)	Country	Research focus	Main results	Sign of the association
Sinkin et al. *JAPP* (2008)	USA	To study the relationship between the adoption of an eco-efficient business strategy, signalled by the issuance of corporate environmental reports, and the firm value	The authors provide evidence of the association investigated	Positive
Moneva and Cuellar *ERE* (2009)	SPAIN	To investigate the association between environmental reporting and financial performance, distinguishing between financial and non-financial environmental disclosure	The authors provide evidence only of the association between financial environmental disclosure and financial performance	Negative
Déjean and Martinez *AiE* (2009	FRANCE	To investigate the relationship between voluntary environmental disclosure and the cost of capital	The authors provide evidence of the association investigated	Negative
Griffin and Sun *JAPP* (2012)	USA	To investigate the association between voluntary environmental disclosure and firm value	The authors provide evidence of the association investigated	Positive
Clarkson et al. *JAPP* (2013)	USA	To examine the association between voluntary environmental disclosures and (1) share price; (2) cost of equity capital	The authors provide evidence of the association 1, no evidence of the association 2 investigated	1. Positive
Matsumura et al. *AR* (2014)	USA	To examine the effects on firm value of voluntarily disclosing carbon emissions	The authors provide evidence of the association investigated	Negative
Plumlee et al. *JAPP* (2015)	USA	To investigate the relationship between the quality of a firm's voluntary GRI-compliant environmental disclosures and (1) share price; (2) cost of equity capital	The authors provide evidence of the association 1 investigated, partial evidence of the association 2 investigated	1. Positive 2. Negative

(continued)

Table 8.2 (continued)

Authors/ journal (year)	Country	Research focus	Main results	Sign of the association
Hassan *BSE* (2018)	Multi-country S&P Global 1200 companies	To investigate: (1) whether corporate environmental disclosure affects firm value; (2) whether organizational visibility mediates such association	The author provides evidence of the association 1, partial evidence of the association 2	1. Positive

Source: Our elaboration

8.6 Analysing the Value Relevance of the Non-financial Risk in the Italian Context

In this section we test the research hypothesis, that is, the NF risk disclosure is value relevant for investors, in the sample identified in Chap. 3, that is, the 51 largest Italian listed companies disclosing their financial risk-related information in the Italian context.

As the value relevance studies rely on the basic assumption of stock market efficiency, i.e. that stock prices pick up the effects of all relevant information, their inferences may be misleading if the stock market under analysis is not efficient. In this respect, the study by Kristoufek and Vosvrda (2014) compares the efficiency of 41 stock indices worldwide based on the correlation structure of the returns (long-term and short-term memory) and local herding behaviour (fractal dimension). Their results show that Italy attains 11th place out of the 41 indices in the efficiency index.

The data related to financial risk disclosure have been taken from the annual report of the company. We measured the quality of NF risks disclosure with a self-constructed index, presented in Chap. 4 of this book.

The year considered is 2017 alone, as the first year of implementation in Italy of the EU Directive. For this reason, to test our first research hypothesis, we employed an ordinary least squares (OLS) regression model.

The equation regression we used to formalize the relationship is a modified Ohlson Model (1995) OM, in which the other variable information (ν) is proxied with the financial risk-related information disclosure.

To mitigate heteroscedasticity, all variables were deflated for a scale factor, and then the deflated variables were substituted for the undeflated variables in the valuation model. In the main model, as deflator the number of shares was selected, which is by and large the most used deflator in value relevance regressions and also because it was supported by Barth and Clinch (2009). In addition, the recent article of Shen and Stark (2013), comparing the performances of the basic Ohlson (1995) model (where market value is regressed on book value and earnings alone), against the extended valuation models (where market value is regressed on many of the accounting variables found to be associated with it) provide evidence that the extended model generally provides less bias and a more accurate valuation model compared to the basic model. Therefore, consistently with Barth and Clinch (2009) and Shen and Stark (2013), we decided to use an extended model scaled by the number of shares.

Consistent with Kothari and Zimmerman in their 1995 article, who emphasized that the slope coefficients are less biased in price models than in returns model (Kothari and Zimmerman 1995), it was decided to use level models to obtain more economically sensible and less biased coefficients, and it was decided to manage the specification problems ascribed to level models by using standard error estimates that are robust to heteroscedasticity problems.

Equation (8.1) defines the modified OM we use to test H3:

$$P_i = \delta_0 + \delta_1\,\mathrm{EPS}_i + \delta_2\,\mathrm{BVPS}_i + \delta_3\,\mathrm{LD254}_{\mathrm{QUALi}} + \delta_4\,\mathrm{LEV}_i + \delta_5\,\mathrm{IND}_i + \gamma_i \tag{8.1}$$

In Eq. (8.1), P is the share price (market value divided by the number of shares), $\mathrm{LD254}_{\mathrm{Quali}}$ is our self-constructed index with measure the quality of disclosure of NF risks qualified according the Italian Legislative Decree 254/2016, whilst LEV and IND are the control variables of Eq. (8.1). As for the control variables, we selected them after a careful review of the literature (De Villiers and Marques 2016; Hassan 2018; De Villiers et al. 2019; García-Sánchez et al. 2019). As control variables we include the financial leverage (LEV) of the firm, and the industry to which the sampled firms (IND) belong, as firms with less debt belonging to some more sensitive industries like oil and gas, industrial and basic material sectors (Chan and Welford 2005) are more likely to disclose risks to their stakeholders. In the first step, we also included SIZE, measured with natural logarithm of total assets, as a control variable. When executing the regression model, we realized that variable SIZE has quite high VIF (about 4) as compared to other variables. Moreover, by Pearson's product-moment correlation test, we found that SIZE and PROV are highly correlated. Hence, we dropped SIZE off the models, also considering that BV is also a firm size measure (Hassan 2018) and that the model used is a share price specification, able to mitigate the scale effect (Barth and Clinch 2009).

Consistent with Hassan (2018) and Landau et al. (2020), a log transformation of all continuous variables (except for the quality NF risk disclosure index) was used when appropriate to reduce the impact of outliers on the current analysis.

Table 8.3 summarizes all variables included in Eq. (8.1).

The focus of Eq. 8.1 is on coefficient δ_3, which reflects the association between financial risks and share price. If the coefficient δ_3 is found to be significantly different from zero, it can be postulated that NF risks affect the market value of a firm.

In detail, a positive and statistically significant coefficient indicates that NF risks information disclosed by firms are considered value relevant by investors. Companies enhance their transparency, improving their risk reporting level and quality. This lowers information asymmetry, and investors transfer this in the share prices, which increases (*convergence* hypothesis).

Table 8.3 Description of variables

Variables	Description
P	Natural logarithm of value share price (market value/number of shares)
BVPS	Natural logarithm of book value per share
EPS	Natural logarithm of earnings per share
LD254_QUAL	Quality of NF risk disclosure subjected to the legislative decree 254
LEV	Natural logarithm of LEVERAGE
IND	IND = 1 if the company is incorporated in manufacturing industry; IND = 0, otherwise.

Source: Our elaboration

Table 8.4 The results of Eq. (8.1)

	Equation 8.0		Equation 8.1	
	Est.	S.E.	Est.	S.E.
Intercept	−0.695*	0.290	−2.316***	0.230
EPS	2.209***	0.359	0.751**	0.247
BVPS	0.578***	0.092	0.381***	0.056
LD254_Qual			0.552***	0.059
IND	0.638.	0.334	0.031	0.174
LEV	−0.678.	0.345	−0.182	0.175
R^2	*0.787*		*0.935*	
Adj. R^2	*0.778*		*0.930*	

Significance codes: '***' 0.001 '**' 0.01 '*' 0.05 '.' 0.1

Equation 8.0 Basic Ohlson model without other information variable

Equation 8.1 Modified Ohlson model with additional information of $LD254_{Quali}$

Source: Our elaboration

A negative and statistically significant coefficient instead confirms that NF risk-related information disclosures are value relevant for investors, but in this case the investors, perceiving a major risk faced by companies, incorporate this bad information in the share prices of companies that go down.

Table 8.4 presents the results of regression Eq. (8.1).

The Eq. (8.1) regression results are statistically significant at small *p*-values (<0.001), thus providing sufficient evidence to conclude that the model as a whole has statistically significant predictive capability.

The results of Eq. (7.1) provide evidence of a positive significant association between NF risks and firm market value.

About the goodness of fit of Eq. 8.1, which includes the NF risks as other information variable, enhances the R-squared, meaning that the variation in the share price is explained by the traditional accounting variables EPS and BVPS and the disclosed information of NF risks.

As far as we are aware, it is the first value relevance study on NF risks within the Italian context and abroad. For this reason, we cannot compare our study with other value relevance NF risks studies. We just can compare our result with other NFI value relevance studies. Coherent with Cormier and Magnan (2007), the disclosure of NF risk-related information, as any other typologies of NFI, increases the transparency of corporate information and helps investors to have a complete framework of the NF side of the firm (objectives, activities, risks and outputs), and this translates into an improvement of the market value.

References

Aerts, W., Cormier, D., & Magnan, M. (2008). Corporate environmental disclosure, financial markets and the media: An international perspective. *Ecological Economics, 64*(3), 643–659.

Al-Tuwaijri, S. A., Christensen, T. E., & Hughes, K. E., II. (2004). The relations among environmental disclosure, environmental performance, and economic performance: A simultaneous equations approach. *Accounting, Organizations and Society, 29*(5–6), 447–471.

Amir, E., & Lev, B. (1996). Value-relevance of non-financial information: The wireless communications industry. *Journal of Accounting and Economics, 22*(1–3), 3–30.

Anderson, J., & Frankle, A. (1980). Voluntary social reporting: An iso-beta portfolio analysis. *The Accounting Review, 55*(3), 467–479.

Aureli, S., Gigli, S., Medei, R., & Supino, E. (2020). The value relevance of environmental, social, and governance disclosure: Evidence from Dow Jones sustainability world index listed companies. *Corporate Social Responsibility and Environmental Management, 27*(1), 43–52.

Barth, M. E., & Clinch, G. (2009). Scale effects in capital markets-based accounting research. *Journal of Business Finance and Accounting, 36*(3–4), 253–288.

Berthelot, S., Coulmont, M., & Serret, V. (2012). Do investors value sustainability reports? A Canadian study. *Corporate Social Responsibility and Environmental Management, 19*(6), 355–363.

Bewley, K. (2005). The impact of financial reporting regulation on the market valuation of reported environmental liabilities: Preliminary evidence from U.S. and Canadian public companies. *Journal of International Financial Management and Accounting, 16*(1), 1–48.

Blacconiere, W. G., & Northcutt, D. (1997). Environmental information and markets reactions to environment legislation. *Journal of Accounting Auditing and Finance, 2*(2), 149–178.

Blacconiere, W. G., & Patten, D. M. (1994). Environmental disclosures, regulatory costs, and changes in firm value. *Journal of Accounting and Economics, 18*(3), 357–377.

Bowerman, S., & Sharma, U. (2016). The effect of corporate social responsibility disclosures on share prices in Japan and the UK. *Corporate Ownership and Control, 13*(2), 202–216.

Cahan, S. F., De Villiers, C., Jeter, D. C., Naiker, V., & Van Staden, C. J. (2016). Are CSR disclosures value relevant? Cross-country evidence. *European Accounting Review, 25*(3), 579–611.

Cardamone, P., Carnevale, C., & Giunta, F. (2012). The value relevance of social reporting: Evidence from listed Italian companies. *Journal of Applied Accounting Research, 13*(3), 255–269.

Carnevale, C., & Mazzuca, M. (2014). Sustainability report and bank valuation: Evidence from European stock markets. *Business Ethics Quarterly, 23*(1), 69–90.

Carnevale, C., Mazzuca, M., & Venturini, S. (2012). Corporate social reporting in European banks: The effects on a firm's market value. *Corporate Social Responsibility and Environmental Management, 19*(3), 159–177.

Chan, J. C., & Welford, R. (2005). Assessing corporate environmental risk in China: An evaluation of reporting activities of Hong Kong listed enterprises. *Corporate Social Responsibility and Environmental Management, 12*(2), 88–104.

Cho, S., Lee, C., & Pfeiffer, R. (2013). Corporate social responsibility performance and information asymmetry. *Journal of Accounting and Public Policy, 32*(1), 71–83.

Clarkson, P. M., Fang, X., Li, Y., & Richardson, G. (2013). The relevance of environmental disclosures: Are such disclosures incrementally informative? *Journal of Accounting Public Policy, 32*, 410–432.

Clarkson, P., Li, Y., & Richardson, G. (2004). The market valuation of environmental expenditures by pulp and paper companies. *The Accounting Review, 79*, 329–353.

Cormier, D., & Magnan, M. (2007). The revisited contribution of environmental reporting to investors' valuation of a firm's earnings: An international perspective. *Ecological Economics, 62*, 613–626.

De Klerk, M., & De Villiers, C. (2012). The value relevance of corporate responsibility reporting by south African companies. *Meditari Accountancy Research, 20*(1), 21–38.

De Klerk, M., De Villiers, C., & Van Staden, C. (2015). The influence of corporate social responsibility disclosure on share prices: Evidence from the United Kingdom. *Pacific Accounting Review, 27*(2), 208–228.

De Luca, F., & Phat, H. (2019). Informativeness assessment of risk and risk-management disclosure in corporate reporting: An empirical analysis of Italian large listed firms. *Financial Reporting, 2*, 9–41.

De Villiers, C., & Marques, A. (2016). Corporate social responsibility, country-level predispositions, and the consequences of choosing a level of disclosure. *Accounting and Business Research, 46*(2), 167–195.

De Villiers, C., Ma, D, & Marques, A. (2019). *CSR disclosure, dividend pay-outs and firm value: Relations and mediating effects.* Paper presented at the European accounting association congress, Paphos, Cyprus, 29–31 May 2019.

Déjean, F., & Martinez, I. (2009). Environmental disclosure and the cost of equity: The French case. *Accounting in Europe, 6*(1), 57–80.

Dhaliwal, D. S., Li, O. Z., Tsang, A. H., & Yang, Y. G. (2011). Voluntary non-financial disclosure and the cost of equity capital: The case of corporate social responsibility. *Accounting Review, 86* (1), 59–100.

Dhaliwal, D. S., Radhakrishnan, S., Tsang, A., & Yang, Y. G. (2012). Nonfinancial disclosure and analyst forecast accuracy: International evidence on corporate social responsibility disclosure. *Accounting Review, 87*(3), 723–759.

Doni, F., Bianchi Martini, S., Corvino, A., & Mazzoni, M. (2019). Voluntary versus mandatory non-financial disclosure: EU directive 95/2014 and sustainability reporting practices based on empirical evidence from Italy. Meditari Accountancy Research, Vol. ahead-of-print No. ahead-of-print. https://doi.org/10.1108/MEDAR-12-2018-0423.

El Ghoul, S., Guedhami, O., Kwok, C., & Mishra, D. (2011). Does corporate social responsibility affect the cost of capital? *Journal of Banking and Finance, 35*, 2388–2406.

Freedman, M., & Patten, D. M. (2004). Evidence on the pernicious effect of financial report environmental disclosure. *Accounting Forum, 28*(1), 27–41.

García-Sánchez, I.-M., Hussain, N., Martínez-Ferrero, J., & Ruiz-Barbadillo, E. (2019). Impact of disclosure and assurance quality of corporate sustainability reports on access to finance. *Corporate Social Responsibility and Environmental Management, 26*(4), 832–848.

Gietl, S., Göttsche, M., Habisch, A., Roloff, M., & Schauer, M. (2012). Does CSR reporting destroy firm value? Empirical evidence on GRI-aligned European firms. *Financial Accounting eJournal, 4*(148). Retrieved March 1, 2019, from http://papers.ssrn.com/sol3/papers.cfm?abstract_id=2183601.

Gregory, A., Tharyan, R., & Whittaker, J. (2014). Corporate social responsibility and firm value: Disaggregating the effects on cash flow, risk and growth. *Journal of Business Ethics, 124*(4), 633–657.

Griffin, P., & Sun, Y. (2012). Going green: Market reaction to CSR newswire releases. *Journal of Accounting Public Policy, 32*, 93–113.

Hassan, O. (2018). The impact of voluntary environmental disclosure on firm value: Does organizational visibility play a mediation role? *Business Strategy and the Environment, 27*, 1569–1582.

Hassel, L., Nilsson, H., & Nyquist, S. (2005). The value relevance of environmental performance. *European Accounting Review, 14*(1), 41–61.

Hughes, K. E. (2000). The value relevance of nonfinancial measures of air pollution in the electric utility industry. *The Accounting Review, 75*(2), 209–228.

Jain, A., Jain, P. K., & Rezaee, Z. (2016). Value-relevance of corporate social responsibility: Evidence from short selling. *Journal of Management Accounting Research, 28*(2), 29–52.

Kaspereit, T., & Lopatta, K. (2016). The value relevance of SAM's corporate sustainability ranking and GRI sustainability reporting in the European stock markets. *Business Ethics: A European Review, 25*(1), 1–24.

Kothari, S., & Zimmerman, J. (1995). Price and return models. *Journal of Accounting and Economics, 20*, 155–192.

Kristoufek, L., & Vosvrda, M. (2014). Measuring capital market efficiency: Long-term memory, fractal dimension and approximate entropy. *The European Physical Journal B, 87*(162), 1–9.

Landau, A., Rochell, J., Klein, C., & Zwergel, B. (2020). Integrated reporting of environmental, social, and governance and financial data: Does the market value integrated reports? *Business Strategy and the Environment, 29*, 1750. https://doi.org/10.1002/bse.2467.

Leopizzi, R., Iazzi, A., Venturelli, A., & Principale, S. (2020). Nonfinancial risk disclosure: The 'state of the art' of Italian companies. *Corporate Social Responsibility and Environmental Management, 27*(1), 358–368.

Li, Y., & McConomy, B. J. (1999). An empirical examination of factors affecting the timing of environmental accounting standard adoption and the impact on corporate valuation. *Journal of Accounting, Auditing & Finance, 14*(3), 279–314.

Manes Rossi, F., Nicolò, G., & Levy Orelli, R. (2017). Reshaping risk disclosure through integrated reporting: Evidence from Italian early adopters. *International Journal of Business and Management, 12*(10), 11–23.

Matsumura, E. M., Prakash, R., & Vera-Muñoz, S. C. (2014). Firm-value effects of carbon emissions and carbon disclosures. *The Accounting Review, 89*(2), 695–724.

Miralles-Quiros, M. D. M., Miralles-Quiros, J. L., & Arraiano, I. G. (2017). Are firms that contribute to sustainable development valued by investors? *Corporate Social Responsibility and Environmental Management, 24*(1), 71–84.

Moneva, J. M., & Cuellar, B. (2009). The value relevance of financial and non-financial environmental reporting. *Environmental Resource Economics, 44*(3), 441–456.

Ohlson, J. A. (1995). Earnings, book values, and dividends in equity valuation. *Contemporary Accounting Research, 11*(2), 661–687.

Plumlee, M., Brown, D., Hayes, R. M., & Marshall, R. S. (2015). Voluntary environmental disclosure quality and firm value: Further evidence. *Journal of Accounting Public Policy, 34*, 336–361.

Reverte, C. (2016). Corporate social responsibility disclosure and market valuation: Evidence from Spanish listed firms. *Review of Managerial Science, 10*, 411–435.

Richardson, A., & Welker, M. (2001). Social disclosure, financial disclosure and the cost of equity capital. *Accounting, Organizations and Society, 26*, 597–616.

Rossi, F., & Harjoto, M. (2019). Corporate non-financial disclosure, firm value, risk, and agency costs: Evidence from Italian listed companies. *Review of Managerial Science*. https://doi.org/10.1007/s11846-019-00358-z.

Schadéwitz, H., & Niskala, M. (2010). Communication via responsibility reporting and its effect on firm value in Finland. *Corporate Social Responsibility and Environmental Management, 17*, 96–106.

Servaes, H., & Tamayo, A. (2013). The impact of corporate social responsibility on firm value: The role of customer awareness. *Management Science, 59*(5), 1045–1061.

Shen, Y., & Stark, A. W. (2013). Evaluating the effectiveness of model specifications and estimation approaches for empirical accounting-based valuation models. *Accounting and Business Research, 6*, 660–682.

Sinkin, C., Wright, C. J., & Burnett, R. D. (2008). Eco-efficiency and firm value. *Journal of Accounting and Public Policy, 27*(2), 167–176.

Truant, E., Corazza, L., & Scagneli, S. D. (2017). Sustainability and risk disclosure: An exploratory study on sustainability reports. *Sustainability, 9*, 636.

Yeldar, R. (2012). *The value of extra-financial disclosure. What investors and analysts said?* https://www.globalreporting.org/resourcelibrary/The-value-of-extra-financialdisclosure.pdf

Chapter 9
The Mediating Role of Non-financial Risk

9.1 Introduction

In the chapter we systematize the three regression equations identified in Chaps. 5, 7 and 8, to hypothesize a mediating role of the NF risk on the association between financial risk and market value. To test this hypothesis, we run three regression equations simultaneously and analyse the beta coefficients to investigate whether NF risk fully mediates the risk market value association in the Italian context. As far as we are aware, this is the first value relevance study which does not ignore the relationships between the two kinds of risk, financial and non-financial, which we investigated in Chap. 5. This chapter ends with the main limits, future research directions and implications deriving from the results of our simultaneous equations model.

9.2 The Mediating Effect in Non-financial Information Literature

Mediation effects have been tested especially in the psychological literature (Hayes 2013; Hayes and Scharkow 2013; Preacher and Kelly 2011) and then used in the accounting and management literature (e.g. Newman et al. 2017, Newman et al. 2019; De Villiers et al. 2019; Hassan 2018).[1]

[1]It is important to distinguish the mediation from the moderation (interaction) effect. A moderator (Z) is a variable that affects the strength and/or direction of the relationship between an independent variable (X) and a dependent variable (Y). Moderation is tested constructing a new variable as the product of scores on X and Z (interaction term) and including this interaction term as a predictor in a regression model along with both X and Z as predictors. If the interaction term is significantly

S. Veltri, *Mandatory Non-financial Risk-Related Disclosure*,
https://doi.org/10.1007/978-3-030-47921-3_9

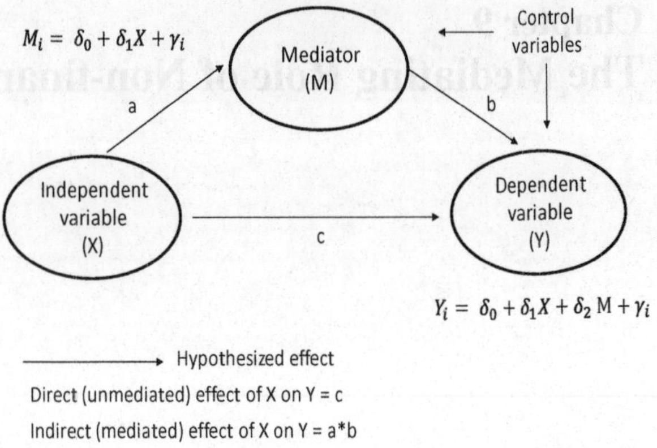

Fig. 9.1 The basic mediation model. Source: Our elaboration

Figure 9.1 illustrates the basic mediation model.

From a theoretical point of view, a mediator explains how or why an independent variable is related to a dependent variable. The focus is therefore on understanding the mechanism, causal chain of events or the underlying process. Mediation, in fact, is also known as an indirect effect of X on Y through M. In other words, it answers the question: "how does X affect Y?" (Hayes 2013).

In a basic mediation model, an independent variable (X) is hypothesized to influence a mediator (M) which, in turn, influences the dependent variable (Y). Theoretically speaking, the mediation effect could be partial or full. In the association investigated, we can identify a full mediation if (1) there is evidence of mediation and (2) the direct effect is non-significant. This means that all of the relationship between X and Y is transmitted through the mediator. Instead, we can identify a partial mediation if (1) there is evidence of mediation and (2) the direct effect is statistically. In empirical studies, partial mediation is more commonly observed than full mediation.

In NFI literature, two recent empirical studies have focused on the mediating effect of a variable able to explain the association investigated. The first one is the article of Hassan (2018) that, investigating the relationship between corporate environmental disclosure (CED) and firm value, hypothesizes that CED affects firm value through the mediation of the organizational visibility, that is, only firms that attract high attention from financial analysts and high institutional holdings record positive association between CED and firm value. The authors provide empirical evidence of their hypothesis, using a modified Ohlson (1995) model and a simultaneous equation model applied to a sample of S6P Global 1200 companies from 2010 to 2015, only when they measure organizational visibility with analyst coverage. Instead, the authors provide no evidence that organizational visibility mediates the association between CED and firm value when they measure organizational visibility with institutional ownership.

different from zero, there is evidence of moderation, that is, the effect of X on Y depends on the values of Z (Baron and Kenny 1986; Dawson 2014).

Table 9.1 Mediating effects in NFI empirical studies

Authors/ journal (year)	Country	Research focus	Main results	Model used
Hassan BSE (2018)	Multi-country S&P Global 1200 companies	To test the mediating effect of organizational visibility on the association between corporate environmental disclosure and firm value	The author provides evidence of the mediation role of organizational visibility when measured with analyst coverage	Modified Ohlson model
De Villiers et al. *EAA conference* (2019)	The 500 largest European firms	To test the mediating effect of the dividend pay-outs on the association between unexpected CSR disclosure and firm value	The author provides evidence of the mediation role of the dividend pay-outs on the association investigated	Modified Ohlson model

Source: Our elaboration

Table 9.1 illustrates the main features in terms of country investigated, focus of the research, main results and model used of the two main empirical studies investigating a mediation effects in NFI literature.

The other study we would like to quote is the study of De Villiers et al. (2019), which hypothesizes that the association between CSR disclosures and the share price of firms is mediated by dividend pay-outs. Using a modified Ohlson (1995) model applied to a large multi-country sample of industrial firms included in the Financial Times 2010 classification of the 500 largest European firms for 2007–2013, the authors find that unexpected CSR disclosure (i.e. the unexplained part or error term of a CSR disclosure prediction model) is positively associated with the share price of firms. The association is not direct but fully mediated by dividend pay-outs, suggesting an indirect effect of unexpected CSR disclosures on firm value.

9.3 Hypothesizing a Mediating Effect in our Research

In Chap. 5, we hypothesized (and tested) a complementary relationship between financial and NF risks. We operationalized our hypothesis in a regression Eq. (9.1) in which financial risks (measured with IAS 37 provisions) are the dependent variable and NF risks (measured by a self-constructed quality risk index on the basis of the Italian Legislative Decree 54/2016) are the independent variable. Our results provide evidence that these two kinds of risk disclosed are related, as the coefficient of financial risk is significant and negative, meaning that the substituting effect prevails over the complementary effect. Starting from this, we hypothesize that the NF risk could be a potential mediator of the association between financial risks and market value (deflated by the number of shares), to test employing a modified Ohlson (1995)

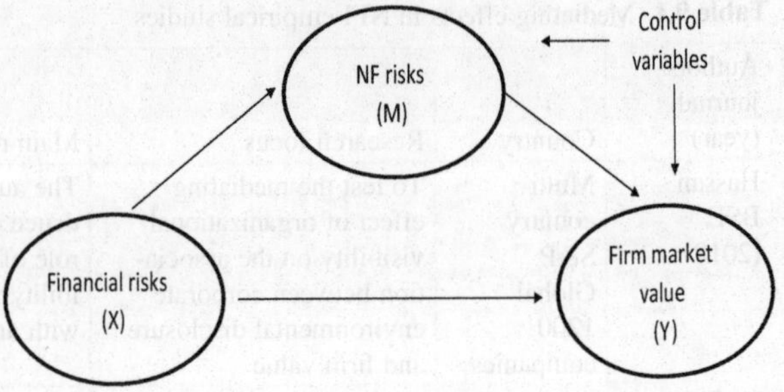

Fig. 9.2 The mediating role of NF risks. Source: Our elaboration

model, according to which market value is affected by accounting fundamental variables (earnings per share, book value per share) and the financial risks as other information variable. Control variables have been included to rely on unbiased regression coefficients.

We stated the fourth research hypothesis as follows:

H4 NF risks mediate the association between financial risks and firm market value.

Figure 9.2 graphically presents the mediating hypothesis at the basis of our H4.

9.4 The Design of the Research

In this section we test research hypothesis 1, that is, the NF risk disclosure mediates the relationship between financial risks and firm market value in the sample identified in Chap. 3, that is, the 51 largest Italian listed companies disclosing their financial risk-related information in the Italian context.[2] The year considered is 2017 alone, as the first year of implementation in Italy of the EU Directive.

To test whether the NF risk disclosure could be a mediator of the association financial risks/market value, we use the following simultaneous equations, following Mackinnon et al. (2002) and Mackinnon and Dwyer (1993):

$$\mathrm{LD254_{QUAL}} = \varphi_0 + \varphi_1\,\mathrm{PROV} + \varphi_2\,\mathrm{EPS} + \varphi_3\,\mathrm{BVPS} + \varphi_4\mathrm{LEV} + \varphi_5\mathrm{IND} + \varepsilon_t \tag{9.1}$$

$$P_i = \sigma_0 + \sigma_1\,\mathrm{EPS}_i + \sigma_2\,\mathrm{BVPS}_i + \sigma_3\,\mathrm{PROV}_i + \sigma_4\,\mathrm{LEV}_i + \sigma_5\,\mathrm{IND}_i + \kappa_i \tag{9.2}$$

[2] As the value relevance studies rely on the basic assumption of stock market efficiency, i.e. that stock prices pick up the effects of all relevant information, their inferences may be misleading if the stock market under analysis is not efficient. In this respect, the study by Kristoufek and Vosvrda (2014) compares the efficiency of 41 stock indices worldwide based on the correlation structure of the returns (long-term and short-term memory) and local herding behaviour (fractal dimension). Their results show that Italy attains 11th place out of the 41 indices in the efficiency index.

$$P_i = \beta_0 + \beta_1\,\mathrm{EPS}_i + \beta_2\,\mathrm{BVPS}_i + \beta_3\,\mathrm{PROV}_i + \beta_4\,\mathrm{LD254}_{\mathrm{QUAL}i} + \beta_5\,\mathrm{LEV}_i + \beta_6\,\mathrm{IND}_i + \omega_i \quad (9.3)$$

In Eqs. (9.1, 9.2, 9.3), *P* is the closing market value per share, BVPS is the book value per share, EPS is the earnings per share, PROV is the financial risks (proxied with the "Provision for risks and uncertainties" under IAS 37, LD254_QUAL is our self-constructed index which measure the quality of disclosure of NF risks qualified in accordance with the Italian Legislative Decree 254/2016, whilst LEV and IND are the control variables, selected after a careful review of the literature (De Villiers and Marques 2016; Hassan 2018, De Villiers et al. 2019; García-Sánchez et al. 2019) and identifying respectively financial leverage (measured as the total debt to total equity ratio) and industry.[3]

We tested Eq. (9.1) in Chap. 5 but without the control variables, as our aim was to provide evidence of an association between the financial and NF risks. We decided to include control variables also in Eq. (9.1) as they control for having unbiased coefficients and also because it is part of a system of equations and all of them should be controlled for the same control variables.

In Eqs. (9.2 and 9.3) we followed prior studies (De Villiers et al. 2019; Reverte 2016; Hassan 2018) and, coherently with them, we used a modified Ohlson (1995) model. The premise of this model is that the accounting measures that explain most of the cross-sectional variation in share prices are book value per share and earnings per share. Other (non-accounting) variables of interest can be added to this basic regression model to test whether these variables add explanatory value to the equation (i.e. are incrementally value relevant) and whether this variable is significantly related to share price. In detail, we proxied the other information variable with the financial risk-related information disclosed, consistently with value relevance literature on risk, in the Eq. (9.2), whilst in Eq. (9.3) we include the financial risk as proxy of the other information variable and the NF risk as mediator variable.

Equations (9.2 and 9.3) are level equations calculated on a per share basis. As for the first character, consistently with Kothari and Zimmerman, who in their 1995 article emphasized that the slope coefficients are less biased in price models than in the returns model (Kothari and Zimmerman 1995), it was decided to use level models to obtain more economically sensible and less biased coefficients, and it was decided to manage the specification problems ascribed to level models by using standard error estimates that are robust to heteroscedasticity problems. As for the second character, all variables in Eqs. (9.1, 9.2, 9.3) have been deflated for a scale factor to mitigate heteroscedasticity, all variables, and then the deflated variables are substituted for the undeflated variables in the valuation model. In the main model, as

[3]In the first step we include SIZE, measured with natural logarithm of total assets, as control variable. When executing the regression model, we realized that variable SIZE has quite high VIF (about 4) as compared to other variables. Moreover, by Pearson's product-moment correlation test, we found that SIZE and PROV are highly correlated. Hence, we dropped SIZE off the models, also considering that BV is also a firm size measure (Hassan 2018) and that the model used is a share price specification, able to mitigate the scale effect (Barth and Clinch 2009).

deflator the number of shares was selected, which is by and large the most used deflator in value relevance regressions and also because it has been supported by Barth and Clinch (2009) and Shen and Stark (2013).[4] Therefore, consistent with Barth and Clinch (2009) and Shen and Stark (2013), we decided to use an extended model scaled by the number of shares.

Equation (9.2) was run in Chap. 7, providing evidence of a negative association (divergence effect) between financial risks and firm value. The purpose of Eq. (9.2) is to establish a relationship between financial risk disclosure and firm value that may be mediated.

Equation (9.3) is thus the equation of the full research model, including as variables affecting market value, beyond the accounting fundamentals earnings and book value also financial and NF risk disclosure. The data related to financial risk disclosure have been taken from the annual report of the company, whilst we measured the quality of NF risks disclosure with a self-constructed index, presented in Chap. 4 of this book.

Different from an interaction effect, the mediation effect implies a causal sequence among our variables of interest (Mackinnon et al. 2002), namely, that the financial risks influence NF risks and NF risks influence MVPS. If φ_1 and β_4 are significant, while β_3 is insignificant in Eqs. (9.2 and 9.3), then the mediator (NF risks) has a full mediation effect, meaning that the influence of financial risks is indirect and fully mediated by NF risks. On the contrary, if φ_1 and β_4 are significant, and also β_3 is significant, then NF risk has a partial mediation effect, meaning that financial risks have both direct and indirect effect on the share price.

9.5 Main Results[5]

Consistent with Hassan (2018) and Landau et al. (2020), a log transformation of all continuous variables (except for the quality NF risk disclosure index) was used, when appropriate, to reduce the impact of outliers on the current analysis. Table 9.2 summarizes all variables included in Eqs. (9.1, 9.2, 9.3).

---

[4]In addition, the recent article of Shen and Stark (2013), comparing the performances of the basic Ohlson (1995) model, where market value is regressed on book value and earnings, against the extended valuation models, where corporate value is modelled as a linear function of accounting variables hypothesized to be associated with company value provide evidence that the extended model generally provides less bias and a more accurate valuation model compared to the basic model.

[5]The section is based on a work written with Francesco De Luca and Ho-Tan-Phat Phan (Veltri et al. 2020).

Table 9.2 Description of variables

Variables	Description
P	Natural logarithm of value share price (market value/number of shares)
BVPS	Natural logarithm of book value per share
EPS	Natural logarithm of earnings per share
PROV	Natural logarithm of provision for risks and uncertainties
LD254_QUAL	Quality of NF risk disclosure subjected to the Legislative Decree 254
LEV	Natural logarithm of LEVERAGE
IND	IND = 1 if the company is incorporated in manufacturing industry; IND = 0, otherwise

Source: Our elaboration

9.5.1 Descriptive Statistics

Table 9.3 gives details of descriptive statistics for firm level variables included in Eq. (9.3). The table also provides VIF and correlation matrix to detect eventual collinearity among variables which could bias coefficients. We conclude that multicollinearity is not detected in our model, as the higher correlation coefficient among dependent variables is 0.78 (Chen and Rothschild 2010) and the higher VIF value is 2.6 (Lin 2008).

9.5.2 Regression Results

The regression models (1), (2), (3) were assessed for the linear model assumptions using the global test (Peña and Slate 2012) on 4 degrees-of-freedom at the level of significance of 0.05. This global test procedure for validating the four assumptions, namely, linearity, homoscedasticity, uncorrelatedness and normality. The (untabulated) tests report that all of the assumptions concerning the appropriateness of the linear models are met. Table 9.4 presents the results of regression Eq. (9.1, 9.2, 9.3).

Equation (9.1) investigates whether the NF risk is a potential moderator of the association between financial risks and firm value, exploring whether financial risks (PROV) affect NF risks (LD254_QUAL). With respect to Eq. (9.1) run in Chap. 5, Eq. (5.1) reported in Table 9.4 includes the control variable leverage and industry.

Equation (9.2) included in Chap. 7 of this book is also reported in Table 9.4 as our aim is to establish whether there is an association between financial risks and share price, which may be mediated. The results of Eq. (9.2) show that financial risks significantly and negatively affect share price, consistent with results from prior studies (Kravet and Muslu 2013; Campbell et al. 2014; Filzen 2015). The negative association shows that financial risks disclosure, proxied with IAS 37 Provisions, Contingent Liabilities and Contingent Assets (PROV) are informative for investors,

Table 9.3 Descriptive statistics for firm-level variables, VIFs and correlation matrix

	Mean	S.d.	VIF	*P*	EPS	BVPS	LD254_QUAL	PROV	IND	LEV
P	1.997	1.235		1.000						
EPS	0.906	0.278	2.436	0.782[a]	1.000					
BVPS	1.196	1.081	1.716	0.786[a]	0.564[a]	1.000				
LD254_QUAL	5.588	1.278	2.635	0.915[a]	0.718[a]	0.611[a]	1.000			
PROV	−3.854	2.157	1.325	−0.427[a]	−0.366[a]	−0.196	−0.452[a]	1.000		
IND	0.451	0.503	1.258	0.335[b]	0.402[a]	0.185	0.283[b]	−0.272	1.000	
LEV	0.991	0.487	1.159	−0.340[b]	−0.314[b]	−0.198	−0.256	0.224	−0.280[b]	1.000

Source: Our elaboration
[a]Correlation is significant at the 0.01 level (2-tailed)
[b]Correlation is significant at the 0.05 level (2-tailed)

Table 9.4 Testing the mediator role of NF risks (LD254_QUAL)

	Equation 9.2		Equation 9.1		Equation 9.3	
	Est.	S.E.	Est.	S.E.	Est.	S.E.
LD254_QUAL						
Intercept			2.716	0.571		
PROV			−0.133*	0.059		
P						
Intercept	−0.530	0.383			−2.035***	0.270
EPS	1.827***	0.385	2.175***	0.573	0.623*	0.254
BVPS	0.578***	0.088	0.359**	0.131	0.380***	0.055
LD254_QUAL					0.553***	0.058
PROV	−0.090*	0.024			−0.016	0.024
IND	0.031	0.174	−0.066	0.261	0.069	0.101
LEV	−0.182	0.175	−0.011	0.259	−0.176.	0.100
R^2	*0.816*		*0.620*		*0.941*	
Adj. R^2	*0.795*		*0.578*		*0.933*	
F	*39.96****		*14.71****		*116.4****	
Df	*45*		*45*		*44*	

Significance codes: '***' 0.001 '**' 0.01 '*' 0.05 '.' 0.1
Equation 9.2 Modified Ohlson model with additional information of PROV
Equation 9.1: effect of PROV on LD254_QUAL
Equation 9.3 Modified Ohlson model with additional information of PROV and LD254_QUAL
Source: Our elaboration

reflecting the actual risks the firm faces, and thus increasing users' risk perception (divergence argument).

Equation (9.3) is the full model that shows the impact of financial risks on share price after controlling for NF risks. It shows that financial risks do not affect share price after adding NF risks and in contrast with the results of Eq. (9.1). It also shows that NF risks is positively and significantly associated with share price, consistent with H3.

The acceptance of the three research hypotheses indicates that NF risks, measured by LD254_QUAL, play a full mediation role, as the coefficient of financial risks became insignificant when NF risks is added to the regression testing the association between financial risks and market value per share.

All regression models are statistically significant at small *p*-values (<0.001) provided by F-tests. This provides sufficient evidence to conclude that the models as a whole have statistically significant predictive capability. The result also shows the improvements in the F-statistic of Eq. 9.3 (166.2) over Eq. 9.1 (39.96). About the goodness of fit, Eq. 9.3 which includes the NF risks as mediator, enhances the R-squared 0.816 to 0.941, meaning that 94.1% of the variation in the *P* that is explained by the traditional accounting variables EPS and BVPS and the disclosed information of both financial and NF risks.

9.6 Testing the Mediation Effect

Figure 9.3 graphically illustrates the results of our research hypothesis 1 in detail that NF risks play a fully mediating role in the association between financial risks and firm market value.

The φ_1 and β_4 coefficients are both statistically significant and in the direction predicted. This provides some evidence in favour of mediation. However, the existence of the mediation effect should be tested. In other words, to test for mediation effect, it is necessary to examine the statistical significance of the indirect effect. There are many statistical tests to investigate the existence of an indirect effect (Hayes and Scharkow 2013). Some of these tests (e.g. the Sobel Z test) assume the indirect effect is normally distributed, but, unfortunately, the indirect effect is rarely normally distributed.

We therefore used non-parametric bootstrapping (with confidence intervals), because it does assume the indirect effect is normally distributed and yields the most accurate results[6] (Tingley et al. 2014). Using bias-corrected bootstrapping with 1000 resamples the indirect effect is −0.0737 (i.e. the product of $\varphi 1$ and $\beta 4$, with a 95% CI: −0.158 to 0.000). With the increased number of resamples from 1000 to 5000, our results are confirmed, with a 95% CI: −0.162 to 0.000. Since the 95% CI does not include 0, the indirect effect is statistically significant (i.e. mediation is supported). In detail, Fig. 9.3 shows that the direct effect (−0.08) is not statistically significant, indicating that the significant influence of financial risks in share price is fully mediated through NF risks and suggesting that financial risk has an indirect effect on the market price of firms. Thus, results show evidence consistent with the existence of a causal sequence among our variables of interest, as higher financial risks negatively affect NF risks, ultimately causing lower share prices.

9.7 Discussions of Results

Risk disclosures are among the most important types of NFI valued by investors. Nevertheless, the empirical literature is silent about the implications of these disclosures for market firm value.

Our book addresses this research gap, by testing the value relevance of NF risk-related information adding both financial and NF risks disclosure proxies to a

[6]To conduct a bootstrap test, a random sample of size N should be taken with replacement from the data (each bootstrap sample is thus the same size as the original sample); then using the bootstrap sample calculates the desired estimates and repeat k times (usually at least 1000 times). The result is an empirical sampling distribution from the bootstrapped samples. The percentile bootstrap is the 2.5 and 97.5 percentiles of the empirical sampling distribution to form a 95% confidence interval (CI) for the estimate. The confidence interval gives a range of plausible values for the estimate. If the 95% confidence interval does not contain zero at the selected level of confidence, it means that the result is statistically significant ($p < 0.05$).

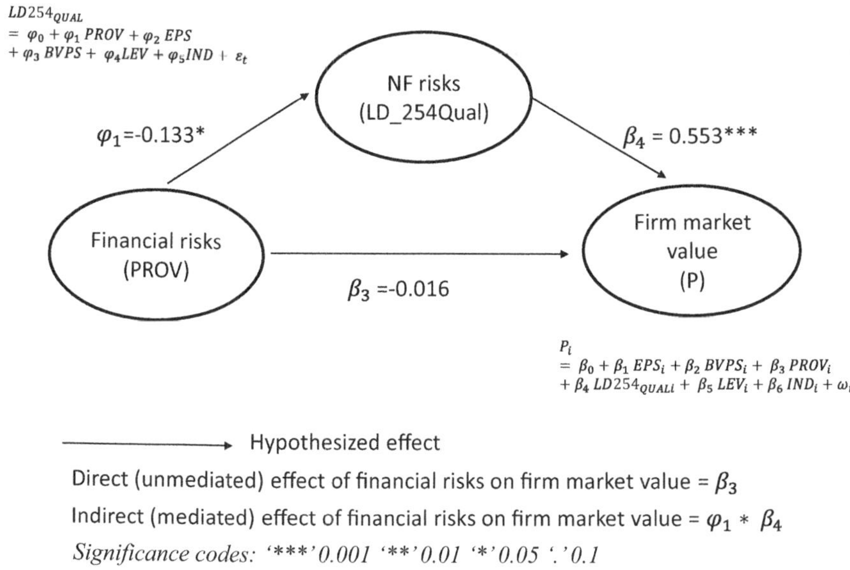

Fig. 9.3 The mediating role of NF risks. Source: Our elaboration

modified Ohlson (1995) model. This is the first contribution of our findings, to enrich the empirical literature on the value relevance of NF variables in a mandatory context.

As far as we are aware, in fact, this is the first value relevance empirical study of the NF risks in a mandatory context, and the results also provide an insight into what role the State can play (or is willing to play) in the regulation of NFI and in detail of NF risk disclosure. In detail, the research was carried out in the mandatory Italian context after the enactment of the 254/2016 Decree implementing EU Directive on non-financial diversity information. In this way, our findings provide evidence that quality NF risk disclosure is incrementally value relevant in a mandatory context, so supporting mandatory disclosure of NFI. Our results also allow understanding that the choices made by the Italian legislator in implementing the EU directive support an NF risks disclosure value relevant for investors.

Our findings provide evidence of the direct effect of NF risks disclosure, measured by a self-constructed index employing a manual meaning-oriented content analysis to capture the quality of NF risks disclosure as required by the 254/2016 Decree, on firm market value, and this is also an original point of our research, whereas the majority of exiting researches focus on coverage indexes. In the Italian context, only the article of Leopizzi et al. (2020) uses a content analysis to measure qualitatively NF risks disclosure, but without ending up with a comprehensive score.

Another original point of our research is the hypothesis of the existence of a relationship between financial and NF risks, which finds its basis in the deep conviction that these two types of risk are different, meaning that they provide information with different features to the stakeholders, yet are related, and, to the best of our knowledge, this research is the first to not ignore the relationship with risky financial and NF information, backward-looking and forward-looking risk information.

We also provide evidence of the value relevance of financial risk information and share price in the Italian context, scarcely investigated from this point of view and above all, providing evidence of a divergence hypothesis, coherently with Kravet and Muslu (2013), that is, there is a negative association between financial risks disclosure, measured by IAS 37 "Provisions risks and uncertainties" (PROV), and firm market value, suggesting that the requirement mandated by IAS 37 on financial risks was successful in generating timely disclosure of bad news.

Finally, our findings also complement the literature providing evidence not only of the direct effect of NF risks disclosure on the company market value but also of its fully mediating effect of NF risks on the association between financial risks disclosure and share prices. To assess the existence of a mediating effect for NF risks, we employed a system of simultaneous equations which test the association between financial risks and share price, the association between financial risks and non-financial risks and then the role of NF risks as a mediator of the financial risks/firm market value association.

9.8 Main Limitations of the Study and Future Research Directions

The main limitation is the size of the sample due to the shortage of data, as the sample includes only large Italian listed companies, and the lack of width, being data related to one year, the first after the enactment of the Decree. This makes the research exploratory in nature, even if it should be underlined that major post-implementation effects usually emerge in the first year of validity of new laws.

Other limits lie in the applied models both to measure the quality NF disclosure index, owing to the subjectivity that is inherent in content analysis methodology, to the subjectivity in the choices of the measures of the quality items and to the interpretation of the estimators that, in the econometric model applied to a short panel of data, can generate large differences.

With the aim to generalize the findings, therefore further research should be addressed with the data several years later (greater time horizons) or of many countries, especially for European countries, given that the new regulation is the result of a European Directive or for companies other than large listed companies also obliged to disclose NF risks.

Future research directions could also focus on the disclosure of corporate activities implemented to face and manage risks, as requested at supranational (COSO 2018) and national level (Legge di bilancio 145/2018) and not only on the risk disclosure.

Lastly, suggestions for further research should also include a comparison analysis in terms of value relevance between the previous voluntary disclosure and the mandatory disclosure after the EU Directive.

9.9 Main Implications of the Study

The improvement of company disclosure of social and environmental information (including information about risk) represents one of the eight areas in which EU policy has put forward an action agenda, so, despite the difficulty of generalizing the results for a bigger context such as the EU, our results could have policy implications, as they provide relevant evidence for European policymakers of the positive effect of quality mandatory NF risks disclosure in rebuilding trust between companies and investors. Moreover, this study, providing evidence of the incremental value relevance of PROV, confirms the push toward the IASB for a possible project to amend aspects of IAS 37 Provisions, Contingent Liabilities and Contingent Assets, to provide a more detailed scheme of risk and uncertainties profile to reach the best estimate of a provision in the light of shareholders' expectations.

Our results could also have practical implications. In fact, our findings could help investors with regard to the identification of NF risk-related information considered critical for investment decisions and could also help companies to recognize the relevance of disclosing NF risk-related information to maximize company value, helping companies mandated to follow the best practices and to adopt an approach able to face the trade-off between being transparent or secretive and companies not obliged to fulfil NF risk disclosure to understand the importance of disclosing (and managing) this kind of information.

References

Baron, R., & Kenny, D. (1986). The moderator-mediator variable distinction in social psychological research: Conceptual, strategic, and statistical considerations. *Journal of Personality and Social Psychology, 51*, 1173–1182.

Barth, M. E., & Clinch, G. (2009). Scale effects in capital markets-based accounting research. *Journal of Business Finance and Accounting, 36*(3–4), 253–288.

Campbell, J. L., Chen, H., Dhaliwal, D. S., Lu, H., & Steele, L. B. (2014). The information content of mandatory risk factor disclosure in corporate filings. *Review of Accounting Studies, 19*(1), 396–455.

Chen, C. F., & Rothschild, R. (2010). An application of hedonic pricing analysis to the case of hotel rooms in Taipei. *Tourism Economics, 16*(3), 685–694.

COSO. (2018). Committee of Sponsoring Organizations of the Treadway Commission, *Enterprise risk management applying enterprise risk management to environmental, social and governance-related risks*. Retrieved June, 2019 from https://www.coso.org/news/Pages/new-guidance-addresses-resiliency-against-esg-risks.aspx

Dawson, J. (2014). Moderation in management research: What, why, when and how. *Journal of Business and Psychology, 29*, 1–19.
De Villiers, C., & Marques, A. (2016). Corporate social responsibility, country-level predispositions, and the consequences of choosing a level of disclosure. *Accounting and Business Research, 46*(2), 167–195.
De Villiers, C., Ma, D., & Marques, A. (2019). *CSR disclosure, dividend pay-outs and firm value: Relations and mediating effects*. Paper presented at the European accounting association congress, Paphos, Cyprus, 29–31 May 2019.
Filzen, J. J. (2015). The information content of risk factor disclosures in quarterly reports. *Accounting Horizons, 29*(4), 887–916.
García-Sánchez, I.-M., Hussain, N., Martínez-Ferrero, J., & Ruiz-Barbadillo, E. (2019). Impact of disclosure and assurance quality of corporate sustainability reports on access to finance. *Corporate Social Responsibility and Environmental Management, 26*(4), 832–848.
Hassan, O. (2018). The impact of voluntary environmental disclosure on firm value: Does organizational visibility play a mediation role? *Business Strategy and the Environment, 27*, 1569–1582.
Hayes, A. (2013). *Introduction to mediation, moderation, and conditional process analysis*. New York: Guilford Press.
Hayes, A. F., & Scharkow, M. (2013). The relative trustworthiness of inferential tests of the indirect effect in statistical mediation analysis: Does method really matter? *Psychological Science, 24*, 1918–1927.
Kothari, S., & Zimmerman, J. (1995). Price and return models. *Journal of Accounting and Economics, 20*, 155–192.
Kravet, T., & Muslu, V. (2013). Textual risk disclosures and investors' risk perceptions. *Review of Accounting Studies, 18*(4), 1088–1122.
Kristoufek, L., & Vosvrda, M. (2014). Measuring capital market efficiency: Long-term memory, fractal dimension and approximate entropy. *The European Physical Journal B, 87*(162), 1–9.
Landau, A., Rochell, J., Klein, C., & Zwergel, B. (2020). Integrated reporting of environmental, social, and governance and financial data: Does the market value integrated reports? *Business Strategy and the Environment, 29*, 1750. https://doi.org/10.1002/bse.2467.
Leopizzi, R., Iazzi, A., Venturelli, A., & Principale, S. (2020). Nonfinancial risk disclosure: The 'state of the art' of Italian companies. *Corporate Social Responsibility and Environmental Management, 27*(1), 358–368.
Lin, F. J. (2008). Solving multicollinearity in the process of fitting regression model using the nested estimate procedure. *Quality and Quantity, 42*(3), 417–426.
Mackinnon, D., & Dwyer, J. (1993). Estimating mediated effects in prevention studies. *Evaluation Review, 17*(2), 144–158.
Mackinnon, D., Lockwood, C., Hoffman, J., & West, S. (2002). A comparison of methods to test mediation and other intervening variable effects. *Psychological Methods, 7*(1), 83–104.
Newman, A., Schwartz, G., Cooper, B., & Sendjaya, S. (2017). How servant leadership influences organizational citizenship behavior: The roles of LMX, empowerment, and proactive personality. *Journal of Business Ethics, 145*, 49–62.
Newman, A., Cooper, B., Holland, P., Miao, Q., & Teicher, J. (2019). How do industrial relations climate and union instrumentality enhance employee performance? The mediating effects of perceived job security and trust in management. *Human Resource Management, 58*, 35–44.
Ohlson, J. A. (1995). Earnings, book values, and dividends in equity valuation. *Contemporary Accounting Research, 11*(2), 661–687.
Peña, E. A., & Slate, E. H. (2012). Global validation of linear model assumptions. *Journal of the American Statistical Association, 101*, 341–354.
Preacher, K. J., & Kelley, K. (2011). Effect size measures for mediation models: Quantitative strategies for communicating indirect effects. *Psychological Methods, 16*, 93–115.
Reverte, C. (2016). Corporate social responsibility disclosure and market valuation: Evidence from Spanish listed firms. *Review of Managerial Science, 10*, 411–435.

Shen, Y., & Stark, A. W. (2013). Evaluating the effectiveness of model specifications and estimation approaches for empirical accounting-based valuation models. *Accounting and Business Research, 6*, 660–682.

Tingley, D., Yamamoto, T., Hirose, K., Imai, K., & Keele, L. (2014). Mediation: R package for causal mediation analysis. *Journal of Statistical Software, 59*(5), 1–38.

Veltri, S., De Luca, F., & Phat, H. (2020). Do investors value companies mandatory nonfinancial risk disclosure? An empirical analysis of the Italian context after the EU Directive. *Business Strategy and the Environment*. https://doi.org/10.1002/bse.2497.

The manufacturer's authorised representative in the EU is Springer Nature Customer Service Centre GmbH, Europaplatz 3, 69115 Heidelberg, Germany. If you have any concerns regarding our products, please contact ProductSafety@springernature.com

Printed and bound by CPI Group (UK) Ltd, Croydon, CR0 4YY
30/09/2026
02225513-0020